The Origins of Christianity
in Bohemia

The Origins

Sources and Commentary

Marvin Kantor

Northwestern University Press

Evanston, Illinois

# of Christianity in Bohemia

Northwestern University Press
Evanston, Illinois 60201

Copyright © 1990 by Marvin Kantor. All rights reserved. Published 1990 by Northwestern University Press.

Printed in the United States of America

95 94 93 92 91 90   6 5 4 3 2 1

Library of Congress Cataloging-in-Publication Data

Kantor, Marvin.
   The origins of Christianity in Bohemia : sources and commentary / Marvin Kantor.
      p.   cm.
   Includes bibliographical references.
   ISBN 0-8101-0874-7
   1. Czechoslovakia—Church history.   2. Czechoslovakia—Church history—Sources.   I. Title.
BR1050.C9K35   1990   90-38056
274.37'103—dc20   CIP

Contents

Preface

A WORD SHOULD BE SAID about the works chosen for inclusion in this book and the translations that follow. My aim was to produce a detailed picture of the literature that resulted from the unique coexistence of two literary languages, Church Slavonic and Latin, and deals with the two principal figures of early Bohemian spirituality, Saint Ludmila and Saint Wenceslas. A secondary goal was to provide a view of the literary spectrum of the era of early Christianity in Bohemia, a period that witnessed the development of original prose and poetic works, and creative translations. Since I thought it would be impractical to attempt exhaustiveness, I excluded works in genres that are already represented. Most conspicuous among these are the Eight Prayers of the *Jaroslav Prayer Book* (*Molitvennik Jaroslavskij*) and the *Vita of Saint Procopius*.

As concerns the translations, my primary objective was accuracy, and a special effort was made to translate as precisely as possible everything found in the texts. When necessary, I consulted other manuscripts of individual works and pursued discussions with colleagues about textual difficulties and possible clarifications. I trust I have not taken too many liberties with any of the manuscripts and/or committed an inordinate number of errors. The solutions offered on the following pages are my own and I accept full responsibility for them.

For the translation of biblical allusions, paraphrases, and quotations, I utilized the King James Version of the Holy Bible. As I have pointed out in the past, to have rendered such passages in a more modern English version of the Bible would clearly have avoided certain archaisms, but at the expense of the text's medieval essence. However, it must be acknowledged that such a distinction in style cannot be discerned in the original monuments.

It should be noted that all verbatim or nearly verbatim biblical quotations are indicated on the pages of the text, where chapter and verse are cited. References to biblical allusions and paraphrases are confined to the notes.

I would like to extend a word of thanks to Henry R. Cooper, Jr. for reading and commenting on my manuscript, and to Ladislav Matějka for his many suggestions and criticism.

Finally, I wish to express my appreciation to the Office of Research and Sponsored Programs of Northwestern University for providing funds in aid of this project; and to the Fulbright program, which is funded by the United States Information Agency (USIA) and administered by the Council for the International Exchange of Scholars (CIES), for making it possible for me to work in Prague.

✝ Introduction

The Church of Saints Peter and Paul, tenth century. Budeč.

✝

Historical Background (Beginnings–1100)

S ITUATED FAR FROM THE ANCIENT centers of civilization and culture, Bohemia, Moravia, Slovakia—the three lands that make up contemporary Czechoslovakia—rarely found their way into the works of classical Greek and Latin writers. Early medieval sources, primarily German chronicles, also fail to shed adequate light on events in these lands before the tenth century. Therefore much of the information about their beginnings, the origin of their inhabitants, and the rise of the states has to be gleaned from old myths and legends as well as from archeological findings. This material, however, has been manipulated and interpreted at will, which often has led to the creation of new myths. As a result, there is a great deal of disparity in the interpretations of the prehistory of Bohemia, Moravia, and Slovakia.

During the so-called Wanderings of Nations, the ethnic formation of Europe was shaped by mass displacements of peoples. As we know, the Slavs were not excluded from this process. And although *Chronica Boemorum* by the Czech Latinist Cosmas of Prague (d. 1125) tells us that the land which was to become Bohemia was uninhabited before the arrival of the Czechs, we know now that the earliest traceable inhabitants were not Czechs but Celts. Their presence is suggested by the names of rivers like the Elbe, "white" (*Labe* = "swan"), and by the etymology for the very name of Bohemia, which is derived from the tribal name of the Celtic Boii. Around 100 B.C. the Celts were displaced by the Germanic tribes Marcomanni and Quadi. And during the fifth century Slavic tribes arrived in this territory from the east while the Germanic tribes moved toward the west and north.[1]

Toward the end of the sixth century, central Europe found itself in the grip of the Avars, who threatened the Frankish Empire in their push westward. As Avar fortunes began to wane during the following century, the Slavs, led by a Frankish nobleman named Samo, revolted

3

against them. It seems that Samo was originally sent to the Slavs to assure them of Frankish support. Under his leadership the Slavs were victorious, and they recognized him as their ruler. But then Samo refused to submit to Frankish claims of supremacy over the Slavs, and from the ensuing conflict he emerged as the head of an independent Slavic state. However, Samo's state disintegrated after his death in the mid-seventh century.[2] Little more is heard about the Slavs of Bohemia until the end of the eighth century, by which time Charlemagne had destroyed the Avars and the Czechs had brought most of Bohemia under their control.

As the ninth century dawned, the entrenched pagan beliefs and customs of the Slavs in central Europe were about to yield to the surge of Christianity. The drive to evangelize these pagans would come from the south and west where, respectively, Roman and Frankish missionaries were poised for the task. Thus the Czechs, as well as their eastern neighbors, the Moravians and Slovaks, became the targets of their proselytizing endeavors. It seems that the Franks considered all of central Europe their preserve.

During the first part of the ninth century a Slavic ruler, Mojmir, managed to form the first central European dynastic state, which would come to be known as Great Moravia.[3] As the century progressed this state grew in power, influence, and size under Mojmir's successor, Rostislav. However, his independence and success—which extended the Moravian state to the borders of the Bulgarian Empire—aroused the resentment of both the Franks and Bulgarians. They concluded an alliance in the hope of subduing Rostislav's realm. In turn, Rostislav allied himself with the Byzantine Empire. The outcome was the most significant occurrence in the early cultural history of all the Slavs: the Christian mission to Moravia led by Constantine and Methodius in 863. The *Lives* of Constantine and Methodius eloquently recount this event.[4]

The brothers were born in Thessalonica of Byzantine Greek parents. It is clear that they were bilingual, as the emperor's words to them testify: "You are both Thessalonians and all Thessalonians speak pure Slavic" (*Life of Methodius*, see chap. 5). Constantine displayed extraordinary intellectual powers at an early age and was summoned to the imperial court to study; Methodius became the governor of a Slavic province, a career he subsequently abandoned to become a priest. Because of his erudition, Constantine was called upon to accompany a diplomatic mission to the Arabs (to mitigate the persecution of Christians in the Arab Empire) and, together with Methodius, to go on a religious mission to the Khazars (to explain Christian doctrine). The main work of the brothers began in 863, when the Byzantine emperor, Michael III, sent them to Moravia at the request of the Moravian prince Rostislav in order to give religious instruction to the local Slavic population in their own language. The words of the Moravian prince make this clear: "Though our people have rejected paganism and observe Christian law, we do not have a teacher who can explain to us in our language . . ." (*Life of Constantine*, see chap. 14).

Since questions of church and state were closely intertwined at this time, Rostislav's appeal to Byzantium was also motivated by political needs. Apparently, Frankish missionary activity bore an excessively worldly aspect and constituted a threat to the independence of Great Moravia.[5] Therefore, an equally important consideration was to create a church capable of resisting German political expansion. Whereas the Western Church insisted on the use of Latin as a *lingua sacra*, the Eastern Church had a tradition of allowing the vernacular. Therefore, the most important contribution of the Byzantine mission was the introduction of the Slavic tongue into the language of the church and the law. No one before Constantine had thought to give the Slavs an alphabet and a literary language, and to teach them to write it by using translations from the New Testament and Byzantine law. Constantine's alphabet, Glagolitic, was an entirely new invention and showed his keen ability to analyze and represent the phonological structure of the Slavic language very precisely. The subsequent success of the Byzantine mission was to have a profound effect on the future of Christianity among all the Slavs. No doubt it played a crucial role not only in Great Moravia itself but also in the early life of the church in Bohemia in the west and Slovakia in the east.

Thus the Great Moravian Empire became noteworthy above all for its attempt to create the first Slavic dynastic state in central Europe[6] and for its contribution to the development of the first Slavic literary language and literature. Constantine created the first systematically written Slavic language—which came to be known as Old Church Slavonic—as a tool for his mission to the Western Slavs in

Great Moravia. This language, to paraphrase Horace G. Lunt, did not represent a specific regional dialect but was a generalized form of early Eastern Balkan Slavic, which cannot be localized. Moreover, Old Church Slavonic as a written *lingua sacra* was based on late Common Slavic, the language spoken by all Slavs before they became differentiated into separate nations, and was therefore readily understandable to Moravians.[7] Thus Constantine's codification was supradialectal in structure, and, because it was a literary language modeled after New Testament Greek, it had to be learned; however, for any speaker of a regional Slavic dialect, this task was immeasurably simpler than learning (and using) a foreign language like Greek or Latin.[8]

The first period of the Slavic Church in central Europe was rather short-lived. Rostislav's successor, Svatopluk, was not sufficiently supportive of the achievements of the Byzantine missionaries. After the death of Methodius in 885, the activities of the Slavic Church were terminated and eastern missionaries were replaced by western ones. Shortly afterward, Svatopluk died (894) and the state began to collapse. The Magyar invasion put an end to Great Moravia, driving a wedge between the Western and Southern Slavs that still exists today.

During Moravia's brief flowering, Bohemia found itself deep in its shadow. Bits and pieces of information about certain events in Bohemia are provided by German chronicles. Thus, the *Annals of Fulda* report that in 845 fourteen Czech chieftains went to Regensburg in Bavaria requesting Christian instruction. They were received by King Louis, who had them baptized. This, no doubt, was a private initiative undertaken by the individuals concerned and not part of a mass conversion of the populace. The reporting of this isolated incident is further indication of the sporadic nature of such occurrences. In 874 Svatopluk's subjugation of Bohemia again brought some more unwanted attention to this area. But toward the end of the century we find names of individual rulers entering the records. The *Annals of Fulda* tell us that in 895 two Bohemian princes, Spytihněv and Vitěslav—representing the Přemyslide and Slavník dynasties (that is, the western and eastern parts of Bohemia)—came to Regensburg, to King Arnulf, to pledge their allegiance to the Frankish Empire. In a political sense, this was the birth of the medieval state of Bohemia. Only in the tenth century would Bohemia step into the limelight.

The emergence of Bohemia as a state is the topic of many legends, one of the most prominent of which concerns the rise of the Czech dynasty, the Přemyslides.[9] It tells how the princess of the land, Libuše, following a prophecy, chose the peasant Přemysl to be her husband and future ruler of the Czechs. This legend is echoed in several works of literature dealing with the early Christian princes of Bohemia (for example, *Legenda Christiani* and *Diffundente sole*) as well as in *Chronica Boemorum* by Cosmas of Prague. Indeed, it was Cosmas who constructed a genealogy for the dynastic line of the Přemyslides and dated the baptism of their first Christian convert, Bořivoj.

Moreover, the Latin legend *Diffundente sole* (see part 4, chap. 6) asserts that Methodius himself also baptised Bořivoj's wife, Ludmila. Clearly the "Methodian connection" in the literature concerning the conversion of Bohemia tried to link the Bohemian and Moravian evangelizations and to view Bohemia as the cultural and political heir of Great Moravia. The semimythical Bořivoj has been treated by some writers as a historical figure, and the parameters of his life have been given thus: birth, ca. 855; marriage to Ludmila, ca. 873; baptism, ca. 874; and death, ca. 891.

We find ourselves on firmer historical ground with Bořivoj's successor, Spytihněv (d. 915). He is considered by some sources to be the first historically attested Christian among the Přemyslides, although the year of his baptism is not confirmed anywhere. Having pledged his allegiance to the Frankish Empire, Spytihněv made Bohemia an ally of Bavaria, a tie that was mutually beneficial owing to the potential Magyar danger. However, it also opened Prague to greater influence from Bavaria and the Western Church. Yet, by this time some of the exiles from Moravia apparently had found their way into Bohemia along with their Church Slavonic books, so that the Church Slavonic tradition of the Eastern Church began to coexist in Bohemia with the Latin tradition of the Western Church. And adding to the intricacies of the situation was Saxony, with its pretensions to ascendancy over all Germans.

Little is known about Spytihněv's reign. However, it is commonly accepted that he built the Church of Saints Peter and Paul at Budeč, north of Prague, where his nephew Wenceslas (Václav) was educated. Moreover, Spytihněv either built or rebuilt the Church of the Virgin

Mary at Prague Castle—clear indications that Christianity continued to develop under his tutelage. He was succeeded by his brother, Vratislav (d. 920), of whom little is known. Apparently he built the first stone church in Prague, which was consecrated to Saint George. It is assumed that Vratislav was killed while defending his land against the Magyars. He was survived by two underage sons, several daughters, and his widow, Drahomira, who became regent for the eldest boy, Wenceslas.

The image of Wenceslas that emerges from the legends after his death is surely much larger-than-life than the man. And though historically he might not have been more important than Edward the Martyr of the English royal house, as R. W. Seton-Watson writes, the myth transcended mundane facts and placed him not only alongside the greatest of Czech national heroes but at their head. For this is how Saint Wenceslas is remembered.

According to tradition, Wenceslas, the first of seven children, was born around 907 at Stochov near Libušin. There is no record of his baptism, but it is thought to have been performed by a Slavic priest (Paul?), the same man from whom Wenceslas learned Slavic letters at the urging of his grandmother, Ludmila. At an early age, according to the legends, he was sent by his father to the school at Budeč, where he was entrusted to the priest Učen (Uenno). The legends are unanimous in praising Wenceslas's accomplishments. However, domestic problems soon compelled him to leave his studies and assume political control of the land. After the death of his father, the reins of power, as mentioned above, had been placed in the hands of his mother, Drahomira, while his grandmother, Ludmila, remained in charge of his education. This fact apparently caused friction between mother and mother-in-law. Drahomira suspected that her authority over Wenceslas was being undermined and that he was being corrupted by priests. Some sources explain this as a conflict between Drahomira's paganism and Ludmila's Christianity and as the cause of Ludmila's violent death—for she was assassinated at her castle in Tetín in a palace revolt (921). Bohemia now had its first Christian martyr.

The interregnum under Drahomira was marked by unrest. In the end Wenceslas's rights were upheld, and finally he ascended the throne (925). According to the *Lives*, he banished his mother to Budeč, had the relics of his grandmother returned to Prague, and recalled the priests who had been driven from the land.

About this time Saxony became the major rival of Bavaria and the dominant power in central Europe. It has been suggested that Wenceslas chose not to resist the Saxon king and to become his vassal because he believed in the concept that the head of the empire was ipso facto the head of all Christian rulers. At any rate, when the Prague cathedral was completed (926–29), it was consecrated to the patron saint of Saxony, Saint Vitus, rather than to Saint Emmeram of Bavaria, as originally planned. Wenceslas's politics apparently incurred the wrath of a faction headed by his brother, Boleslav (Boleslas), which was to prove fatal to the young monarch.

The precise cause of conflict between Wenceslas and his brother is difficult to pin down: internal strife, family quarrel, envy, ineptitude—any one or all might serve as an explanation. What seems clear from the legends is that the brothers were diametric opposites, with differing personalities, preferences, and life-styles. Whereas Boleslav was ambitious, domineering, and worldly, Wenceslas was retiring, humble, and ascetic (a characterization especially evident in some of the Latin legends). All the sources attest to the latter's commendable Christian virtues—his sense of justice, solicitude for the needy, orphans, and widows, and generous support of the clergy and founding of churches; none mentions any abilities as a political leader or military commander. Indeed, what emerges from the pages of the *Lives* (for example, *Crescente fide, Legenda Christiani, Second Church Slavonic Life*) is the picture of a man under the thumb of priests, retiring, neglectful of and perhaps even insensible to the affairs of government. Christianity had not eliminated the necessity for a strong leader. Wenceslas appears to have lacked this important dimension. Left to his own devices, he would have preferred to become a monk and withdraw to a monastery. It remains a matter of speculation whether the conflict between the brothers was caused by Wenceslas's pro-Saxon policy as opposed to Boleslav's favoring of Bavaria. And just as conjectural is whether or not Wenceslas's own fervent commitment to Christianity resulted in an effort to convert the country in a manner that brooked neither delays nor compromises. Whatever the actual cause of the animosity, it resulted in the assassination of Wenceslas. Lured to his brother's residence at Stará Boleslav under the pretext of celebrating the consecration of a new church in honor of Saints Cosmas and Damian, Wenceslas was murdered. His death, traditionally placed on 28 September 929 (though some critics argue that 935 corresponds more closely with contemporary chronology), gave Bohemia its second Christian martyr and national saint. Wenceslas began to be invoked as a consoler, healer, and liberator, and became the protector of Czech armies. He is also known to the English-speaking world, thanks to John Mason Neale's Christmas carol, "Good King Wenceslas."[10]

Boleslav turned out to be an able ruler. Christianity gradually spread across the country under the influence of Prague. He soon made amends for his complicity in the killing of his brother and had the latter's relics brought to Prague and interred in the Church of Saint Vitus (4 March 932). After the death of Henry I, he assumed a more independent attitude toward the German Empire, refusing, for example, to pay the annual tribute. Nevertheless, Boleslav was again obliged to recognize the sovereignty of Otto I, and Bohemia's political future was more or less (though not as yet formally) fixed vis-à-vis the empire henceforth. It would enjoy autonomy and could develop its own national and economic life—but within the empire. Boleslav went on to play an active role in the affairs of the empire and, after the battle of Lechfeld (955),[11] brought Moravia, Slovakia, Silesia, and Cracow under his control—a move that extended his borders into Poland. At this time Boleslav gave his daughter, Dubravka, in marriage to the Polish ruler, Mieszko I, to whom he also sent Christian missionaries. And it was Boleslav who began negotiations to found a new bishopric in Prague, which finally came into being (972–73) during the reign of his son, Boleslav II (967–99). Despite the fact that Boleslav enjoyed good relations with the empire and the pope, his new bishopric could not remain independent of the German Church, being subordinated to Mainz-on-the-Rhine. Perhaps a small concession was made in the appointment of the new bishop, Thietmar (Dětmar), a Saxon from the Benedictine monastery of Corvey, who was well acquainted with the Slavic world and even spoke Slavic.

Continuing his father's work, Boleslav II fostered Christian institutions and promoted the hegemony of the Přemyslide princes of Prague in association with the Slavníks. The prominent role played by the princely house of Libice in eastern Bohemia had hitherto been, apparently, in concord with the Přemyslides. Indeed, owing to the mutual cooperation between the Přemyslides and Slavníks, Bohemia was able to annex Moravia, Slovakia, Silesia, and Cracow. Also, the first native Bohemian to become bishop of Prague was the Slavník Adalbert (Vojtěch), who succeeded Thietmar in 982. However, this peaceful collaboration was not destined to last. Conflict with Poland over the possession of Silesia and Cracow put the two houses at odds. Boleslav wished to claim this region for Bohemia, but Soběslav, the ruling Slavník prince and Adalbert's brother, sympathized with Poland. Adalbert was caught in the middle of this political rivalry and proved ineffectual in bridging the gap. Deprived of the support of Boleslav and weakened as chief administrator of the church in Bohemia, he left Prague (989) for Italy with plans ultimately to make a pilgrimage to the Holy Land. He spent some time at Monte Cassino, the center of the Benedictine order, and in Rome, where he became a monk the following year. From there he was persuaded to return to Prague (992) after Boleslav's campaign against the Poles ended badly. A brief period of cooperation ensued between prince and bishop; but the Slavníks' persistent support of Poland undermined his position once again. He left Prague for the last time in 995.

Adalbert became the founding bishop in Gniezno (Poland) and his brother, Gaudentius (Radim), the first archbishop of Poland (1000). He died a martyr's death in Prussia in 997 as a missionary to the pagan population. With Adalbert gone and Soběslav away in Germany with his army helping the emperor, Boleslav was determined to put an end to what he viewed as Slavník treachery. He ordered the destruction of Libice, where every man, woman, and child was massacred. Thus perished the house of Slavník, and now the Czech Přemyslides alone ruled the lands of Bohemia. In 999 Boleslav II died, and Bohemia declined rapidly.

For approximately the next thirty years Bohemia was beset by internal dissension, and Prague had to contend now with the Germans, now with the Poles. Boleslav III (999–1003) and Oldřich (1012–34) could not prevent the loss of most of the territories that their predecessors had gained. At the close of these bleak years (1032–33) an important center of Slavic letters arose in the monastery of Saints Mary and John the Baptist on the Sázava River. On a land grant from Oldřich, it was built by Procopius, who established the Benedictine rule after becoming its first abbot. Here the Cyrillomethodian tradition and Byzantine orientation were perpetuated. Church Slavonic manuscripts were copied, and most probably new translations were made from Latin into Church Slavonic. The cause of the Slavic Church was further strengthened by Oldřich's appointment of a native, Šebíř (Severus), as bishop of Prague.

Oldřich was succeeded by the grandson of Boleslav II, Břetislav I (1034–55), who regained part of Moravia, which henceforth would remain linked with Bohemia. And it was he who removed Adalbert's relics from Gniezno, after subduing the Poles (1039), and brought them to Prague. Břetislav also favored Church Slavonic and continued to support Sázava. After the death of Procopius (1053), his nephew, Vitus, became abbot. However, the use of the Slavic liturgical language came to depend on the patronage of the ruler of Bohemia.[12] And the consequences of the schism between the western and eastern branches of the church in 1054 boded ill for the future of the Slavic liturgical language in the lands of the Roman Empire. It became more and more difficult to retain the traditions of the Slavic Church within the Western Church because Rome insisted on uniformity of rite.[13]

A sharp break occurred with the ascension of Břetislav's son, Spytihněv II (1055–61), who turned out to be inimical toward the Slavic monks at Sázava. The reasons for his hostility are uncertain. One suggestion is that Spytihněv wished to appease Pope Gregory VII, who disapproved of the Slavic liturgy. Indeed, accusations against the Slavic monks—similar to those that had been leveled at Constantine and Methodius—were aired once again, claiming that the monks were being drawn into a sect of heretics because of their Slavic writings.[14] Hence, the Slavic monks were driven out of Sázava and expelled from the land. They found refuge in the monastery of Saint Andrew at Vyšehrad located in Hungarian-occupied Pannonia and apparently maintained contact with Kiev and Constantinople.

Affairs in the political life of Bohemia now became very complicated, since the ruling family had grown very large but there were still no laws of succession. This resulted in a constant struggle for primacy that would plague Bohemia for a century and a half. Břetislav I had adopted the principle of seniority,[15] a precarious guide because successive princes invariably wished to secure the throne for their eldest sons. Vratislav II (r. 1061–92), Břetislav's second son, did not acknowledge his brother's rights. Gathering his forces, he completed the conquest of Moravia and in 1061 took Prague. With Vratislav on the throne, the fortunes of the Slavic liturgical language were temporarily reversed. He invited the Slavic monks to return to Sázava. Emmeram (the son of Procopius) became their new abbot. Indeed, Vratislav attempted to secure the continuing existence of the Cyrillomethodian tradition in Bohemia. Choosing what he thought to be a propitious moment—after differences between him and Pope Gregory VII over his support of Henry IV were settled—he dispatched an embassy to Rome (1078–79) that sought to obtain canonical recognition of the Slavic liturgical language. Such acceptance was not without precedent. Some two hundred years earlier popes Hadrian II (868) and John VIII (879) had given their *nihil obstat* to the Church Slavonic liturgy in Great Moravia. However, that was a time when the winds of reconciliation were wafting between Byzantium and Rome; now there were gusts of rancor. The international atmosphere was not in the least mitigated by the domestic one. The hostilities between Vratislav and his brother Jaromir, the bishop of Prague and a Latinist, were bound to harm the Slavic cause. Indeed, recognition was denied in a bull of Gregory VII (1080), a decision that virtually doomed the Slavic liturgical language in Bohemia.

The Slavic monks spent their last years at Sázava under Božetěch, who became their new abbot in 1085. He was a talented artist and sculptor who is thought to have decorated the churches of the monastery. Only fragments of this artistic endeavor remain, but Božetěch is generally credited with founding a school of Czech religious art. In 1095, Sázava received part of the relics of the first Russian martyrs, Boris and Gleb. But the inevitable end of Sázava as a center of Slavic culture came during the reign of Břetislav II (1092–1100). Being a Latinist, he had no intention of harboring an activity that had failed to gain papal recognition. In 1096–97 the Slavic liturgical language was forbidden at Sázava and its monks were expelled for the last time. By 1100, the Slavic Church officially ceased to exist in Bohemia. The older tradition preserved an amazing mixture of Church Slavonic terminology and early Czech in the spiritual hymn *Hospodine pomilui ny*, which is one of the proofs of the popularity of the Church Slavonic tradition in Bohemia. There was a brief but distinctly artificial revival of Church Slavonic in the fourteenth century under Charles IV (1346–

78), for which the pope gave special dispensation, apparently in the hope of securing the support of the king of Bohemia for a crusade against the Turks. Croatian monks had to be summoned in order to recreate the Church Slavonic tradition in Bohemia.

During the last decade of the eleventh century, Sázava became a Benedictine monastery of the Latin rite. Evidently the very recollection of the Cyrillomethodian tradition in Bohemia was considered heretical. With the disappearance of the last vestiges of its Byzantine cultural inheritance, Bohemia was completely absorbed into the Latin sphere of influence. In the twelfth century, Latin replaced Slavic as the language of both the liturgy and the literature, which was subsequently partly supplemented by German. And it was not until the end of the thirteenth century that the Czech literary language started to develop.

The ecclesiastic problems of the state proved easier to solve than the political ones. By violating the principle of seniority in favor of his brother Bořivoj, Břetislav II plunged Bohemia into a protracted civil war.

Bohemian Literature in Church Slavonic and Latin

The Ludmila and Wenceslas Legends

As a result of the persecution of Slavic liturgy and literary language in Bohemia and the subsequent triumph of Latin language and literature, virtually all of the original Church Slavonic texts that were written during the tenth and eleventh centuries were destroyed. What is known of this tradition is derived primarily from later Russian and Croatian compilations that found their way abroad and survived in their respective literary heritages and/or from local Latin monuments that reworked the Bohemian compositions. Unfortunately, these sources cannot completely account for all the perished manuscripts, whose existence, in some cases, is simply a matter of postulation. An example of this is the nonextant first work of Bohemian Church Slavonic literature, the *Life of Ludmila*, dating, perhaps, from as early as late in the decade in which she was murdered. This work is believed to have served as the model for, and been partially preserved in, the

Church Slavonic extract known as the *Prologue Life of Saint Ludmila* and to have been reshaped in the Latin legend about her passion, *Fuit in provincia Boemorum*. Furthermore, the latter work was adapted and incorporated into Christian's *Vita et passio sancti Wenceslai et sancte Ludmile avie eius*.

Bohemian literature begins by introducing a genre which was unknown to Slavic literature at that time—namely, the lives of princes. The first links in a chain of legends that would follow later in Russia (for example, the narratives about Boris and Gleb) and Serbia (the works about Stephen Nemanja) were the aforementioned *Life of Ludmila* and the so-called *First Church Slavonic Life of Saint Wenceslas*. Today most scholars agree that this legend arose in Bohemia and was written shortly after Wenceslas's death. This legend of Saint Wenceslas is the only original Bohemian work that survived in its entirety. It was preserved in Croatia and Russia, where it experienced retouches of form and content. The cult of Saint Wenceslas penetrated into Russia before the end of the eleventh century, a fact attested to by the occurrence of his name in the Russian princely house and by the existence of a service to him in Russian ecclesiastic manuscripts since 1095. Here, too, his more complete *Life* was extracted for an abbreviated one arranged according to the calendar, namely, the *Prologue Life of Saint Wenceslas*.

The *First Church Slavonic Life of Saint Wenceslas* represents the literary link in the cultural continuity between Great Moravia and Přemyslide Bohemia. It is clearly the work of an author fully trained in the Cyrillomethodian tradition. The legend's Moravo-Bohemian language, its style and conciliatory treatment of historical personages mark it as a typical product of this school. It is an unadorned tale that treats Wenceslas as a pious and just man—not a saint—and portrays Boleslav as a victim of evil advisors—not himself evil. This picture of the main protagonists, coupled with the linguistic archaisms, is further testimony in favor of the work's early composition in Bohemia during the reign of Boleslav I. However, those scholars who denied the cultural continuity between the Slavic states in question placed this legend at various later dates: for example, ca. 980 (Králík); ca. 1000 (Urbánek); at Sázava (Fiala, Novotný, Vacek); toward the end of activity at Sázava (Bartoš, Kalandra). Indeed, Novotný and Urbánek even considered this legend a translation from Latin. All of the surviving manuscripts are of a late date: the Croatian Glagolitic manuscripts are from the fourteenth and fifteenth centuries; the Russian Cyrillic manuscripts, from the sixteenth and seventeenth centuries. Of the former [16] there are three complete copies in breviaries from 1379, ca. 1400 and 1459, and two fragments. The question as to which of the versions, the Croatian or the Russian, is the closest to the initial text of the original legend has been disputed among historians and philologists. For example, Jakobson and Weingart came to opposite conclusions.[17]

The first Latin legend about Saint Wenceslas is known by its opening words, *Crescente fide* (the original of which is not preserved), and is thought by the majority of scholars to date from shortly after the death of Boleslav I (d. 967). Dobrovský dated this work between the twelfth and thirteenth centuries and considered Gumpold's *Vita* to be its source. This opinion was later reechoed by F. Vacek and after him by J. Slavík.[18] It is now generally assumed that the author of this legend based his work on the older Church Slavonic legends about Ludmila and Wenceslas, that is, the *Life of Ludmila and the *First Church Slavonic Life of Saint Wenceslas*, which he supplemented by adding historical and legendary details derived from local traditions. Another generally accepted assumption is that the author was a Czech and that the work originated in Bohemia. This appears to be confirmed by the fact that the legend was well known in Bohemia and was utilized by other Czech authors. For example, it served as a source for Christian's work, and it was transcribed by a native—the so-called Bohemian Recension of *Crescente fide*.

With the spread of the cult of Wenceslas to the Latin west, *Crescente fide* became known in Bavaria, where it was rewritten (hence the Bavarian Recension), somewhat abridged and altered. There are a number of hypotheses about the relation between the two recensions. The most noteworthy discrepancy between them reflects the politics of the Western Church. The distinction of the first Christian prince among the Czechs is accorded not to Bořivoj, whose alleged baptism by Methodius connected the Bohemian princely house to Cyrillomethodian Christianity—a memory they were striving to erase—but to his son, Spytihněv, who placed Bohemia under Bavarian ecclesiastic jurisdiction. Wenceslas's cult also penetrated to Italy, where his biography (the Bavarian Recension) served as the source for Gumpold's *Vita* and for the *Vita* written by the monk Laurentius of

Monte Cassino. It is assumed that the latter work was compiled between the years 989–97 from material provided primarily by Bishop, later Saint, Adalbert, who came to Monte Cassino in 989. This work was not known in Bohemia.

The Bavarian Recension of *Crescente fide* is found in an eleventh-century Munich manuscript, while the Bohemian Recension is preserved in the Stuttgart *Passionale*, dating from the first half of the twelfth century.[19]

It is possible that the Latin legend *Fuit in provincia Boemorum* is older than *Crescente fide*; however, its date is uncertain. Chaloupecký believed it was the oldest of the Latin literary works that originated in Bohemia. On the other hand, Králík dated it to the second half of the eleventh century, while Třeštík attributed both *Crescente fide* and *Fuit* to the activity of the monks of Regensburg to whom, he felt, the cultural life of tenth-century Bohemia was indebted. The role played by Regensburg certainly has to be taken into account, since it was the diocese to which the Přemyslides belonged and which controlled the ecclesiastic affairs of Bohemia at that time. The postulated Church Slavonic *Life of Ludmila*—ostensibly written after her translation from Tetín to Prague (925)—aimed, it is assumed, to promote her canonization. This work, however, would not have been sanctioned by the Western Church. In order to have her sanctity recognized there, a Latin Vita had to be written. The extent to which *Fuit* reflects the nonextant Church Slavonic *Life of Ludmila* cannot be ascertained. Chaloupecký's assertion that it is a nearly verbatim translation of the original Church Slavonic text still awaits substantiation.[20]

Fuit is preserved in numerous manuscripts (twenty-four), the oldest of which, the Dresden Manuscript, dates from the end of the twelfth century. This particular manuscript is thought to have been produced at the Sázava monastery.[21]

Around the year 980, Gumpold, the bishop of Mantua, was commissioned by Emperor Otto II (967–83) to write a Vita of Saint Wenceslas. Since the Italian author was not familiar with the local tradition concerning the saint, he drew much of his material from an earlier Latin work, *Crescente fide*. The facts that there is no mention of Bořivoj in Gumpold's *Vita* (which begins with the words *Studiorum igitur genera*), and that Spytihněv is credited with being the first

Christian prince of Bohemia, seem to indicate that the author was familiar with the Bavarian Recension. Gumpold's work is preserved in many manuscripts from the eleventh and twelfth centuries. The most famous is the Wolfenbüttel manuscript—dedicated to the wife of Boleslav II, Emma (d. 1006)—which was later utilized by Christian, and still later (in the thirteenth century) served as one of the sources for two other Latin Vitae about Saint Wenceslas that are known by their opening words as *Oportet nos* and *Ut annuncietur*.

Some scholars have suggested that *Ut annuncietur* was originally written in Slavic and was used by the Slavic translator of Gumpold's *Vita* for certain details (for example, the prisoner miracles). This is a moot point, since no Slavic manuscript has ever been found, and is a view that was rejected emphatically by Vašica.[22] However, Gumpold's *Vita* became known in Bohemia and gave rise to the so-called *Second Church Slavonic Life of Saint Wenceslas* (sometimes also referred to as the Nikol'skij Legend).[23]

The most noteworthy (and controversial) of all the Bohemian Latin legends is the *Vita et passio sancti Wenceslai et sancte Ludmile avie eius* by Christian, a monk from the Břevnov monastery. It is more commonly known as *Legenda Christiani* (i.e., *Christian's Legend*, hereafter *CL*). Though in a contemporary sense it is not an entirely original work because of the author's exploitation of other literary models—*Crescente fide*, Gumpold's *Vita* (*Life of Ludmila?*, *Life of Constantine?*, *Life of Methodius?*, *Life of Naum?*, other ??)—it is nevertheless unique. In the dual legend of Wenceslas and Ludmila, Christian created a totally new, organic literary work. This characterization of *CL* might well meet with objections from those scholars who view this work as a chronicle—namely, a "historia sacra et prophana." Indeed, much scholarly effort has been expended to determine the scope of filial dependence of the Wenceslas and Ludmila legends and their chronological framework. The question of whether Christian borrowed or conceived on his own the material from which he wove his text acquires less importance when viewed in the light of the Middle Ages' perception of literary originality. For imitation, indeed copying, was not considered plagiarism but an indication of the author's erudition and stylistic resourcefulness. We can certainly give Christian full credit for that. A more detailed discussion of this work follows below.[24]

Just as Christian used Gumpold's *Vita* et al. to create a new Latin legend about Wenceslas and Ludmila, so an anonymous Bohemian author used it to compose a new Slavic legend, the aforementioned *Second Church Slavonic Life of Saint Wenceslas* (the name given to it by Pekař). This text shared a similar fate with the *First Church Slavonic Life*. It, too, did not survive in the country of its origin[25] but managed to find its way to Russia, where it was transcribed from Glagolitic into Cyrillic. However, this legend was not known to exist until 1904, when the Russian Slavist N. K. Nikol'skij discovered it preserved in two redactions: the Kazan' Manuscript, dating from the early sixteenth century, and the Petersburg Manuscript from the second half of the same century. Analyses of these manuscripts revealed that they were indeed based on Gumpold's *Vita* (with some researchers claiming as much as two-thirds of it to be direct translation). However, these manuscripts also contained parts that appear to have been drawn from *Crescente fide*, a fair amount of rephrasing of the underlying source, as well as wholly original supplements. The differences between the Church Slavonic redactions and Gumpold's Latin legend were noted in detail by Nikol'skij in his extensive introduction to the publication of these works.

The search for the source of these differences and supplements has led scholars to assume the existence in Bohemia of (an)other unpreserved Wenceslas legend(s) in Latin (even, possibly, [an]other Church Slavonic one[s]), containing some or all the details which this work and other works—both contemporary and later—utilized, viz., the sermon *Licet plura* (Nikol'skij); the Laurentius *Vita* and *Oportet nos* (Urbánek); and *Ut annuncietur* (Vašica).[26] For example, the marriage motif—not mentioned in any other text save *CL*, where it is noted in passing—is richly developed only by this Slavic author. Sobolevskij, who conducted a systematic investigation of Church Slavonic translations from Latin, was inclined to consider the translator-author of this work to be the same person who translated the *Sermons* (*Besědy*) of Gregory the Great. Characteristic of both translators was a propensity for verbatim translation, often at the expense of comprehensibility. Indeed, the language of the "Slavic Gumpold" is extraordinarily convoluted in places because of his attempt to render verbatim the Latin sentence structure, with its sophisticated means of syntactic dependency.

It has been generally assumed that Gumpold's *Vita* was known in Bohemia not long after its composition, and was translated either at the turn of the century—that is, 994–1000 (Sobolevskij, Chaloupecký, Pekař, Vašica) or during the eleventh century (Nikol'skij). Some Czech scholars (Urbánek, Bartoš, Graus, Králík) have viewed this work as originating at the Sázava monastery.[27]

The rise of the cult of Saint Wenceslas also occasioned the creation in Church Slavonic of a liturgical service and canon in his honor. This work, known as the *Service and Canon in Honor of Saint Wenceslas*, is now generally regarded (in agreement with Sobolevskij and Pekař et al.) as having originated in Bohemia, probably toward the end of the tenth century but certainly not later than the eleventh. Some scholars had considered it to be either of South Slavic origin (Novotný, Vondrák, and Vašica, who later changed his mind to Bohemian) or Russian (Krofta, Serebrjanskij, Weingart).[28] It was preserved in Russia in two manuscripts of liturgical menologies dating from the eleventh and twelfth centuries (the latter being a copy of the former). The older manuscript, the *Novgorod Liturgical Menology* (1095–96), represents the oldest copy of a manuscript associated with the Wenceslas cycle.

In creating his eulogy on the martyrdom and translation of Saint Wenceslas, the author adhered closely to the Byzantine models in this genre. Such models were known in both Moravia and Bohemia. However, since no specific Greek model has ever been found for this work—if indeed it ever existed—it should be regarded as an original Church Slavonic work. Also supporting this assumptiom is the kinship of language this monument shares with the *Kievan Leaflets* and themes it shares with both the *First and Second Church Slavonic Lives*. It presents further evidence of the cultural link between Great Moravia and Bohemia. Moreover, its similarities (in motifs, stylistics, and so on) with the Church Slavonic *Canon of Saint Demetrius of Thessalonica*—which was certainly composed in Great Moravia by either Constantine (Vašica) or Methodius (Jakobson)—as well as with the Greek canon of the same saint (the Slavic translation of which is preserved in the same menology where the *Service and Canon of Saint Wenceslas* is found), seem to substantiate cultural continuity between these two Slavic States.[29]

Closely connected with ancient Bohemian hagiography are several Church Slavonic abbreviated legends—namely, the *Prologue Life of Saint Wenceslas, Prologue Life of Saint Ludmila,* and *Prologue Translation of Saint Wenceslas.* All of these texts have been preserved in East Slavic recensions (primarily Russian), the earliest dating from the late thirteenth or early fourteenth century. The history of these monuments is exceedingly complex and still awaits a definitive solution, as do the date and place of their origin. A detailed analysis of these works was made by J. Serebrjanskij, who examined ninety-eight prologues for the month of September (for the Lives) and sixty-nine for the month of March (for the *Translation*), dating from the thirteenth/ fourteenth to the fifteenth centuries. That, however, still left many extant manuscripts (particularly of a later date) unexamined. He came to the conclusion, to summarize briefly, that (1) these legends were written after the *Service and Canon* came to Russia; (2) the two Lives are closely related and were probably composed by the same author at the same time (second half of the twelfth or beginning of the thirteenth century) after reworking the Church Slavonic legends of these saints; (3) the *Life of Saint Wenceslas* was influenced by the Church Slavonic **Life of Ludmila* (which underlies the prologue version about her) and the *Second Church Slavonic Life*; (4) the Russian *Narrative* (*Skazanie*) about Boris and Gleb was used as a model; and (5) the date of composition and underlying source of the *Translation* is the same as the *Life of Saint Wenceslas* but its author is not. More recently, however, the date of origin of these monuments has been moved back to late in the eleventh century because of evidence based on internal analysis. Previous datings purportedly were based primarily on the history of the monuments' composition. It was pointed out that there was a compositional connection between the abbreviated form of the saint's life (i.e., the *Prologue*) and the *Service and Canon*. For example, liturgically the reading of an abbreviated life was required as the *synaxarion* after chanting the sixth canon. In Russia, the Byzantine *synaxarion* was called "Prologue." Nevertheless, as stated above, the date and place of origin of these prologue works are controversial and have been assigned to different times (from the tenth to thirteenth centuries) and to different places (Bohemia, the Sázava monastery in Bohemia, and Russia).

The most enigmatic of the prologue legends is the *Life of Saint Ludmila*. Of all the details reported therein, many correspond with facts (with some minor deviations) recorded only in such Latin legends as *Fuit, CL,* and *Diffundente sole*. Of these, only *CL* contains them all. However, *CL* could not have served as the only source for this Prologue because of the contradictory information it contains (cf., e.g., the number of daughters or Bořivoj's age when he died) as well as information that is unique to this work alone (e.g., the exact hour of Ludmila's death, her place of burial). Moreover, the emphasis in the *Prologue* is on the glorification of Ludmila, whose faith influenced Bořivoj, that is to say, Bořivoj became a Christian only after marrying her. The uniqueness of this work, which, apparently, was an abbreviated version of a more elaborated *Life*, reflects the underlying, original source that was, it is believed, the nonextant Church Slavonic *Life of Ludmila*. It also suggests the existence of this saint's cult.

Although Serebrjanskij singled out the influence only of the Church Slavonic *Life of Ludmila* and *Second Church Slavonic Life* on the *Prologue Life of Saint Wenceslas*, Weingart has shown that it was based extensively on the *First Church Slavonic Life*, with which it often has nearly verbatim correspondence. The same can be said for the *Prologue Translation*, which utilized only the concluding portion of the *First Church Slavonic Life*. An interesting feature of all three prologues is that they retain vestiges of great antiquity.[30]

The great schism (1054) that split the Eastern and Western churches resulted in even greater intolerance of the Slavic liturgy in Bohemia and of the saint most closely connected with its Cyrillomethodian beginnings, Ludmila. Veneration of her, it seems, was to be consigned to oblivion. It is reported that in 1100, Heřman, the bishop of Prague, did not want to hear talk of her sanctity. Apparently in response to this attitude, a Bohemian author, writing in Latin, composed an apology for Ludmila in the form of a homily known as *Factum est*. It is assumed to date from the late eleventh century, though the oldest preserved manuscripts are from the second half of the fourteenth. Pekař praised this work as the most beautiful Bohemian legend, while Chaloupecký considered it the most poetic work produced in Bohemia during the Middle Ages. In it the author defends the veneration of Ludmila, whom he extols as the first intercessor for and patroness of the Czechs.

For a long time *Factum est* was regarded as part of another legend, *Diffundente sole*. However, not only is this homily found as a separate work in the majority of manuscripts (ten out of seventeen), but it differs from *Diffundente* both in source material and in its style of rhythmic prose. The homily is drawn almost entirely from *CL*, which it reworks in a more florid manner. It is interesting to note that Jakobson believed that its probable Church Slavonic prototype inspired the eulogy to Olga in the Russian *Primary Chronicle*.[31]

Latin legends about Saint Wenceslas that were written during the Gothic period at the peak of the Middle Ages began to synthesize details found in earlier legends with new motifs. One of the first works of this type is *Oriente iam sole*. In his time Pekař considered it the prototype for all the subsequent legends about Wenceslas of the thirteenth and fourteenth centuries. The later discovery of a manuscript of another legend from about the same date, *Ut annuncietur*, makes his assertion problematic. Be that as it may, *Oriente* still represents a very important development in the evolution of the cycle of legends about Saint Wenceslas. It was written in the middle of the thirteenth century (ca. 1250), allegedly by an anonymous priest from the Saint Vitus cathedral in Prague, and has been preserved in numerous manuscripts from the thirteenth to fifteenth centuries. Being some three hundred years removed from the historical events, the author drew freely from the earlier legends, *Crescente fide*, Gumpold, and especially *CL* (*Ut annuncietur* exhibits a reworking of the same sources). However, he supplemented the details from these sources with flights of fancy from his own imagination and, more importantly, added a new dimension to the portrait of Wenceslas—one that would be emulated in the future. For the first time Wenceslas appears not merely as a Christian saint celebrated for his exemplary life and glorious miracles, but also as a protector and liberator of his nation, that is, as *dux perpetuus*. And this new aspect would be amplified and popularized in the last *Vita* (ca.1355) about Saint Wenceslas written by the king of Bohemia, Charles IV, which drew on all the available sources but emphasized Wenceslas's chivalry and statesmanship. Thus Charles shaped Wenceslas in his own image and juxtaposed himself to the saint as the accomplisher of what Wenceslas had inaugurated.

A number of themes that were introduced by the author of *Oriente* corrupted the historicity of events and persons. For example, in this work we hear that Wenceslas's life was a struggle against paganism; that his mother, Drahomira, was an unregenerate pagan and an accomplice in his murder; that he received the relics of Saint Vitus as a gift and therefore built a church in his honor; that he obtained independence for his country which formerly was a tributary of the empire; and so on. Also, several of the miracles added to the text are of a completely different nature than the older, borrowed ones—for example, the resurrection of a dead girl. Finally, *Oriente* remained true to the Latin concept of Bohemian ecclesiastic history at the time of its writing, a fact that resulted in the Slavic contribution being conveniently passed over in silence.[32]

The work that caused almost as much controversy as *CL* is the legend *Diffundente sole*. However, no new arguments have been advanced recently that would contradict its late-thirteenth- or early-fourteenth-century origins. In its essence *Diffundente* is an apology for the use of the Slavic liturgical language, and as such it anticipates the revival of Slavic letters under Charles IV. This work is preserved in seven manuscripts, the oldest of which dates from the late fourteenth or early fifteenth century. All of these manuscripts are combined with the homily *Factum est*.[33]

The chronology, hypothetical and real, of the works discussed above can be summarized as follows:

Life of Ludmila—920s?

First Church Slavonic Life of Saint Wenceslas—930s

Crescente fide—970s

Fuit in provincia Boemorum—tenth century ?

Gumpold's *Vita*—980s

Laurentius's *Vita*—late tenth/early eleventh century

Legenda Christiani—990s

Second Church Slavonic Life of Saint Wenceslas—late tenth/early eleventh century

Service and Canon in Honor of Saint Wenceslas—late tenth century

Prologue Life of Saint Ludmila—late eleventh century

Prologue Life of Saint Wenceslas—late eleventh century

Prologue Translation of Saint Wenceslas—late eleventh century

Factum est—late eleventh century

Oportet nos—late eleventh/early twelfth century

Ut annuncietur—mid-thirteenth century

Oriente iam sole—mid-thirteenth century

Diffundente sole—late thirteenth/early fourteenth century

Charles IV's *Vita*—mid-fourteenth century

Other Church Slavonic Works

Among the legends translated from Latin into Church Slavonic that Sobolevskij published at the turn of the century (1903) was the *Life of Saint Vitus*, the Sicilian child martyr of the fourth century and patron saint of Bohemia since the tenth. In Sobolevskij's opinion, this legend (the oldest copy of which is preserved in Cyrillic among the East Slavic manuscripts of the twelfth-century *Uspenskij sbornik*) was translated from Latin during the ninth century in Great Moravia. Shortly before Sobolevskij's work appeared, Vajs discovered a Glagolitic fragment in Prague dealing with the life of this saint (the *Office in Honor of Saint Vitus*), which he published (1901). Since he was not aware of Sobolevskij's manuscript, he came to the conclusion that the *Office* had been translated from Latin in the fourteenth century by a Croatian Glagolitic scribe working in Prague. Almost a half-century later Vašica discovered, in a Latin breviary of Benedictine nuns in Prague, a Latin fragment corresponding closely to Vajs's Glagolitic fragment. Moreover, he pointed out the parallels between the Cyrillic Church Slavonic *Life* of the twelfth century and Vajs's Glagolitic fragment. His analysis of the Cyrillic *Life* and the Glagolitic *Office* showed that there was a clear relation between the two manuscripts, and he concluded that both texts used an older common source whose prototype dated from tenth-century Bohemia.

Additional proof of the common ancestry of these manuscripts was provided by L. Matějka (1973), who in turn discovered in Zagreb, in a *Passionale martyrum* of the tenth century, a manuscript of *Passio sancti Viti* whose text corresponded almost verbatim to more than ninety percent of the Church Slavonic *Life* found in the *Uspenskij sbornik*. Matějka's conclusion was that the Cyrillic *Life of Saint Vitus* preserved in the *Uspenskij sbornik* must be closely related to the Latin text that was used for the Church Slavonic translation contained therein. Furthermore, the Prague Glagolitic *Office* (Vajs's fragment) and the text in the *Uspenskij sbornik* (collectively referred to by him as the *First Church Slavonic Life of Saint Vitus*) have a common Church Slavonic ancestor that was translated from a Latin text related to the Zagreb *Passio sancti Viti*.

Shortly after Matějka's discovery, G. Kappel (1974) published a Latin text of the *Life of Saint Vitus* based on a variety of Latin manuscripts in the Vienna National Library and the Collegiate Library at the Heiligenkreuz monastery that appeared to be textually even closer to the earliest Slavic version. And Mareš considered the unknown protograph of Kappel's later text to be the direct source of the Church Slavonic legend in the *Uspenskij sbornik*.

The so-called *Second Church Slavonic Life of Saint Vitus* (in Matějka's terminology)—which is much younger and is textually different from the *First Church Slavonic Life of Saint Vitus*—is preserved in the form of an *Office* in Croatian Church Slavonic breviaries of the thirteenth and fourteenth centuries (Vatikanski 6 [1379], Pašmanski, Ljubljanski, Novoljanski, and so on). Its exact protograph is not known. However, the text in the Latin breviary printed in Venice in 1521 corresponds closely to the *Second Church Slavonic Life of Saint Vitus* (as does the text in *Legenda aurea sive Chronica Lombardica*).[34]

What still remains problematic and controversial with regard to the *First Church Slavonic Life of Saint Vitus* is where and when did it arise, and how did it reach the East Slavs. It is quite plausible that Bohemia of the tenth and eleventh centuries provided the proper climate and logical setting for the origin of the Church Slavonic translation of the *First Church Slavonic Life of Saint Vitus*. And though some researchers (Havránek, Weingart) have suggested an eleventh-century dating, the translation is more widely thought to have taken place in tenth-century Bohemia. The place and date of the translation of Vajs's Glagolitic fragment is still being questioned by Mareš.[35]

Not directly related to the above but nevertheless noteworthy is the publication by Mareš of a hitherto unknown work about Saint

Vitus, the *Prologue Life of Saint Vitus*. He considers this work to be a mechanically abbreviated version of the more complete *Life* in the *Uspenskij sbornik*. However, Matějka believes that it is an East Church Slavonic adaptation of the Cyrillic *Life of Saint Vitus* and that it deviates enough from its underlying source to be regarded as a separate work. He thus calls it the *Third Church Slavonic Life of Saint Vitus*.[36]

Whereas many manuscripts preserved in other Slavic regions are presumed to have originated in Bohemia, there is one manuscript about which there is no doubt with regard to its origins, the *Prague Glagolitic Fragments*. Although the text is brief and somewhat distorted, it nevertheless comprises the only direct evidence of the Cyrillomethodian literary heritage in Bohemia proper. In fact, its ancient Bohemian origins were never doubted by its discoverer and publishers, and since that time its linguistic peculiarities have been viewed as characteristic for Church Slavonic monuments of Bohemian provenance. Furthermore, the discovery of these *Fragments* brought about a reexamination of the primacy of Cyrillic over Glagolitic.

The *Fragments* were discovered in the Prague capitular library in 1855 by K. A. C. Höfler, pasted to the inside jacket of a Latin manuscript. They were published two years later by him and P. Šafařík (*Glagolitische Fragmente*, Prague, 1857). In the introduction, Höfler dated the Latin manuscript in which the *Fragments* were found to the eleventh century. Šafařík followed with a detailed analysis of the partially deteriorated *Fragments* from which a facsimile and transcriptions were made into Cyrillic and Latin. He came to the conclusion that the *Fragments* originated in the "Bohemo-Moravo-Pannonian" region and were written sometime between 862 and 950. Since these *Fragments* preserved a portion of an Office of the Eastern Rite that was originally translated from Greek (evening prayers of a Good Friday Office?), some of its earlier investigators could not believe that they were of Bohemian origin or were in use there. Therefore, they were either considered to be of Bulgarian origin (Pastrnek, Vondrák, Jagić [Bulgaro-Russian]), or were ascribed to a much later period—namely, the fourteenth century during the revival of the Church Slavonic (Glagolitic) tradition in Bohemia under Charles IV (Makušev, Voskresenskij). However, there were several older scholars who anticipated the contemporary view about the *Fragments*. For example, I.

Sreznevskij believed that they were either completely or at least partially transcribed from a manuscript of Russian provenance, and N. Grunskij refuted their Bulgarian origins and later date (his point of view was subsequently adopted by Jagić and Vondrák). Grunskij also pointed out the prominent part the Czech language (that is, the Bohemian recension of Church Slavonic) played in the *Fragments* (in particular, fol. 2), and the manuscript's similarity in paleography and language with the *Kievan Leaflets*.

The majority of contemporary scholars now maintain that the *Prague Glagolitic Fragments* date from the eleventh century and are indeed of Bohemian provenance. Weingart believed that fol. 2 was older than fol. 1 (both not being from the same manuscript), and could be dated to the first half of the eleventh century (fol. 1 to the end of it). As concerns the *Fragments*'s prototype, Mareš assumed that a Russian manuscript from the eleventh century was the probable model for the last Bohemian copy. This view was supported by Havránek. If that was indeed the case, it would be the first and only known document to have been transcribed from Cyrillic into Glagolitic. Such a supposition is not at all inconceivable, for it has been shown that Cyrillic was known and used in Bohemia (Horálek). Moreover, the ties between Sázava and Kievan Rus' have been well established. An interesting feature of this monument is the intermingling of three different linguistic elements—literary Church Slavonic, Czech, and Russian.[37]

The problem of determining the date and origin of the oldest Czech spiritual hymn, *O Lord, have mercy on us*, is very complicated and still remains unresolved. For a long time tradition ascribed this hymn to Vojtěch (Bishop Adalbert). It was first mentioned in the thirteenth century, when three separate entries in Czech-Latin chronicles (under the years 1249, 1279, and 1283) recorded only the hymn's first line. The entire hymn was preserved in manuscripts from 1380 and 1397, the latter being musically notated. Though the first manifestations of Slavic musical culture undoubtedly began to take shape in Great Moravia, the evidence in support of this is controversial. And this makes debatable the question of whether or not the Cyrillomethodian Byzantine musical heritage was transferred to Bohemia.

It is not unreasonable to assume that the first hymnal (musical) monuments in Bohemia would develop out of the traditions of the Slavic liturgy. Also, a book of church hymns known as the *Hirmolo-*

gion—translated, it is assumed, from Greek into Church Slavonic at the time of the Moravian Mission—was known from musically notated Russian manuscripts. These hymns could have served as a model for the Czech hymn. Another possible model could have been the hymn *Encomium to Gregory the Theologian*. It is attributed to Constantine or one of his disciples and reveals a close structural correspondence to the Czech hymn.

In a detailed analysis and reconstruction of the Czech hymn, Jakobson came to the conclusion that its original redaction was Church Slavonic, and that it was close in its linguistic and poetic composition to other such monuments of the Cyrillomethodian legacy. Mareš's most recent reconstruction of the Czech hymn agrees with Jakobson's in its most essential feature, namely, the hymn's original octosyllabic meter. Mareš also attributes this work to the Cyrillomethodian tradition of Church Slavonic poetry. Furthermore, the results of Racek's musical study of the genesis of the Czech hymn has corroborated Jakobson's reconstruction. Racek showed that the tripartite structure of the melody corresponded exactly to the three parts of the text. However, Jakobson does not date the Czech hymn but alludes to the correctness of the pioneers of Czech literary scholarship who found in this work either "a remnant of the Slavic liturgy perhaps from the time of Bořivoj" (Jungmann), or "an ancient song composed perhaps as early as the ninth century" (Vlček). For his part, Mareš dates this work to the tenth century.

In contrast to Jakobson's and Mareš's view is V. Flajšhans's earlier assessment of the Czech hymn. He did not believe that Church Slavonic poetry had struck firm roots in Bohemia and dated this work to the thirteenth century. Weingart, who viewed it as an admixture of Czech and Church Slavonic, also suggested a later date, placing it in the second half of the eleventh century. Such a wide range in dating (ninth to thirteenth centuries) is perhaps inevitable when the earliest surviving copies of the text date from the late fourteenth century—a fact that apparently has detracted from the monument's antiquity in the minds of certain scholars.[38]

The last of the works included in this book are two prayers, *Prayer Against the Devil* and *Prayer to the Holy Trinity*. These prayers, particularly the latter one, are of especial interest for the history of the beginnings of Christianity in Bohemia, since they include the "newest" martyrs and missionary saints from Bohemia, Poland, and Russia as well as from England, Germany, and Scandinavia. However, from an artistic standpoint these monuments are among the least interesting. They do not display great literary merit and are made up, in essence, of a series of supplications addressed to a wide variety of saints venerated in the East and West. Of greater interest is the language of the monuments, which in places shows great antiquity, and the material they offer to students of devotional literature. They are representative of a special genre, litany prayer, one of the basic types of prayers found in ancient Christian liturgies that arose in both the Eastern and Western churches. Although these prayers are preserved only in Russian manuscripts dating from the thirteenth to sixteenth centuries, they are undoubtedly from a much earlier period and probably originated in the Slavic West. The general assumption is that they had their origins in Bohemia, where they were translated from Latin into Church Slavonic while this language was still being used for the liturgy and ecclesiastic literature. Sobolevskij believed that these prayers could be dated to the time of Procopius and the flourishing of the Sázava monastery. And although Dvornik has also dated these prayers to that period, the actual time of their composition, as Ingham notes, is not at all certain.[39]

The Debate

Within a third of a century from its inception as a political entity, and while only rudimentarily Christian, Bohemia produced two native saints in the persons of its earlier rulers, Ludmila and Wenceslas. Their murders during a time of exacerbated political strife were soon considered martyrdoms, and they joined the hallowed ranks of Christian dignitaries. Indeed, they were accorded the unique honor of becoming the first Christian martyrs among the Slavs and also the first Slavic sovereigns to be canonized. As their cult spread—eventually reaching beyond the borders of Bohemia—it provided material for accounts of their lives. And the works written about these individuals, who initially exemplified Bohemian spirituality and inspired a sense of national self-awareness, marked the beginning of Bohemian literature.

It is perhaps not surprising that from the very outset two literary traditions were engendered, for it appears that Bohemia received at least as much of its Christianity in Cyrillomethodian form as it did in Latin. Whether at any given point during the approximately two-century life of the Slavic-language church in Bohemia Slavic itself held sway over Latin, or vice versa, cannot be determined. However, a striking feature of this literature was the production of both Slavic and Latin versions of the same subject matter, but often with differences in detail. Unfortunately, none of these works has reached us in manuscripts that could be directly ascribed to their original author; nor have any manuscripts come down to us from the period of their alleged composition. As a result, numerous controversies have ensued, which to date have not been resolved to the complete satisfaction of all the specialists in the many disciplines that became involved in the debate: archeology, history, linguistics, and literature. The major question has been whether (and if so, how, and to what extent) Bohemian Christianity and its Church Slavonic usage are connected with the Cyrillomethodian traditions of Great Moravia. In other words, was there continuity in the cultivation of the Slavic liturgy and the Slavic literary language between Great Moravia and Přemyslide Bohemia, revealing the latter as the cultural and political heir of the former?

At the center of this issue lies the question of the authenticity and dating of a Latin work by the monk Christian, *Vita et passio sancti Wenceslai et sancte Ludmile avie eius* (*CL*). For before the discovery of Church Slavonic works of Bohemian provenance in the nineteenth century, the premise of a Cyrillomethodian tradition in Bohemia was predicated on the opening chapters of *CL*, which speak about: (1) the conversion of Moravia by Constantine; (2) the latter's successful defense of the Slavic liturgical language before the pope; (3) the career of Archbishop Methodius and his relations with Svatopluk; (4) the baptism of Prince Bořivoj by Methodius; and (5) the founding of the first Christian churches in Bohemia. Furthermore, the problem of determining the relationship of *CL* to the other works dealing with Wenceslas and Ludmila became pivotal to the entire discussion. Hence, the following survey is a summary of the debate to date.[40] For specific individual issues—for instance, the person of Christian, the baptism of Bořivoj, the relationship between the Přemyslides and

Slavníks, and so on—the works mentioned in the notes can be consulted.

The opening words of the prologue to CL, the dedication of the work to the author's ostensible contemporary living relative, Bishop Adalbert (Vojtěch), appear to fix the date of its composition in the last quarter of the tenth century (the oldest extant manuscript is dated ca. 1340). This prompted the first publisher of CL in 1677, the Jesuit exponent of the Counter-Reformation in Bohemia, Bohuslav Balbín (1621–88), to proclaim that it was older than Cosmas's Chronica Boemorum (twelfth century) and an invaluable source of Bohemian history. Balbín considered the right of the Czechs to celebrate the Mass in the vernacular a legacy of the Moravian Mission.

However, the Age of Reason, with its new standards of scholarship and emphasis on facts, brought a sharply different view into focus. The credibility of CL was attacked by J. F. (Gelasius) Dobner (1719–90) and Josef Dobrovský (1753–1829) and labeled a later falsification. In Dobner's view, the cultural level of Bohemia in the tenth century was rather primitive. Nonetheless he believed that the Slavic liturgy had been instituted there, although he could not accept the validity of Christian's outspoken criticism of his father "the fratricide" (since he considered Christian the son of Boleslav I),[41] nor the sophistication of the work. Dobner concluded that CL was a late-twelfth-century compilatory falsification. Dobrovský, who is credited with being the father of modern Slavic studies, went even further than Dobner in his criticism of CL, calling it a worthless compilation of the late thirteenth or early fourteenth century. According to Dobrovský, Cosmas's Chronica Boemorum was the oldest Bohemian historical work, and he unequivocally rejected the notion of the existence of the Slavic liturgy and Slavic literature on Bohemian soil before the founding of the Sázava monastery in the eleventh century. Moreover, he argued that the Vita of Saint Wenceslas written by Gumpold (ca. 973–83), the bishop of Mantua, was not only the oldest life dealing with Wenceslas but also the source from which all the other lives about this saint originated. The source of the tale about Bořivoj's baptism by Methodius Dobrovský traced to the Latin legend Diffundente sole, which he condemned for its mythmaking.[42] Dobrovský's views were to have a strong influence on a number of subsequent scholars.

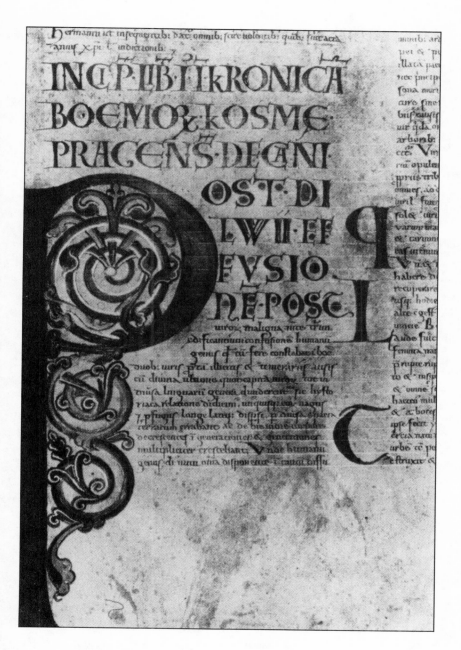

Chronica Boemorum by Cosmas of Prague, twelfth century.

In 1827, the Russian Slavist A. Vostokov, while examining systematically the manuscripts of the Rumjancev Museum (present-day Lenin Museum), discovered a manuscript dealing with Saint Wenceslas that he assumed was a translation from Latin. He published it under the heading *The Slaying of Saint Wenceslas, Prince of the Czechs*. It never occurred to Vostokov that the manuscript he had in hand was not a translation but an "original" Church Slavonic text, or that Slavic literature had existed in ancient Bohemia. Vostokov's view was not alien to Czech scholarship either. For a considerable time after the disclosure of Macedonian linguistic features in the oldest Glagolitic texts, scholarly attention was focused on the Bulgarian part of Church Slavonic culture and was diverted away from central Europe, as Roman Jakobson has noted. It turned out that the manuscript Vostokov found (which became known as the *First Church Slavonic Life of Saint Wenceslas*) was the first link in the chain of lives about Wenceslas and was written shortly after the saint's death. Its overall simplicity, broad use of Bohemianisms and archaic linguistic construction, knowledge of contemporary reality and treatment of the "dramatis personae" marked it as a monument of the early tenth century. Subsequently, opinions diverged as to which of the recensions of this legend, the so-called Vostokov Variant or the Croatian-Glagolitic Variant, most closely resembled the lost original protograph, and found R. Jakobson arguing in favor of the former while M. Weingart defended the latter.

The significance of Vostokov's find did not go unnoticed by Czech scholarship, but it failed to alter the views of such scholars as F. Palacký and P. Šafařík, who basically adhered to Dobrovský's position regarding the Slavic liturgy in general and *CL* in particular. On the other hand, W. Wattenbach was moved by Vostokov's discovery to accept the possibility of the existence of the Slavic liturgy in tenth-century Bohemia. J. Emler, the publisher of *Fontes rerum Bohemicarum* (which included a number of ancient Latin and Slavic legends) was induced to conclude, as Ludvíkovský noted, that "the liturgy originally introduced into Bohemia was Slavic and it indeed survived past the introduction of the Latin liturgy, until the end of the eleventh century." Nevertheless, both Wattenbach and Emler essentially endorsed Dobrovský's falsification theory vis-à-vis *CL*, which in their opinion all but recapitulated all the other legends dealing with Ludmila and Wenceslas. Wattenbach's endorsement of Dobrovský's view is surprising, because he had discovered at the Austrian Heiligenkreuz monastery a twelfth-century Latin life (*Subtrahente se*) describing the assassination of Ludmila, which turned out to be an adaptation of chapter 4 of *CL*. Emler, on the other hand, also followed Dobrovský with respect to the place he accorded Gumpold's *Vita* in the Wenceslas cycle of lives. It is interesting to note that the discovery in Russia of the *First Church Slavonic Life of Saint Wenceslas* was followed shortly thereafter by a series of other manuscript finds—some not entirely new—namely, the *Prologue Life of Saint Ludmila*, the *Prologue Life of Saint Wenceslas*, the *Prologue Translation of Saint Wenceslas*, and, around the middle of the century, the hitherto unknown *Canon in Honor of Saint Wenceslas*, which was discovered by I. Sreznevskij and I. Kuprijanov. However, Dobrovský's point of view had become the "official" position in Czech scholarship, and it would remain so throughout the nineteenth century.[43]

An intrinsically new ideology appeared on the scene early in the twentieth century. It impugned Cosmas as the authority on Bohemian history and challenged the dogma of Dobrovský. In 1900, the Russian philologist A. Sobolevskij showed that a group of Slavic texts (for example, *Kievan Leaflets*, *Life of Saint Vitus*, and so on) were translations from Latin and had originated during the Great Moravian period of the Slavic Church. After digesting the criticism of his opponents, he changed his opinion several years later and considered these texts to be of Bohemian provenance. Furthermore, in 1904, another Russian, N. Nikol'skij, discovered a Slavic rendition of the Latin *Vita* by Gumpold (which was to become known as the *Second Church Slavonic Life of Saint Wenceslas*). Finally, the most decisive challenge was posed by J. Pekař who, in an exhaustive study (1906) of all the available legends, reestablished *CL* as an authentic historical source of the tenth century. Pekař's rehabilitation of *CL* lent credence to the theories of earlier researchers (e.g., Šafařík) that works such as the *First Church Slavonic Life*, the *Canon in Honor of Saint Wenceslas*, the *Prague Glagolitic Fragments* et al., were of Bohemian origin. His study reached the following conclusions: (1) the *First Church Slavonic Life* was the primary source for the literary tradition concerning Saint Wenceslas; (2) the oldest preserved text was *Crescente fide*, specifically its Bavarian version; (3) the fragments *Subtrahente se* (Wattenbach's discovery), and the *Recordatus* text (on the translation of Ludmila to Prague), as well as part of *Diffundente sole*, were excerpted from *CL*. In Pekař's opinion, there was nothing in *CL* that contradicted its late-tenth-century origin. As concerns Christian's sources, Pekař acknowledged that the author could have utilized an ancient Slavic legend as the model on which the Latin legend, *Fuit in provincia Boemorum*, was based. According to Pekař, this particularly pertains to *Crescente fide* and Gumpold's *Vita* (although these sources could not account for all the information contained in *CL*). Indeed, it was this very variety of sources that had prompted earlier scholars to condemn *CL* as a compilation and a fake. Pekař, on the contrary, credited Christian with reshaping and welding diverse material into an integrated whole.[44]

The studies of both Sobolevskij and Pekař found proponents and opponents. Not finding any phonological proof of the Western origins of the texts (for example, in the *Kievan Leaflets*), G. A. Il'inskij's review of Sobolevskij's work rejected his conclusion. He maintained that the Slavic translations of the Latin manuscripts could have been made anywhere with the participation of Czech monks. The philologists V. Jagić, F. Pastrnek and V. Vondrák felt, in sum, that the search for traces of the Slavic liturgy in Bohemia had gone too far afield, a view which in its essence put them closer to Dobrovský in their skepticism with regard to the existence of the Slavic language and literature in tenth-century Bohemia. Their position is perhaps best revealed in Jagić's telling metaphor apropos the Slavic liturgy in Bohemia: "It was always merely a tender indoor flower that was bound to be damaged by any rough gust of wind." It is noteworthy that subsequently Jagić changed his position quite radically after his study of the *Kievan Leaflets*. The historians B. Bretholz and V. Novotný refused to accept the legitimacy of *CL* and maintained that it was a twelfth-century forgery. Novotný would go only so far as to acknowledge the possibility that there were, sub rosa, some negligible manifestations in Bohemia of the Slavic liturgy before the founding of the Sázava monastery. However, the reviewers of Pekař's study (including Novotný) were unable to refute Pekař's theories.

In celebration of the one-thousandth anniversary (1929) of the death of Wenceslas, Pekař prepared an extensive, partially reformulated, study of Old Bohemian history in which he modified and updated his earlier work on *CL*. Other supportive studies were contributed on various aspects of the question dealing with the Slavic liturgy and Slavic literature in Moravia and Bohemia, for example, N. Serebrjanskij's work on the *Prologue Lives* of Ludmila and Wenceslas and their origin, R. Jakobson's study of the Old Czech paraliturgical hymn and the beginnings of Church Slavonic culture among the Western Slavs, and J. Vašica's study on the relation of the *Second Church Slavonic Life* to Gumpold's *Vita* and other Latin legends, et al. Associated with this millennial celebration was the publication of a comprehensive compendium of studies entitled *The Saint Wenceslas Memorial* (*Svatováclavský sborník*, 1934), in which Pekař's reformulation was published. Other studies contained therein also supported Pekař's position on the antiquity of Church Slavonic culture in Bohemia, for instance, the archeological studies of J. Cibulka and K. Guth, and M. Weingart's detailed reconstruction and analysis of the *First Church Slavonic Life of Saint Wenceslas*, a work that he proclaimed older than both *Crescente fide* and *CL*—hence the oldest and the first original work of Bohemian literature.[45] However, soon another dimension would be added to the debate.

In the second volume of *The Saint Wenceslas Memorial* (Prague, 1939), a disciple of Pekař, the historian V. Chaloupecký, published a detailed study entitled "The Tenth Century Sources of Christian's Legend about Saint Wenceslas and Saint Ludmila" ("Prameny X století Legendy Kristiánovy o svatém Václavu a svaté Lidmile"), which essentially attempted to increase the credibility of *CL*. Despite its numerous valuable insights, it did not succeed in laying the argument to rest. Many of the author's views—especially on the history of the Slavic liturgy—were overstated, and the work's principal hypothesis was disproved and rejected by both followers and opponents of Pekař. It appears to have been the cause of the recrudescence of Dobrovský's dating of *CL* because of the emphasis placed on its compilatory nature. Chaloupecký (as Pekař and others before him) regards the unpreserved Church Slavonic *Life of Saint Ludmila* (the assumed model for the Church Slavonic *Prologue Life* and Latin legend *Fuit in provincia Boemorum*, which he considered the oldest preserved Latin legend) as the cornerstone of Bohemian literary and historical tradition. Furthermore, he fully agrees with Pekař on the question of the authorship and dating of *CL*, and correctly separates the homily on

Saint Ludmila (*Factum est*) from the legend *Diffundente sole*. Nevertheless, he totally ignores Pekař and an earlier study by B. Ryba that had substantiated the opposite view and declares the legend *Diffundente sole* to be the source of *CL*—as had Dobner and Dobrovský at the dawn of Slavic literary studies—and dates it to the latter half of the tenth century. Chaloupecký repeated his mistakes in a later publication of translations of Church Slavonic and Latin legends which he annotated (see *Na úsvitu křesťanství*, Prague, 1942).

In a review of Chaloupecký's study, J. Vilikovský convincingly demonstrated once again that the legend *Diffundente sole* was extracted from *CL* and was most probably compiled as late as the fourteenth century as a preface to a homily on Saint Ludmila. Ludvíkovský asserts that Chaloupecký's firm conviction of the cultural and political continuity between Great Moravia and Přemyslide Bohemia, and especially his belief in the results of the linguistic research of R. Jakobson and J. Vašica, which coincided in time with the German occupation of Czechoslovakia, might explain his overemphasis on the Slavic idea. These three scholars shared a remark- ably similar view of the wellspring of Bohemian culture, one fervently expressed in V. Mathesius's preface to *What Our Country Gave to Europe and Mankind* (*Co daly naše země Evropě a lidstvu*, Prague, 1939).[46]

The early post–World War II years witnessed the appearance of two major studies devoted to Bohemian antiquity and its literary traditions. They refueled the debate. In entirely different ways, both works turned pronouncedly against Chaloupecký and Pekař. The first, by Z. Kalandra, is in part a daring comparative examination of myths applied to early Bohemian historiography. Kalandra departs completely from the traditional approaches and rejects the historical and literary analysis of the materials in question.[47] He also rejects *CL*, considering it a compilation and an early-fourteenth-century fake. Furthermore, he condemns the *First Church Slavonic Life of Saint Wenceslas* as a falsification, and attempts to prove that Cosmas's *Chronica Boemorum* is older than *CL*. Another more detailed study by R. Urbánek arrived at the same conclusions after a thorough investigation of all the texts. Here we find the already familiar inversion of the manuscripts and labeling, as well as the theory that the Wenceslas and Ludmila texts are associated with the activity of the Sázava monastery. In fact, the author's picture of tenth-century Bohemia bears a definite resemblance to that of Dobrovský or Novotný.

In a series of reviews, the theses of both Kalandra and Urbánek were rejected by J. Ludvíkovský. In Urbánek's work he found most troublesome the acceptance of Chaloupecký's standpoint on the relation of *Diffundente sole* to *CL*. Yet he did not agree with him on the dating and his identification of the so-called Böddecke Manuscript (the first five chapters of which correspond basically to *CL*) as an independent Ludmilian life of the twelfth century. Urbánek's rehabilitation of Dobrovský's position was supported by some of the former opponents of Pekař, namely, the historians J. Slavík and F. M. Bartoš. The latter went so far as to defend Dobrovský's negative attitude on both *CL* and the Slavic liturgy in tenth-century Bohemia.[48]

From the time Kalandra and Urbánek rekindled the controversy, evidence to establish the Slavonic-Latin symbiosis in tenth- and eleventh-century Bohemia and its cultural and literary links with Great Moravia would increasingly be furnished by philologists (linguists) and archeologists.[49] A small example of this is provided by the publication of the book *Magna Moravia* (Brno, 1964; Prague, 1965) that was dedicated to the eleven-hundreth anniversary of the Moravian Mission. Here we find a series of extensive articles relating to the question under discussion, for example, on the authenticity of *CL* and the literary continuity between Moravia and Bohemia by J. Ludvíkovský, on early Moravian architecture and its influence on the Bohemian by V. Richter, and on the assimilation and development in Bohemia of Moravian Church Slavonic features by R. Večerka. Obviously, a host of linguistic and archeological studies have gone unmentioned. Suffice it to say for the moment that linguistic and archeological evidence from textual analyses and discoveries testifies very strongly in favor of the originality of *CL*, the Cyrillomethodian beginnings of Bohemian Christianity, and cultural and literary continuity.

However, that does not mean that new problems have not arisen or that all aspects of the old dispute have been resolved. There are scholars, such as O. Králík and F. Graus, who agree with the genuineness and tenth-century origins of *CL* but do not accept the notion of Moravian-Bohemian cultural and political continuity. In attempting to bridge the gulf separating Dobrovský's skepticism and the modern rehabilitation of *CL*, as well as the substantiation of Bohemian provenance of numerous Church Slavonic texts, Králík sowed discontent on both sides of the debate. He maintained: (1) that there is no evidence to support the coexistence of the Latin and Slavic liturgy in Bohemia during the first half of the tenth century, the development of which was not possible before the founding of the bishopric of Prague (973) and the establishment of Benedictine monasteries; (2) that the elevation of Adalbert to the bishopric brought about the revival in Bohemia of Cyrillomethodian cultural and literary traditions and the writing of the *First Church Slavonic Life of Saint Wenceslas*; (3) that the Ludmilian legend, *Fuit in provincia Boemorum* (which originated in the eleventh century at Sázava), was extracted from *CL*; and, finally, (4) that Bořivoj's baptism by Methodius was a product of Christian's imagination, concocted to support the idea that Přemyslide Bohemia was a continuation of the Great Moravian Empire.

The general results of Králík's work, and his ideas about the Slavic policy of Bishop Adalbert in particular, were flatly rejected in a jointly written article by the historians Z. Fiala and D. Třeštík. They argued that formulations in support of views that Bishop Adalbert might have had are wholly untenable in the complete absence of evidence—excepting *CL* (which, as we shall see, Fiala rejected). To the philologists Večerka and Ludvíkovský, the most objectionable feature of Králík's work was that he attributed the creation of Slavic literature in tenth-century Bohemia to the initiative of Adalbert and the good offices of his friend, Emperor Otto III. In sum, Večerka rejected Králík's chronology and his notion that the Slavic liturgy and literary activity were novel to tenth-century Bohemia, while Ludvíkovský noted his overestimation of Adalbert's adherence to the Slavic idea and marveled at the very thought that tenth-century Bohemia up to the year 982—according to Králík's line of reasoning— was plunged "into a mist of sterility without culture and literary production." Králík's other theories were also not given a very warm reception.[50]

Another series of discordant notes were sounded by the historian F. Graus. He accepted the authenticity of *CL*, maintaining, however, that it confirmed only the legendary tradition about Constantine and Methodius in Bohemia and not the existence of their cult which, he believed, was introduced as late as the mid-fourteenth century. In his view, the cultivation of the Slavic liturgy and literature in tenth-century Bohemia was "a tendentious fable." And Graus also refuted the political continuity between Great Moravia and Přemyslide Bohemia, viewing this *translatio regni* as having no basis in fact. This stance trod not only on the toes of the philologists but on those of Králík as well. It would not go unanswered.

Though many of the contributions to *Magna Moravia* refuted Graus by simply assuming an opposite view, other studies, for example, those by Večerka and Králík, were aimed specifically at him. It was pointed out (1) that *CL* itself applies (though only once) the epithet "saint" (*beatus*) to both Constantine and Methodius, while the legend *Beatus Cyrillus*—a work that has been dated to the time of Cosmas—uses this epithet consistently; (2) that the ecclesiastic cult of the Thessalonian brothers is documented in the East in *Codex Assemanianus* (late tenth or early eleventh century) and the Ostromir Gospel (1056–57); and (3) that linguistic analysis of the Church Slavonic *Office of Cyril and Methodius* has shown this text to be of Bohemian origin, dating from the tenth or eleventh century. Graus's denial of political continuity was countered with evidence from *CL*, that is, its unique historical aspect—the combining of Moravian and Bohemian history into an integrated whole.

Resistance to the genuineness of *CL* was mounted again in the mid-1970s in several studies by the historian Z. Fiala. He basically sided with the negative evaluations of *CL* and thus linked himself to the chain extending from Dobrovský to Urbánek. For his part in this linkage, he attempted to prove that Christian knew and utilized as his source the legend *Oriente iam sole*, a work that had been solidly placed in the mid-thirteenth century (1250–60). After analyzing the Ludmila and Wenceslas legends in *CL*, the tale about Wenceslas's servant, Podiven, and the miracles associated with Wenceslas, and noting the symmetrical and logical organization of *Oriente iam sole* as opposed to the amorphous and compilatory nature of *CL*, Fiala also reached the conclusion that *CL* is a fourteenth-century falsification.[51]

From the time Sobolevskij published his work at the turn of the century, Slavic philology and linguistics have managed to clarify many of the problems that over the years have evoked skepticism. The results obtained from linguistic analyses of Church Slavonic manuscripts have come down on the side of Pekař and his followers to such an extent that at present the use of the Slavic liturgy and the Slavic literary language in Přemyslide Bohemia is a widely accepted fact among specialists in this discipline. The only skeptic concerning the extent and significance of Church Slavonic literature in Bohemia is the Croatian Slavist J. Hamm. The other aspect of this question—whether there was continuity between Great Moravia and Bohemia in the use of the Slavic liturgy and literary language—has also been resolved to the satisfaction of the great majority of contemporary Slavic philologists and linguists. Opinions have differed about the Church Slavonic monuments that are central to the linguistic end of this question, namely, the Glagolitic *Kievan Leaflets* and *Prague Glagolitic Fragments*. Both of these monuments were held to be of Bohemian provenance, the former of tenth- and the latter of eleventh-century origins. This view has now been generally abandoned with regard to the *Kievan Leaflets*. Because of the highly archaic nature of the vocabulary, script, and the orthography, with the striking Moravianisms/Bohemianisms (e.g., the reflexes of the Proto-Slavic clusters *dj, *tj, *stj, *skj > z, c, šč) that are preserved in this monument, it began to be considered a much older work by such scholars as F. Mareš, V. Tkadlčík et al., and its origins were moved back to Great Moravia. On the other hand, the *Prague Glagolitic Fragments* were clearly shown to be of Bohemian origin, displaying pronounced Czech features in the reflexes of the same Proto-Slavic clusters mentioned above, the third palatalization of velars, and the retention of the Proto-Slavic cluster *dl, and so on. A comparison of the phonological and grammatical features of these two kindred monuments showed that whereas the *Kievan Leaflets* reflect the norms of the Great Moravian literary language—that is, an admixture of adaptation to West Slavic conditions and the retention of South Slavic traits—the *Prague Glagolitic Fragments* added to the former part of the admixture but froze the latter. In other words, the Slavic literary language of Bohemian provenance did not follow the Bulgarian or Croatian line of development but proceeded directly from the Great Moravian.

Further evidence of this was provided by a comparison of the language of Bohemian manuscripts which, as Večerka indicated, basically shows only two layers: Church Slavonic (that is, the codified literary language) and Bohemian (that is, the Moravo-Bohemian adaptation). This certainly would not have been the case had there not been linguistic continuity between the two West Slavic states. For if Church Slavonic had come to Bohemia at some later date from anoth-

Kievan Leaflets, tenth century.

er Slavic environment, the influence of that particular recension of Church Slavonic would surely have left its distinct mark in these manuscripts. That, however, is clearly absent. Moreover, evidence of this Moravo-Bohemian linguistic fusion can be discerned in manuscripts whose protograph was produced in Bohemia despite the heavy influence of the "other" Slavic milieu in which it was copied and/or preserved. For example, West Slavic words from Latin (*mьša, križь*) and Old High German (*rovaniję, vъsodъ*), calques (*vьsemogyjь*), localisms (*rěsnota*)—not to mention the substantial Moravo-Bohemian contribution to the Christian religious terminology of Church Slavonic—seem to project a line leading from the *Kievan Leaflets* to the *First Church Slavonic Life of Saint Wenceslas* and the *Canon in Honor of Saint Wenceslas*.[52] Hence, linguistic analyses of literary monuments that can be related to Bohemia have corroborated the cultural and literary continuity between Great Moravia and Přemyslide Bohemia by establishing that the Church Slavonic literary language of Bohemian provenance was based on the Church Slavonic literary language of the Great Moravian recension.

The possibility of manipulating *CL* appears to have been the common point of departure for the more recent skeptics, Kalandra, Urbánek, and, following in their footsteps, Fiala. Indeed, Fiala has clearly refused to take into serious consideration evidence and new knowledge concerning the problems in question that have been brought to light over the past thirty-five years by Slavic and Latin philology. Indeed, the most convincing evidence for the originality of *CL* was provided by J. Ludvíkovský in a series of studies that focused primarily on the philological aspects of this Latin monument. In a detailed analysis of *CL*, Ludvíkovský noted (1) the decidedly uniform character of Christian's language, style, and syntax throughout the work; (2) that its vocabulary was essentially that of the *Vulgate*, with more than 80 percent of its words attested therein (a feature one would expect from a work that drew its word stock from hagiographic literature, namely, *Crescente fide*, Gumpold's *Vita*, et al.); and (3) that *CL* bears no traces of a reading of Roman classics. Continuing his analysis, Ludvíkovský noted the work's most conspicuous stylistic feature, the device known as *hyperbaton*, a deviation from the regular word order whereby syntactically related words and phrases are separated in order to emphasize them in the sentence. In their time, Pekař cited several *hyperbata*, pointing out that this artful style was favored by writers of the late Middle Ages, while Kalandra condemned them as distasteful inversions and horrendous turns of phrase. Indeed, Christian's style on the whole is much easier to read than the bombastic style of Gumpold (compare the *Second Church Slavonic Life of Saint Wenceslas*) that was so popular during his time. It is quite the opposite of a mechanical conglomeration of numerous texts written by various authors at different times and borrowed without stylistic adaptation, as Urbánek and others concluded.

As a textual critic, Ludvíkovský was aided by Christian's abundant use of *hyperbata* in general and unusual forms of it in particular (for example, replaced prepositions, conjunctions, and relative pronouns). By comparing the Rajhrad manuscript (chap. 4 of *CL*) with the same text found in the Heiligenkreuz monastery (Wattenbach's text), he found that whereas the former was loyal to *CL* (hence, replete with *hyperbata*), the latter converted this device to the colloquial style—a clear indication that the Rajhrad manuscript was older. Since the manuscript from the Heligenkreuz monastery was dated 1181–1200, V. Dokoupil's dating of the Rajhrad manuscript to the mid-twelfth century was justified.[53] Hence, this offered incontrovertible proof that *CL* originated no later than the mid-twelfth century. Moreover, the most compelling evidence for the tenth-century origins of *CL* was provided by Ludvíkovský's analysis of the author's use of prosaic rhythm, *cursus*, found particularly at the ends of clauses and sentences, which in antiquity was based on length of syllable but in Medieval Latin, on pitch. One of Kalandra's arguments against the originality of *CL* was that clause and sentence endings betrayed a knowledge of a rhythmic *cursus* that the papacy brought back only at the end of the eleventh century—which went back to an old tradition that was broken in the seventh century—and that became the rule in the twelfth century under Pope Gregory VIII (Oct.–Dec. 1187). This so-called *cursus Gregorianus* had three characteristic end-rhymes: *cursus planus* (x́x, xx́x); *cursus tardus* (x́x, xx́xx), and most frequently, *cursus velox* (x́xx, xxx́x or x́xx, x́x, x́x). Ludvíkovský's analysis of the entire text of *CL* proved that its *cursus* was not the Gregorian type but one very much like the style found in *Crescente fide*, Gumpold's *Vita*, and other tenth-century authors—and thus corresponding to the sophisticated Latin prose of the Ottonian renaissance of the late tenth century.

Vilikovský's review of Chaloupecký's study "Tenth Century Sources" had already stressed the importance of *cursus* as a means of dating the legend *Diffundente sole*, which the latter had placed in the tenth century and considered the model for *CL*. Ludvíkovský's detailed analysis of sentence endings in this work showed that its *cursus* was *velox* in 70 percent of sentence endings (and more than 80 percent with clauses of the Gregorian type), as opposed to less than 14 percent in *CL*. Hence, the legend *Diffundente sole* could not have been written in the tenth century (Chaloupecký), nor at the end of the eleventh century (Urbánek, Bartoš), but most probably in the thirteenth century (Pekař) or fourteenth century (Vilikovský, Ludvíkovský). And as Ryba's study had shown earlier, the archetype of *CL* could not be so chronologically near to the oldest preserved manuscript (ca. 1340) as Dobrovský, Urbánek, and Bartoš maintained. Therefore, *CL* is an original tenth-century work which, in the words of Ludvíkovský, represents "the most important document relating to the problem of the Moravian-Bohemian cultural and political continuity as it can be chronologically fixed."[54]

Continuing from where Ludvíkovský left off, the historian D. Třeštík finally called for an end to the debate about *CL* in a study titled: "Ten Theses about *Legenda Christiani*" (*Deset tezí o kristiánově legendě*). In a conclusion reminiscent of Pekař's, he states (to paraphrase): given the fact that there is not a single cogent argument against the originality of *CL*, there are no reasons not to recognize the evidence that attests to the legend's origin in the late tenth century (992–94). This same point of view is maintained in Třeštík's most recent works, the last published in 1983.[55] Curiously, nevertheless, he asserts that *CL* is still an open problem, not so much from the point of view of any of the individual skeptics who are already on record, but from a versatile consideration of all their arguments. However, no one since Fiala has as yet ventured forth in print to take up the gage.[56]

✝ Church Slavonic Fragments and Hymns

✝ Prague Glagolitic Fragments

✝

Fol. 1a

 1 Exaposteilarion[1]
 2 The Word
 3   vow   , O Lord,
 4   young   , as God
 5 most bles
 6   being   the Word
 7 Exaposteilarion on Mid-Pentecost[2]
 8 From the life-bearing
 9 ever ready   , O Christ, granting me mercies
10 may there be life for me like running water
11 a wellspring, O Lover of man.
12 Exaposteilarion on the Transfiguration
13 O Christ, God, Thou didst transfigure Thyself on high, having
          shown
14 Thy disciples
15   in radiant cloud   , O Lord,
16 in spirit and through prayers   , O God,
17 save our souls, Most Saintly of the saints.
18 Give thanks to our God,   all of you,
19 the low and the high, the chosen who fear God,
20 as our Lord God is King.[3] Let us rejoice
21 and make merry and render glory unto God.
22 Exaposteilarion to the blind
23 Wash my eyes that have become blind, O Lord, from many
24 sins. Thou illumine and
25 remove the sins from me, who in humility
26 wash myself with my tears.

50

27 Exaposteilarion on the Ascension
28 Thou ascendest to Thy Father, rejoice
29   to disciples in Thy glory.

Fol. 1b

 1 For Thou didst ascend, O Christ
 2 having illumined everything.
 3 Exaposteilarion on Pentecost
 4 Holy Pentecost is coming
 5 We all revere the Holy
 6 Spirit: For It came giving wisdom
 7   the apostles.   Let us all
 8 receive It, and let us
 9 worship It.   Exaposteilarion
10 on the birth of John
11 As the ancient and new
12 intercessor, O forerunner
13 of Christ, by your prompt prayer
14 send us
15 who praise your venerable
16 divine birth
17 Exaposteilarion on the Apostle
18 Peter
19 You both received your power from God,
20 O most wise holy Apostles.
21 O Peter, rock of faith
22 O Paul, firmament of the world,
23 a luminous pair
24 the praise of Rome.   Exaposteilarion on
25 the Dormition of the Mother of God
26 You passed from earth
27 to the heavens, O Mother of God.

Fol. 2a

 1   antiphonon 3[4]
 2 1. Psalm 21,[5] tone 6.[6]

3 Many dogs have compassed me,
4 they smote Thee, O Emperor, on the cheek
5 and question Thee while smiting,
6 and they bore false witness,
7   harken, O God
8 Antiphonon 2, psalm 34,[7] tone 2
9 Refrain after the antiphonon[8]   during Thy evening
10 O Christ, when Thou preached to Thy disciples
11 "one of you betrayed
12 me treacherously."
13 Judas wished not to understand
14 Thee, giving offense to the Lord.
15 Antiphonon 3, psalm 40,[9] tone 8
16 Refrain after the antiphonon: plagal.[10] The law-breaking word
17 they raised against me and Thee,
18 O Lord, leave me not but have mercy on us
19 Kathisma:[11]   plagal tone
20 What kind of cunning, O Judas, instigated you
21 to betray salvation, for you
22 were separated from the Apostles' countenance,
23 for you were deprived of the gift of healing,
24 for you have dined with them,

Fol. 2b

1 for you were rejected from the table, for
2 having washed their feet, you
3 despised your own: O how much good you have forgotten
4 Your praiseless will
5 denounces you, and that
6 immense mercy and great compassion
7 has been breached.
8 The Beatitudes:[12] tone 4
9 Because of the tree was Adam expelled from paradise;
10 through the tree in the form of a cross
11 a brigand settled in paradise
12 for that one was tempted
13 to transgress the commandment

14 of the Creator and the Other
15 was crucified. And they professed God
16 Who was hidden. Remember me, O Saviour, when
17 Thou comest to Thy Kingdom
18 They took from the disciples the Creator of law
19 and placed before Pilate the Righteous One
20 like a criminal in court,
21 crying out: "Crucify the One
22 Who in the desert
23 was filled with manna."
24   us   the righteous[13]

✝ O Lord, Have Mercy On Us

✝

1 O Lord, have mercy on us,
2 O Jesus, have mercy on us!
3 Thou, O Saviour of the whole world
4 Save us and heed
5 Our voices, O Lord!
6 Grant us all, O Lord,
7 Life and peace on earth!
  Kyrie eleison, Kyrie eleison[1]

1 Gospode, pomilui ny,
2 Isuse, pomilui ny!
3 Sъpase vьsego mira
4 Sъpasi ny, i uslyši,
5 Gospodi, glasъ našixъ!
6 Dazь vьsěmъ, Gospodi,
7 Žiznь i mirъ vъ zemi![2]
  Krleš, krleš

✝ Church Slavonic Works about Wenceslas and Ludmila

✝ First Church Slavonic Life of Saint Wenceslas (*Croatian-Glagolitic Redaction*)

First Church Slavonic Life of Saint Wenceslas, 1379. Vatican Library, Rome.

✝

For the Feast of
Saint Wenceslas the Confessor[1]

BEHOLD THAT PROPHETIC WORD WHICH, spoken by our Lord Jesus Christ Himself, has now come to pass: "For it shall be," He said, "in the last days," which we believe are now upon us, "brother shall rise against brother, son against father,[2] and a man's foes shall be those of his household[3] [Matthew 10:36]. For men shall be at variance one against the other, and then shall God reward them according to their works."[4]

There was a prince among the Czechs by the name of Vratislav,[5] his wife was called Drahomira.[6] And they had a son, their firstborn, whom they baptized and gave the name Wenceslas.[7] Now when he reached the age of tonsuring,[8] his father, Vratislav, summoned a bishop by the name of Notar,[9] along with his clerics, for the tonsuring. And upon celebrating a mass for him,[10] the bishop took the boy, placed him on a side step before the altar, and blessed him, saying: "O Lord God, Jesus Christ, bless this boy as Thou hast blessed all Thy righteous ones." And thus with a blessing he was tonsured.

Therefore, through the blessing of that righteous bishop and his prayers, we believe the boy began to grow, sheltered by God's grace. And well did he learn both Slavic and Latin letters.[11]

Then, when his father died, the Czechs appointed Wenceslas, his son, as prince.[12] And Boleslav[13] grew up under him. However, both were as yet young. Thus his mother, Drahomira, fortified the land and ruled the people until Wenceslas came of age. And when he came of age, he himself began to rule his people.

And, verily, with the grace of God, Prince Wenceslas not only mastered letters but he was perfected by faith. According to the words of the Gospel, he rendered good unto all the poor, clothed the naked, fed the hungry, and received wayfarers. He defended widows, had mercy on the people—the wanting and the wealthy—served those

61

who worked for God, and adorned many churches with gold. For he believed in God with all his heart, and he did, as much as he could, all manner of good things in his life.[14]

However, because the Devil entered their hearts, as he once entered the heart of Judas, who betrayed the Lord,[15] Czech men waxed proud and rose up against their lord, Wenceslas, as did the Jews against Christ our Lord. For it is written: "Whosoever rises up against his lord is like unto a Judas."[16]

And they provoked Boleslav, saying: "Your brother Wenceslas wishes to murder you and has taken counsel with his mother and his men."

Evil dogs! Formerly they had counseled Wenceslas to banish his mother without cause.[17]

But understanding the fear of God, Wenceslas feared the words that say: "Honor thy father and thy mother" [Exodus 20:12] and "Thou shalt love thy neighbor as thyself" [Matthew 19:19].

Then, wishing to fulfill God's truth in all things, he recalled his mother, repented earnestly, and in tears said, "O Lord God, lay not this sin to my charge"[18] [Acts 7:60]. And he recalled the words of the prophet David and said, "Remember not the sins of my youth, nor my ignorance, O Lord"[19] [Psalms 25:7].

Indeed, he repented and honored his mother. And she rejoiced in his faith and in his charitable works. For not only did he do good to the poor and the indigent, and to wayfarers and many others, as we have said, but he ransomed those who had been sold.

And he built churches well in all the towns and quite fittingly appointed to them servants of God[20] from many nations, and they conducted divine services day and night, both by God's decree and that of His servant Wenceslas. And God inspired his heart, and he built the Church of Saint Vitus.[21]

However, because Boleslav, his brother, had been incited against him, the Devil now sowed malice in Boleslav's heart—to murder him—so that his soul would not be saved for all eternity. The feast of Saint Emmeram, to whom Wenceslas had made a pledge, arrived.[22] And while he was rejoicing in that day, those evil adversaries summoned Boleslav and held an inimical council with him against his brother Wenceslas,[23] as the Jews once did against our Lord Jesus Christ.

When the churches were being consecrated at the castles, Wenceslas rode out to all of them. On Sunday, during the Feast of Cosmas and Damian,[24] he entered Boleslav's castle.[25] After attending mass, he made ready to go home to Prague. But Boleslav distracted him with malicious intent, saying: "Why are you leaving, brother? You know, I have the very finest ale!"

And he did not refuse his brother, but mounted his horse and began to sport with his servants.[26] We believe that they then informed him, saying, "Your brother wishes to murder you." But he did not believe it, and entrusted this matter to God.

At nightfall those evil adversaries gathered in the courtyard of Hněvysa. And they summoned Boleslav and confirmed with him their devilish plot against his brother. For just as the Jews once came together, plotting against Christ, so also did these evil adversaries gather and take counsel together, how they might murder their lord Prince Wenceslas.[27] And they said, "We shall seize him when he goes to matins."

When morning came, matins were rung. Hearing the bells,[28] Wenceslas said, "Praise to Thee, O Lord, that Thou didst preserve me unto this morn," and rising, he set off for matins. But suddenly Boleslav overtook him at the gates. And Wenceslas looked back toward him and said, "Brother, you were a good host to us last evening."

But because the Devil had inclined Boleslav's ear and corrupted his heart, he drew his sword and replied to him, saying, "Now I wish to be a better host for you." And saying this, he struck him upon the head with his sword. Wenceslas turned to him and said, "What have you plotted, brother?" And seizing hold of him, he cast him to the earth.[29] Then Tuža rushed up and struck Wenceslas on the arm. Wounded in the arm, he released his brother and ran to the church. But two evildoers, Tira and Česta, slew him by the doors of the church.[30] And Hněvysa fell upon him and pierced his ribs with a sword. And immediately Wenceslas gave up the ghost, saying, "Lord, into Thy hands I commend my spirit[31] [Luke 23:46].

And in that castle one of Wenceslas's nobles also was slain, one called Mstina.[32] The others they pursued to Prague; some were slain, while others scattered throughout the land. And they slaughtered infants, gave many women to other men, banished God's servants, and committed all manner of wickedness.[33]

Then Tira said to Boleslav, "Let us go and slay the lady, your mother, and you can mourn your brother and mother at the same time."

But Boleslav replied, "She will not escape before we overtake her with the others." And they left Wenceslas, dismembered and unburied.

A priest, Krastěj, picked him up and, covering him with a sheet, laid him down before the church. When his mother heard that her son had been slain, she came in search of him. And when she espied him, she fell upon his breast, weeping. After gathering all the parts of his body, she dared not take them to her home. Instead, she washed and clothed the body in the priest's lodging, and taking it to the church, placed it there. Frightened that she would be murdered, she fled to Croatia.[34] Boleslav did not find her here.

And he summoned a priest named Paul[35] to perform prayers over the body of Wenceslas. Then they buried the venerable body of Wenceslas, a good and just, God-worshiping, Christ-loving man. And his soul ascended to God, whom he had served in reverence and fear. For three days his blood remained on the ground.[36] Then, on the third day, while all looked on, a church rose up over him[37] so that all marveled.

We yet hope in God that through the prayers of this pious and good man, Wenceslas, a greater miracle will be manifested.[38] For, verily, his suffering may be likened to the suffering of Christ and the Holy Martyrs, since counsel was taken against him as the Jews did against Christ. They dismembered him as they did Peter; and they slaughtered the innocents because of him, as they did because of Christ.

Thus Prince Wenceslas was slain on the twenty-eighth day of the month of September.[39] May God give repose to his soul in His holy place with all the righteous and with those innocent ones killed for His sake.

And God left not His faithful to be profaned among the faithless, but made manifest His grace: He turned hearts of stone[40] to repentance and to understanding of their sin. When Boleslav recalled the many sins he had committed, he prayed to God and all His saints, and translated the body of his brother, the just man Wenceslas, to Prague, saying, "I have sinned and my sin I acknowledge."[41] And Wenceslas was placed in the Church of Saint Vitus, on the right side of the Altar of the Twelve Apostles, where he himself had said he would build a church.

And, verily, the body of the God-loving Prince Wenceslas was translated on the fourth day of the month of March.[42] May God place his soul in the bosom of Abraham, Isaac, and Jacob, wherein all the righteous repose, awaiting the resurrection of their bodies in Christ Jesus our Lord.[43]

✝ Second Church Slavonic Life of Saint Wenceslas (The Kazan' Manuscript)

Мца. септАврА въ. кн. днепочинаетсеапраю
шстмивАчеслАвъмцкрАбъ. хабви, шче.
Спнагапоистинньродымногшшбразныако
моуждшвродтесмртныишвьıчаимьють
хитростиипечали. имижеросовоипода
шбразований. силоiовьнютрьнаботогда
родшбразумьти. инньхитростиисловесь
ипобьтстеи. исделиксакошmomъподвинове
нирасумьтчии. даcmompmiмоглнкышай
квазавьктоучаесюомоужитиивесельраду
ютеслоуюнчати. сейпоистиннькоумомъ
смыслепыпоправъмирьскаачргпй ца. кы
шнижелаетъ. шитаиескопаннанавысотоу
тьстий. горадхомъоучьвгаАмирьскыйкы
шнижелаютъ. нетотьтакошнымтаипровоу
многаждыоуазвлаетъ. многестъаны
аестаростистаростьмногожишотнаа.
нанравьстарыаисешителнаапривлачи
семьременстдоухраворьстий. дрьзаа мрш
етъ. хотАщоупохвальıслашвьрiатиАдрш
гомъдтвлаврагличныйтроухитростьны
атьностаижзьачить. оумьıродителнаа
тоностию, имоучаетъетерижесмотри
нiемъглубиныеписанiемьсловесъпобче
нннтьлисвобшоюшбрагныошчоднытгаъхо
доржестви есмотрениишдашесАчаишипро
читанiемъ подвиханiе. звьздаъ. толи
вьтечениемъанеподвижнырастоАтъ.
исаанликсаковамькрагесекаговеличестви
апочатокъ. етериаиситаинныйпроймь.

ਬ਼

зī. ли.

✝

The Month of September on the 28th Day
The Prologue Concerning Saint Wenceslas,
Martyr for Christ, Commences[1]

Bless us, O Father!

VERILY, ALL MORTAL BEINGS have certain characteristics and various attributes such as solicitude and reason. Thus, through the power of their inner imagination they can comprehend with their mind and intellect, and perceive through their understanding of words and discourse those things that are in any way subject to the senses. And they, in keeping with man's desire, are pleased to bring about the joys of life. One who is truly rational of mind, having scorned worldly amusements, will desire the supernal. Yet another, molded for the pinnacle of honor, with ardency of soul and fear of the worldly, will desire the supernal.[2] The irreverence of youth often incites against morals; torpid old age, an old age attained by long life, leads to the old and salvific morals. The bold dare to engage in the arts, seeking to gain wisdom and the glory of praise; but the indolent draw away from the skillful execution of divers tasks, and their natural intelligence is jaded by refinement. Indeed, some are absorbed in speculation about the profound. Having devoted themselves, perhaps as the pastime of their leisure, to the examination of wondrous discourses on scholarship, they try then to explain with remarkable calculations which immutable course fixes the motion of the stars;[3] which or what sort of measure expands, either through some mystical providence or according to geometric formulas, to include the genesis of the earth's magnitude and the true end of the world;[4] which principle regularly equalizes all supernal quantity by weightiness; what proportions of harmony tune a natural melody;[5] how can a most profound reckoning be made by those who speak of the supernal and heavenly, which they labor prodigiously to investigate in their meditations, when set forth under the notion of truth and falsehood and the equivocal confusion of them. Yet others, encouraged by their perceptiveness, gravitate toward the amusements of song, one wishing to appear more skillful than the other. However, beguiled by their tales, they are not afraid, in their careless yet profaned realm, to conceal the message of truth concerning the deeds of our God's saints, and to remember what so often has been laid before the eyes of mortals by the benevolence of heaven. Thus, it is no wonder that exalted matters have moved the wise men of our era to compose philosophical studies, and away from the notion of simple composition. For many of them, in emulation, have been clinging to pagan writings and little to what has been propagated and expounded in accounts concerning the glory of God in His holy deeds, which were entrusted to posterity, being designated for it. Indeed, claiming and insisting that it is not at all useful, they discard as distorted what to sacred thought is divine, and expressed more calmly, simply, and easily.

Thus, lulled by this facility, many think the human condition continues through restraint, and would rather strive for exalted rhetorical heights through science. And we too have clung to such a form of wise and learned discourse. Nevertheless, by His holy command and through our rusticity, this brief commentary introduces the treasure of the following composition. It soon reveals the name of a memorable man and the memory of his deeds and miracles. And though not perfectly written, it is done at the behest of the victorious emperor and temporal majesty Otto II.[6] For as much as chastisement frightens him who writes imperfectly, how much greater is the dignity that adorns the saint, whose memory and holy deeds determined the arrangement of this discourse.[7]

The Discourse on the Generation and Passion of Prince-Saint Wenceslas Commences

I

It was from the first, enlightened doctrine for all the faithful, after ruinous transgression had come to an end,[8] that the life-giving luster of learning with its brilliant diffusion radiated divinely throughout the entire universe, which had been made gloomy by the darkness of error. And there is sufficiently strong evidence, as we have come to know, that shoots of salvific faith began to grow, and the Church was established and gained strength through this first faith and the sagacity and salvific works of the first theologians. And this was written down in books, widely disseminated, and firmly designated as a faithful guide for the people. However, while some nations, after long and circuitous wanderings, were brought to the rightness of the true way by the holy illumination, nevertheless not all the nations of the world, even those predestined, partook of and received this gift of grace at the same time. Rather, through the dispensation of Majesty on high, this gift fortunately proceeded to other regions, as though conquering diabolical perdition by degrees. And indeed I shall now depict in a most simple style one of these regions, a land inhabited by Slavs. The region to which we direct our attention is harsh and more spiritless in faith than others; yet this land, through the gift of the Holy Spirit, desired, if belatedly, to adhere to the Christian law of confession through blessed conversion.

II

Verily, this land is called Bohemia by the inhabitants themselves. And after the reign of his most serene majesty Henry of blessed memory, king of the Franks and Romans,[9] a man of serene lineage from that land, Spytihněv by name, the son of Bořivoj,[10] was enthroned by virtue of his great strength among his neighbors. He kept the princedom under imperial rule. And he was drawn by the sweet covenant to God's law, he thirsted much for holy water and to be born again through the sacrament, and he purified himself through baptism. Enkindled by his new knowledge, he established churches in blessed memory of God and of His Holy Mother Mary, and of Saint Peter, the Apostle.[11] And after they were built, innumerable miracles occurred in later years by the grace of God.

III

Now, when by the law of human nature the days of his praiseworthy life had been sealed—years exemplary by their beautiful deeds— and he had passed away from this world, his younger brother, Vratislav,[12] who was chosen by all the people, ascended the princely throne. Like his brother, he observed Christian law, erected a church in honor of the victorious warrior, the Blessed Martyr George,[13] and truly believed in God. And after several years when he was departing this world in conformity with human nature, he, while still alive, chose as his successor the child Wenceslas, born a glorious wonder among men, and highly praised. Verily, he was the eldest among the sons, beloved of God and desirous of the heavenly.[14]

IV

For when this wondrously brilliant, handsome, and most beloved child reached the first stage of his blossoming youth, and while his father was still alive, he longed for knowledge of books, and through repeated supplications he conquered his father's heart, mind, and understanding. And he was sent to a town called Budeč, and entrusted to a priest named Učen,[15] to be instructed in the Scriptures. And, verily, by virtue of his ability, he was guided to a quick and matchless understanding; and through his quick learning he mastered the Book of Psalms and the remainder of the other books, and retained them firmly within his memory. Afterward, when his father, as was said, had departed this world, this youth, who in his deeds was like an adult, was elected with the favorable approval of the people, despite his great resistance, to inherit his father's territory under the ascendency of his most serene majesty Otto;[16] and he was duly placed upon the princely throne.

V

It is no wonder that, upon accepting earthly power, the new prince's benevolent nature was oppressed within him by the dire contradictions of his tormented anxiety. For he had formerly resolved in his intimate thoughts that he would contemplate the heavenly more than all else. And although he was indeed master of the temporal domain, he was nonetheless possessed from earliest youth by love for the sweet service of God. Thus, guarding himself against sin, he neglected to punish the iniquities of people entrusted to him, so as not to act according to the severity of the appropriate law. However, after pondering this vexing matter, he wisely perceived the true path, that he would not refuse his temporal duties, nor would he fear in the future that he had perchance disregarded something in striving for the heavenly. He then established just laws among the people, for the poor as well as the rich. And while occupying the princely throne, he would arrange everything by decree. Therefore, he was a prudent overseer, disposed toward mercy: without recompense he saved from destruction those accused of terrible transgressions, and he rejected in sentencing the divers tortures of the pagans. Moreover, he followed not the crowd, was mindful of moral purity, and was not remiss in making generous promises in the presence of the mighty, and then in remembering to fulfill his vows. To wayfarers and the poor and to strangers he gave grand and worthy demonstrations of his love; to orphans he was a father, and to widows a helper, giving assistance from his own possessions. He also comforted exiles, and always showed his wonderful fatherly love toward them. He was modest in all his deeds and an unforgettable lover of patience; in every trouble he was a prudent master; he generously distributed his property upon receiving petitions from the grieving poor, and followed those who were humble and loving. Often he was most severe with himself, but with others he was always gracious, setting an example of eternal life by being compassionate, instructing the ignorant, and strengthening the unlearned.

VI

The blessed youth's manner of living was thus adorned by such holy splendors. And he found such delight in charitable labor that if, when sitting in judgment with his magnates and judges, one of the captured prisoners was found guilty of murder and condemned to death because of his iniquity, and the merciful prince could in no wise object or deliver him from death, he would find some pretext and flee so that he would not be guilty of shedding blood, nor would he hear about the final slaying. And he had this agreement with his worthy page: "If you should hear that my boyars have condemned a man to death, find some pretext and call me from them, that I may not participate in that bloodshed." For he remembered the word of the Gospel, spoken by the Lord, "Judge not, and ye shall not be judged: condemn not, and ye shall not be condemned" [Luke 6:37].

VII

Obeying and loving to the fullest this divine command, the youth, when he had not heard the words of condemnation spoken by any mortal, was not guided by those words. Thus, he would mercifully spare the guilty condemned to execution, and he set them free, striving to bring them to repentance. He destroyed every prison in every castle, and ordered every gibbet throughout his many lands struck down, making a beginning in this himself. And when they heard of his virtuous acts in other lands, many clerics and servants of God were drawn to his kindheartedness, and he received them himself with joyful displays of his love. And by embracing this divine love, he was able to keep them in his presence, attentive and benevolently joyful because of his esteemed affection. Being exercised often, his pure mind was divinely instructed by their frequent instruction, and he reached a wondrous understanding of the Scriptures, both the Latin and the Greek.[17] What he had previously perceived as virtues in his teachers, he himself now manifested in zealous deeds. Because he had compassion for man's every sorrow, he would come with merciful assistance to those who were suffering from disease, and he himself would arrange funeral services for the deceased who were poor, and destitute, and neglected by their neighbors. Moreover, he would impart the good doctrine of the new faith to those living in the old pagan way. Upon seeing how these ignorant people would go to the sanctuaries of idols, and how frequently during the course of the year they hastened to make sacrifices to strange, unknown gods, this blessed youth was quick to abstain—although he was often invited—from attending and from partaking of this unclean food. For he thirsted more than all else to partake at the heavenly table rather than to defile himself with the devilish filth of sacrifices. Moreover, he was sorely distressed over those oppressed by this evil error, and he would often study the Scriptures, since the word of the Apostle commands, "Bear ye one another's burdens [Galatians 6:2]." Others, who were somewhat inclined toward the true path of the higher good, he would instruct in a sweet voice and divert them, promising them the beneficence of the higher gift, that they might renounce the pagan images by which they were deceived and submit with faith to a true vow of sacred conviction. Still others, who were less receptive to salvific instruction, those with hearts hardened and minds slothful in understanding the truth, he, according to the word of the Apostle, "taught well but chastened poorly."[18] Whenever he could, he in truth summoned these servants, the free as well as the unfree, to the Father's table in all its abundance, and he brought them closer to eternal joy, wishing as much as possible that both estates might envision their reward.

VIII

Moreover, he neither neglected nor was wearied by the prayers and works directed toward generous relief of the poor. Although encumbered by secular government, this saintly youth devoted special days during Lent each year to truly wondrous observances of the fasts, in hunger and in prayer. At night he devoted himself to the most lucid of vigils, thinking neither of rest nor slumber. And once the nocturnal calm had settled, he abandoned the bed in his chamber, and concealing it from the others, he arose and silently awakened his page, the chamber-valet. Taking the Scriptures in hand, he would leave the palace without the guard's knowledge. Accompanied only by his page, he would make his way from castle to castle to individual churches, walking barefoot over the sharp crests of hills and along the bottoms of precipices and jagged craters, along rocky trails and terrible ice masses, chanting psalms and other prayers. Verily, while seeking them out, he so mortified his flesh that the splashes of blood which flowed from his tender, lacerated feet marked his trail. And he returned secretly to his home and his bed.

The saint himself avoided revealing his inner understanding. When he sat upon the throne he was dressed in fine, princely robes, but beneath the royal robes his most pure body was clothed in a hair shirt.

When harvesttime came, he would, concealing it from everyone, arise in the middle of the night together with his page, who has been mentioned already, and he would walk barefoot to his fields. And with his own hands he would reap the wheat, tie it into sheaves, and place them upon his own shoulders and those of his page. And he would hide them in a secret corner of his home. There, having threshed and ground the wheat on millstones and sifted it clean with his own holy hands, he sprinkled it with water in the name of the Trinity. And upon making the sign invoking the Trinity, he, together with the page who was serving him, would mix the flour in a vessel with the water that he himself had carried in a bucket from the well. When he had mixed the work of his hands and baked the host,[19] he would send it to the priests in the churches as an offering during services to Our Lord Jesus Christ.

In the fall, upon summoning his worthy, faithful servant, the page and follower to whom reference has already been made, he would climb over the fences of his vineyards at night together with him, unbeknownst to anyone, and fill two baskets with grapes. Placing them upon his shoulders, he returned home with his page and would press the grapes with his own hands, and prepare everything for the divine service. And no one knew about this save that one page, already mentioned frequently. Thus, it was known only to God and that page where the vessels filled with wine were secretly placed. Finding an appropriate time, he would send them around to the churches, to the clerics and priests, along with the host which he himself had baked for church services, and he distributed equally to all.

O how indissoluble are the bonds of undefiled faith encompassing his most pure breast! O how praiseworthy is the obedience of the follower of the most sacred! O how marvelous is the humility of the prince who is not ashamed to submit to the tasks of his servants for the sake of divine love! For in his thoughts he constantly contemplated the heavenly and in his heart perceived the Mystery. And he so revered the sacred and salvific offering of the body and blood of the Lord, and the service, that through this offering of heavenly faith he prepared for the cleansing of sins. And he struggled through faith and zealous service and, in truth, by inwardly preparing the most pure wellspring, he took upon himself the work of a servant, and in this charitable gift he himself became a servant in the sacerdotal order.

IX

Nor would it be fitting to withhold his prophetic vision concerning the priest Paul[20] and his home, about which he himself informed everyone upon awakening, saying:

X

"While I was lying in bed and sleeping, as were some of my pages, my small retinue, and servants, I had a terrible vision in the middle of the night. I saw the home of the priest Paul, as well as the foundations of all the people's dwellings, completely laid to waste from top to bottom. Troubled by this vision, I tossed about and was filled with the inner grief of anxiety for these righteous people. However, I shall pray about this vision to the omniscient, merciful Creator in whom I believe, and thus divine the truth of the message in this vision."

XI

"Verily, the end of the home in my vision signifies the death of my grandmother, the venerable Lady Ludmila.[21] And the destruction of Paul's home foretells the expulsion of our clerics and priests from the land, and the confiscation of their property. For I saw how my mother, a pagan by birth and in the unmingled vileness of her deeds,[22] which are not worthy of mention, consorted with her evil, godless counselors to plot the death of her mother-in-law."

And these words of his, which were brighter than the sun, came to pass. For his evil mother, who was mistakenly named Drahomira,[23] took counsel with impious men and said, "What shall we do about this matter, since he who is to become prince has been led astray by clerics and by my mother-in-law, and is like a monk? I shall destroy her and drive the others from the land."

XII

And immediately she sent her counselors and had her mother-in-law Ludmila strangled. And after this there was a general banishment of clerics, and churches were destroyed throughout the land of Bohemia.[24] And she stationed guards along the streets and said, "Wherever you see a cleric going to my son, cut him down on the spot and do not spare his life." And throughout the land she set up sanctuaries for idols and turned the entire land over to them, making sacrifices to them and forcing her son to them. Being still a child and unable to resist his mother, the holy youth went to the sanctuaries but never defiled his soul with idolatrous filth. For the saint was protected and strengthened by heavenly armor. And when his magnates went to the sanctuaries it appeared that he complied, but his heart's inward profession would disavow their deeds. He was heeded by all the people, the weak as well as the strong: it was his due, because the grace of God was upon him [Luke 2:40]. And he was loved by all, for he was forthright in his words, just in judgment, wise in council, considerate in kindness, and ruled by understanding in all good usages. He would often kneel for the prayers of the Divine Office; he kept small, handwritten books guardedly and secretly on his person beneath his clothes. Withdrawing from the earthly cares of the tribunals, he would, twelve times or more, give himself up to secret prayers in the privacy of the curtain in his chamber. And he would read them through to the end, both at night and during the day, praising Christ in pure profession.

XIII

When the years of the saint's youth had thus passed propitiously, and the prince himself had grown to a manly understanding of the powerful, gradually and manfully he cast off the senseless counsels of the men whom he was following. And having conceived no little hatred toward their ignorant wanderings away from the true God, he summoned his boyars and retinue to the palace one day and began to speak reproachfully to them: "O faithful retinue, but not in Christ! When I was sent by my parents to study the Scriptures, I found in them a lesson of Paul, who said: 'When I was a child, I spake as a child: but when I became a man, I put away childish things'[25] [1 Corinthians 13:11]. In faithfully examining myself through this dictum, since putting into practice the first of all these words, wretch that I am, I wish with a longing heart to attain manhood. However, after my father died, I was still a child—though by birth eldest among my brothers—when I was elected by you to rule. After beginning to rule and reforming the entire government, with God's help I oversaw and strengthened the land greatly against its enemies. And I wish to fulfill the word that the prophet David spoke, 'I understand more than the ancients, because I keep thy precepts' [Psalms 119:100]. But in your hearts you are slothful in your devotion to the higher truth, and in faith you remain separate from me. Hitherto I have been too tolerant of your many iniquitous enticements but I no longer wish to tolerate them. According to the Scriptures, I have done away with the things of my youth,[26] and being a man now, I shall destroy the childish things in my deeds, by the Lord's command. Strengthened by the mercy of the Most High, my desire is to resist and no longer give ear to your untruth. And therefore, let the murmurings of your conspiracy against me cease! Let the conspiracies and gatherings of the cruel and evil among you end! Let the love of peace well up in my domain, both at home and beyond its walls! Let no affair before any court be judged wrongly and contrary to fact! Let no one be confronted henceforth by the errors with which truthful men have been defiled hitherto! If you do not wish to heed the mandate of this law out of fear of the Most

High King, then our anger at the transgressor will be inflamed by divine zeal; and if anyone is found guilty in this, his head shall be struck off!"

And having said this, he banished his mother, at the head of the lawlessness, from his presence and from his land.[27] And after the prince had had his say, the magnates of the land, and the conspirators, and counselors returned to their homes in fear, and their arrogant schemes were put down for a time.

Already, by the grace of God, several uprisings of pagan regions had been subdued under his hand, and a joyful flowering of the Catholic faith burst forth. Churches which had been established according to divine law and recently destroyed because of the disdain of unbelievers were restored on a firm foundation. Clerics exiled from the land were drawn back by merciful generosity. Not only did all of them receive their properties at once but, verily, they were enriched by a multitude of fitting gifts from the estate of this holy man. And all the churches throughout these regions rejoiced under such a prince and were gladdened.

XIV

And when they received word about the benevolence of this holy man, many departed from Bavaria and from Franconia and Saxony—and they came also from other lands—bringing relics and divers books to him, which he purchased with his own gold and silver, and expensive brocades and robes, in true faith, for the benefit of Christianity over the entire land.

XV

And then his brother Boleslav[28]—younger in years, loathsome in the deformity of his mind and the violence of his deeds, incited by the Devil's touch and armed pitilessly with the wrath of malice against divine reason—covetously wished to take his brother's domain into his own hands and to destroy him by violent death with help from impious men of the Devil. However, through divine foresight, the saint learned then of the future plot against him, for it was truly revealed.

At the same time this devout man, having made a vow, planned in his heart to build a church in honor of God and His victorious warrior and martyr, Vitus.[29] And he sent envoys to the bishop of Regensburg[30] and said: "My father established a church in honor of Saint George; at your bidding, I too wish to build a church in honor of Christ's martyr, Saint Vitus." When Bishop Tuto[31] heard this, he raised up his arms to God in heaven, and lifting up praise to Christ, said, "Go and tell my worthy son Wenceslas, 'As you intend, so now your church stands complete in heaven before God.' "

XVI

Upon hearing the bishop's message, Wenceslas arranged for workers. And he himself carried lime on his shoulders, and with his own hands he laid the foundation and finished it. And he summoned the aforementioned bishop and consecrated the church in the name of Saint Vitus. And to the present day many miracles and wonders occur there to the detriment of the Devil.

Now the saint himself wished to turn his reign over to his brother and go to Rome[32] to the holy Apostle Peter,[33] and there renounce this world. Nevertheless, he tarried because of this church, as it was not yet finished to completion. But like one who mows hay during the height of the day's heat and thirsts for water, so also did the saint thirst for martyrdom and for the shedding of his blood, but not at the hands of his brother. Yet through the providence of our merciful God, the Rewarder and Payer of rewards to the faithful, the reward for which he thirsted in other regions God deservedly granted him here in the land of his own forefathers.

Nor are we able to pass over in silence one of his deeds which to mortals was marvelous, to the angels of God, joyful, and to those who fear God, astonishing and altogether unprecedented among the people, a deed that the saint's breast—which was harder than stone—carried in his heart. Indeed, being compelled by his brother and his boyars, he consorted with a woman for the sake of procreating sons, and begot of her a son named Izbrjaslav.[34] And he said to her: "Behold, we have now greatly offended God and have committed iniquity! Let us stop this now, since by our human nature we have conceived a child. Let it be known between us: you have me in place of a brother, and I you in place of a sister." And she agreed to this and pledged herself to it before God and him. Once she sinned with his favorite servant. And when the saint himself saw this, he said, "Why have you lied to God?[35] You were at liberty to marry or not to marry. However, do not divulge this to anyone until I have thought the matter through."[36] And without knowing of his agreement, he arranged a great banquet and gave her in marriage to that same servant, making her his sister.[37]

XVII

Then his younger brother, the aforementioned Boleslav, upon learning that he wished to go to Rome, began secretly to plot much evil against him, and to do much harm. He conspired with evil counselors against this holy man, taking counsel in their homes. And they in no way concealed their plots from the saint, but he silently pondered how this matter would end.

XVIII

And another time his brother summoned his counselors and said, "Consider how we shall destroy him." And they answered him thus: "There is no way you can destroy him while you are in his territory. However, ask permission to go home to your castle,[38] invite him to your home, and there you can destroy him."

And after obtaining his brother's permission, he and his counselors arranged a great, solemn feast, saying it was in memory of the saints Cosmas and Damian.[39] And he sent envoys to his brother and said, "My brother, I have arranged a great celebration in memory of the saints, and I beg your lordship not to refuse to come to us." And the saint answered the envoy, "My brother's celebration is God's celebration, and at his request I shall make ready."

And all this hatred and these intrigues were not concealed from the saint, for he understood everything. And immediately upon joining his retinue, he mounted his horse and began to sport,[40] galloping before them around the courtyard, saying to them: "With you Czechs mounted upon your steeds, would I not be able to find our enemies? But that is not my desire." And having said this, he rode off to his brother.

And with great humility his brother came out to greet him together with all his attendants and dignitaries. His humility, false though it was, gave godly Wenceslas much joy. And they kissed joyously, embraced one another, and then entered the house, rejoicing.

They sat down to dine. And after a time, when several of them had become drunk, the intrigue of those who intended to murder this holy man could no longer remain hidden. With swords concealed beneath their clothing, these malefactors arose three times, and as if stricken by some infirmity, they fell back again and again into their chairs, becoming at length altogether enfeebled in strength and resolve. Because the hour of his suffering, ordained by God, had not yet arrived, they let him go unharmed. And he was not unknowing of the plot or fearful of death, and he found courage in God's protection. Nor did he give way to sorrow when one of his brother's servants whispered into his ear that he should be on his guard, because they were preparing to murder him. Moreover, he did not leave his brother, but like his host offered praise and lovingly entreated those with whom he was sitting to make merry.

And after this, having sat for a time, he rose from the table, filled a goblet with wine, and sweetly addressed them all, raising a peaceable toast, speaking thus: "May Christ salute you all with health. It becomes each of you to drink the toast which I hold in my hand, in the name of the holy archangel, whom we honor tomorrow by fasting on his holy day.[41] And so, may he be willing to receive in peace those of us honoring his majesty with spiritual love into eternal paradise, in the hour when our souls will depart this world. Amen." And after these words he drank joyfully, and with the same love bade all to empty their goblets. And he embraced and kissed them tenderly, without trembling from fear, and departed to sleep on his bed.

XIX

And in this troubling circumstance—with the knowledge that he would bear his coming death willingly for Christ—he spent that night devoutly in prayer and in almsgiving to the poor, sweating in his exertions.

Then his brother said to his men:[42] "In no way can we destroy him because his retinue is with him and is vigilant. However, we know his habit: as soon as he hears the first sounding of the church bell, he leaps from his bed and hurries to church alone, waiting for no one. Let us tell the priest to ring early." And thus it came to pass.

When the holy man heard the bell's signal, he leaped from his bed unmindful of sleep, as was his habit, and ran to the church. Upon entering, he became absorbed in listening quietly to the morning chants and the praises of matins. Then, wearied after many prayers, he left the church to rest at home.[43] Girded with a sword and lying hidden from the dawn's first light in a concealed spot along with several of his cutthroats, the holy man's brother, inscribed as Boleslav of infamous memory, savagely rushed to the attack like a wolf that wants to attack a lamb and viciously tear it apart; and he met him in the middle of the road. But the saint greeted him in a calm, kind voice, saying: "Good health, dear brother! We owe you many thanks for your kindness, because you served us yesterday so honorably, lavishly, and joyfully." He, the madman, did not reply,[44] but quickly drew his sword and struck the saint with all his strength on the top of his head, saying, "And you arrange an even better feast today." However, the sword bounced off and no trace of a wound appeared. He struck a second time, but was unable to harm him in any way. And when he wished to strike him a third time, the sword fell from the hands of this astonished servant of the Devil. Then Saint Wenceslas grasped the sword by the hilt and, holding it above him, seized his disarmed, sinful brother's hair, shook him by the head, and said: "You see, my brother, how I could turn the onset of your rage against you! Where am I prohibited from becoming the spiller of my brother's blood? But, brother, I do not wish to be held accountable at the Last Judgment for your blood, shed by my hands. Take the sword and the damnation for yourself; and do not tarry with the matter at hand. Go and summon those who have instigated you, but do not sin by shedding a brother's blood yourself."[45]

As soon as the impious brother received his sword, he cried out loudly, as though engaged in battle, calling for help from his men as follows: "O you rebels, you who have instigated me, are you not going to help me?" And he himself drew back unharmed, as though forced by his brother's assault to retreat. Summoned by his loud cries, his retinue immediately came running, as if ignorant of the offense, seeking the uproar and sensing the rising anger of their prince. And now, after he, the instigator of sin, had struck his holy head for the fourth time and finally split it open, all of them fell upon him with weapons and pierced the saint's limbs with swords and spears. Having torn him apart like wolves, they cast him to the earth, scarcely alive. Again and again they inflicted blows and wounds, and shed innocent blood. And his body, which was free of sin, was torn apart as though by dogs. However, his most pure soul was liberated from the domicile of its bodily confinement by his many wounds and torments, and was raised up by angelic hands in honorable victory and glory. It entered into the eternal joy of the heavenly kingdom on the fourth day before the calends of October,[46] joyfully to behold the Most-High Merciful One, seated forever on the throne among His glorious martyrs.

XX

And his holy body was honorably sealed in a coffin by the few faithful who were there, and after performing all the prescribed rites over him, they buried him in front of the church near the place of his victory.

Then, when Prince Boleslav took power, a reign of great injustice began.[47] And not long after the murder of the saint, being filled with wrath at the faithful, he sent his retinue to Prague and destroyed all the saint's friends and clerics. And seizing his servants, he slaughtered them all and cast their children into the river.[48]

XXI

Immediately after the venerable passion of God's staunch warrior, some servants, following orders, were washing with water the blood that had spattered on the boards of the church wall at the very moment of his martyrdom; and they wiped it away completely. Upon coming there the following day, they saw that no less blood was there than before; it was on the wall in the same place and had spread farther. Frightened not a little by this sight, they again brought water and very quickly washed and wiped it away. Coming on the third day to make certain that it was still so, they looked and saw that the wall was no less bespattered with blood; and they looked more than three times. And they marveled much over this. They then ceased the work of washing. And that same wall, even to this day, shows this venerable trace of spattered blood.

XXII

However, in stories and oft-repeated accounts, it has been revealed that after the victorious resistance of Christ's warrior, all those who spilled his blood were shaken by the wrath of the Most High.

Title page of the Wolfenbüttel Manuscript of Gumpold's *Vita* of Saint Wenceslas. Princess Emma (the wife of Boleslav II) is kneeling at the feet of Saint Wenceslas, upon whom Christ is bestowing a martyr's crown, eleventh century.

Some were possessed by the Devil's power and were never after seen in this world; some changed their human ways and, no longer speaking, barked like dogs, gnashing their teeth and imitating fighting dogs. Then they ended their lives evilly, for their wretched bodies wasted away.[49] Moreover, his brother also, as many of our predecessors relate, had to be supported in the arms of his men and servants because of the frequent attacks on him by demons. And after coming to himself, he would say: "You are the ones who have done this to me, because I listened to you and pursued his golden head; and now it has marked me." Nevertheless, all of them, as we have said, finished their lives evilly before their prince.

XXIII

Since his venerable body still rested where he was slain, after three years had passed it was revealed to some of the faithful in dreams at night that it would be fitting—for it was God's will—to bring the holy body from that place to the Church of Saint Vitus the Martyr, which he himself had built, there to give it a most honorable burial. They believed the vision even though deep in slumber. But they remained silent, honestly fearing the prince's rage. However, when this same vision appeared again and again, frightening them greatly, they were unable to conceal it longer, and they told the prince what had been revealed to them. And as if startled from a deep sleep and frightened not by fear of God but by shame before men, the prince directed priests to go by night and to bring the saint's body without anyone knowing.

Upon arriving at the holy place with the help of prayers, they placed the coffin containing the venerable body of the martyr on a cart, and they set off along the way by which they had come, wishing to fulfill the prince's order during the night. But when they came to a little river called Rokytnice,[50] God caused such a strong flood in the river that it destroyed the bridge and swept the planks away. They stood opposite this, seeking where they might find wood to build a raft. And not finding any, they pondered what they might do. And while they were absorbed in meditation and woe, they suddenly looked up and saw a miracle, for God's power intervened: the horses with the cart were standing on the other side, untouched by even a single drop of water. Miraculous tidings like those for the Apostle Peter: Peter walked on the sea at God's command,[51] but the body of the saint was brought across in the wink of an eye. Who can reckon how it was carried across? Only the power of God carried it across. They themselves marveled at His miracle for a time, and following the holy body, they swam on horseback across the river and soon came to the place mentioned previously. Praising God, they entered the church secretly at night, as his brother had commanded. However, it was illuminated by the power of God so that all the people saw them, and they glorified God.

Abundant prayers poured forth after the doors were locked securely, and after lighting candles, they opened the holy coffin and looked inside. And lo, the body was incorrupt and still intact, and healed of all its wounds save one—the wound from his brother's sword from which they could see warm blood still flowing.[52] O praiseworthy dignity of a man of God, and miraculous accession to preeminence! The blessed Wenceslas was here honored by that which honored Jonah. Just as Jonah once was swallowed by a whale and after three days vomited out upon dry land unharmed, so also after three years did the earth, at God's command, surrender this body which even more wondrously was neither decayed nor decomposed but healed of its wounds.[53]

And when the saint's body was again encased, it was accompanied by the faithful and by the clerics with praise and hymns. They laid the venerable body on the south side beneath the very approach to the altar, in deference to his holy memory. And since God's omnipotence frequently manifested itself in countless miracles and signs, this became a gathering place for all the faithful. But for unbelievers it caused dread and fear, for the worthy deeds of such a man manifest themselves frequently.

The time of this translation was the fourth indiction, the month of March, on the fourth day,[54] and it has been celebrated over the years since his death. The sad recollection of this spiritual tale tells in due course about those who were impediments and who still can be understood as such. But because of his dignity, the mercy of God afterward revealed the glory of the saint to the entire universe.

XXIV

Some men were arrested, falsely accused and bound, and brought before a judge in the palace. At the prince's command they were thrown into prison, where they were shackled by the hands and feet and cruelly placed under guard. And in the middle of the night, being in irons and pressed and tormented by the irons with which they were shackled, they all cried out in prayer with bitter, heartrending sighs, saying: "O sovereign God, Comforter of the sorrowing and miraculous Creator of heaven and earth, look upon us who are condemned to death, and by virtue of the prayers of Thy beloved martyr Wenceslas who while living in this world was a merciful protector of the unfortunate, deign to deliver us unfortunate ones from our impending doom."

And when their prayer was finished, the half of the prison in which the guards were standing watch grew dark, and the torches of the guards inside were extinguished; but the other half where the captives lay was lit up as though by a light brighter than the sun. And lo, suddenly a voice from heaven sounded in the ears of the prisoners: "Arise and leave this place." Now, because they were struck by both great fear and joy, they moved their shackles silently. And immediately the chains and irons broke and fell off, their hands and feet were freed, and they ran joyfully through the open doors of the prison, freed by God's command.[55] And they made it known to the people, praising Christ and His holy martyr, Wenceslas.

XXV

Among the prisoners was a pagan as yet uncleansed by the grace of baptism. But once cleansed and delivered from death by the prayers of the blessed Wenceslas, he converted to the Catholic faith and cleansed himself through the salvific ablution of baptism. And he established himself with all his love in God's faith, and promised to turn his only begotten son, whom he loved like his own soul, over to God's service in the clergy of the Church of the Blessed Martyr. And when all this was fittingly accomplished, having lived many years believing in God and serving Him, he himself reposed in the Lord.

XXVI

And after this miracle had occurred, another miracle no less remarkable followed; it happened to a youth from among his valets who, of all his servants, was the most trustworthy in secret matters. The saint himself truly loved him during his lifetime, and this writing has mentioned him previously. Separated from his beloved lord, he was often overcome by grief, sorrowing for days on end. And he would tell everyone about his many good deeds, many of which he himself had witnessed. But his prince, inflamed by a violent and reckless rage, ordered him hanged.[56] And after two years had passed, as the reports of truthful men bear witness, the hanged man appeared no different than any living and healthy person, for the gray hair and fingernails on his body were still growing and glossy. And while he was hanging these many days, an eagle sent by God was seen perched above him, guarding the body so that the birds would not prey upon it.[57] And even the withered tree on which he was hanged sprouted and branched out.

XXVII

After this someone was seized by an evil judge and cast into prison. On the following day he was condemned to death, and securely shackled with irons. And, verily, he cried out bitterly, and in secret prayers called upon God's saint, Wenceslas, to help him, saying: "O holy martyr of God, if it is true, as people say, that you can appeal to God On-High, plead for me, who am dying, so that through your supplications I may be spared, sinner that I am, to live until my mortal sins are forgiven."

And when he finished his prayers, immediately, by the grace of God, the chains that were so secure broke, and he was led out of the prison without the guards knowing. However, he was seized again and tightly bound by some pagans standing outside. When he began to relate his earlier prayer to them, their pagan hearts were appeased, and they untied him and released him. And thus he was spared. After this, while passing through all the lands, he praised God and the Blessed Martyr Wenceslas, and extolled them in words.

XXVIII

It is said that in the same town where the saint's body rests, there lived a woman who lost the sight of her eyes, and from birth was crippled in her hands.[58] And when it was the saint's feast day, she entered the Church of Saint Vitus the Martyr and was brought before the grave of Saint Wenceslas, whither she had longed to come. She prostrated herself for a very long time in supplication to him. And after she had finished her tearful supplication, everyone saw that she had been cured by the holy man: she could see with her eyes and returned to her home with healthy hands.

XXIX

And after this a certain man was seized as a guarantor of another's money, and for this he was very brutally bound so the debt would be paid. But while they were absent and the others were conducting their business in the town,[59] they left the bound man in custody, lying on the road near the church. And in the anguish of affliction he raised his hands back toward the church doors and offered this prayer: "O serene commander, venerable martyr, because your purity has already delivered many from the hands of the impious through your appeals to Almighty God, I pray, sinner that I am, that you will not forget me who am bound, but that in your mercy you free me now."

And God's mercy came swiftly, for at the prayer of the blessed martyr the chains fell apart as though cut by an iron tool. And he himself ran into God's church and in prayer gave thanks to God and His saints. And thus he returned a free man.

XXX

In the land of the Franks there was a man, a cripple from childhood, who, because of his disfigurement at birth, was unable to walk and dragged himself along the ground on all fours. One night after lying down he was startled from sleep; a winged man of wondrous beauty standing next to his bed had roused him, the cripple, and revealed a cure to him, saying: "Rise, O lame one, in any way you can, and go to the Bohemian city called Prague, even if you have to give all your possessions for a litter on which to be carried there. And when you arrive, go into the Church of the Holy Martyr Vitus, where the body of the Holy Martyr Wenceslas rests, and upon reciting a prayer there, you will receive a cure for your lameness."

Lost in his dream, he ignored the dreamy command, believing it to be his imagining, and completely ignored the path he had been shown. And on the following night, while resting on his bed, he again saw an old man of equal resplendence standing next to his bed. Reproaching him in this manner, he said to this stubborn and foolish man: "Awake from your sleep and recognize the truth of this vision, which was foretold and through which your body, unfortunate man, shall be cured. Why do you ignore the cure which was revealed to you at my direction?" Having awakened under this severe reproach, the man replied without further inquiry into its truth: "I cannot go there, O gracious and venerable elder."

But when morning came, he acquired a cart, paid the merchants who were traveling by the same road, and was soon brought to his destination. And in accordance with his previous instructions, he was carried into the Church of the Holy Martyr Vitus. Lying on the ground before the altar, he besought God and the saints in prayer. And after he had spent a short time in prayer, by the power of God's succor and the miraculous prayers of the blessed Wenceslas, the veins, which previously were withered, began to crack as though being broken, and they stretched and his heels became firm. And by the grace of God he arose healthy, not supported by anyone, and returned to his home, glorifying God and proclaiming the sanctity of Saint Wenceslas throughout the Frankish lands.

And even to the present day many other miracles occur next to the holy martyr, which God works according to His mercy. And unto Him be the glory and the power, together with the Son and the Holy Spirit, now and always and forevermore. Amen.

✝ Service and Canon in Honor of Saint Wenceslas

Saint Wenceslas. Fifteenth century fresco, St. Sergius Trinity monastery, Zagorsk, Russia.

✝

Service in Honor of Saint Wenceslas
On the 28th Day of the Same Month.[1]
Feast of Our Venerable Father
Chariton the Confessor,
and Saint Wenceslas the Martyr

Kathisma on the day of Saint Wenceslas[2]

Fourth Tone,[3] melody of [4] "Quickly forewarn"

Today in common gladness the angels rejoice together with the people. Heaven and earth triumphantly jubilate in your memory, O saint! And we sinners zealously cry out to you: "Intercede with the Lord for us, who revere your lasting memory; that He deliver us from the snares of our visible and invisible enemies."

Kontakion[5]

First Tone, melody of "Choir of angels"

Being in the presence of choirs of angels, you, O blessed one, delight in divine and ineffable goodness. And drawing gracious gifts of miracles therefrom, you issue the gift[6] of healing to all who turn to your sanctity with faith.

Stichira[7] to Saint Wenceslas

Eighth Tone, melody of "O most glorious"

Brilliantly adorned by most radiant auras, you, O wondrous Wenceslas, shine forth more than the sun for those who are in need, delivering the unjustly bound and banishing every sickness from those who truly call to you for help and lovingly laud your most venerable dormition.

Come all you faithful, let us today spiritually celebrate the most miraculous memory of Christ's servant, Wenceslas. For he received the kingdom of heaven, having left the corrupt service of earth, and on this day[8] he commended his most holy spirit into the hands of the Lord,[9] glorifying God Who made his memory wondrous.

Another Hymn[10]

Melody of "Paradise which is Eden"

Led by love for the highest calling,[11] you, O most blessed one, went to Christ's Church,[12] and there you received the majestic, immortal, and everlasting crown. Like the sun you illumined yourself with it, emitting radiant auras of miracles to the West and to the northern lands[13] which laud your most glorious memory, O unconquerable Saint Wenceslas!

By shedding your most pure blood, O most glorious one, you have adorned Christ's Church with purple majesty. And adorned with it, she[14] assembles all the lands for the feast to celebrate triumphantly your most holy memory, and to cry out with faith unto the Benefactor and Creator of all. Glory to Thee, Christ, who hath made the memory of this saint wondrous.

Another Hymn[15]

Fourth Tone, melody of "As the bravest among"

Let us praise him, all you who have gathered, as the great helper of those in need. For from Christ the Saviour he received the gift of grace to deliver the unfortunate, to console the sorrowing, and to heal every sickness for those who call for help with faith, and who with love keep his most miraculous feast.

Canon[16] of Saint Wenceslas

Sixth Tone, Canticle One
First Verse:[17] As on dry land . . .[18]

Let us be joyfully jubilant with serene souls, O you righteous, glorifying the Saviour on this day in most miraculous memory of Christ's servant, Wenceslas.

You have made yourself worthy of the Lord's sufferings, O glorious one, unjustly slaughtered like an unblemished lamb. Thus, rejoice now, O divinely blessed one, with the choirs of martyrs.

Having accepted death, O mediator of life, you are now in glory by the Lord of Hosts. Render supplication for us, O saint, that we who keep your most miraculous memory may attain this.

Who, O glorious one, will declare the miracles which you performed on earth without number? For always have you given ample healing to all the faithful.

(To the Mother of God)[19]

Raise me up, Our Lady, for by my sinful[20] deeds have I fallen among despoilers and am sinking in death. I implore You: Intercede for me with Your Son and God.

Canticle Three

First Verse: There is no saint like . . .

Ever enkindled by Christ's love for the holy Church, there did you behold your unjust slaughter like a meek lamb.

Your Church is adorned with your bright blood and emits radiant rays of miracles[21] to those who laud your memory, O praiseworthy one.

Illumined from youth by the aura of the Trinity, you were an heir of Christ. Beseech Him to send peace unto our souls.

(To the Mother of God)

The miracle of Your divine birth, O Immaculate One, surpasses the nature of all beings; for supernaturally You conceived God in Your womb and, upon bearing, You did forever remain a virgin.

Canticle Four

First Verse: Christ is my strength, God and Lord . . .

Graciously reared from youth in pure faith, with love you followed the Lord in your pure works. And through hope in Him, you shamed the crafty Enemy.

Radiating brilliance, O holy Wenceslas, illumine with your prayers those who are benighted by sin, for you are at liberty to intercede for us with the choirs of martyrs.

Felled by the sword, O unconquerable saint, you felled the wily Enemy with the sword of passivity. Thus did you receive the crown from the hand of the Almighty.

(To the Mother of God)

Truly ineffable and incomprehensible to those of earth and heaven are the mysteries of Your divine travail, O Mother of God and Ever-Virgin.

Canticle Five

First Verse: By God's light . . .

Through your sufferings, O praised one, you have received a blissful life. O Saint Wenceslas, be a defender of all the suffering, who with faith cry to you for help.

With the most radiant auras of your miracles, O blessed one, you illumined the North, the South, and the West more than the sun.[22] Therefore, O saint, illumine us who celebrate your memory.

To those in need you were a helper, to the poor, food, for the sorrowing, a comfort. Therefore, even after death, O saint, you save all who with faith cry to you for help.

(To the Mother of God)

O gracious Mistress of the world, save those who with all their heart profess You as the Mother of God. For being truly the Mother of God, O Immaculate One, we have Your intercession.

Canticle Six

First Verse: Of life . . .

Through fasting, O wondrous Wenceslas, you acquired a pure life and became a compatriot of the angels. Pray with them for the salvation of our souls.

Leaving your earthly, temporal princedom, you have received a royal adornment from the right hand of the Lord, and wisely acquired the eternal through transient things.

Accept praise, O saint, from pitiable lips that are unable to weave fitting praise for you. And beseech merciful God to grant us much mercy.

(To the Mother of God)

Most pure Mistress, You who gave birth to a Helmsman and Master for earthlings, guide the tormenting confusion of my desires, and grant my heart tranquillity.

Canticle Seven

First Verse: To a season of cooling . . .

Envious of your saintly life, the old evildoer instigated the crazed mob to murder you. But with a clear conscience you cried out incessantly to your Creator: "Blessed God of Our Fathers."[23]

Today Prague, your most glorious city, joyfully rejoices, revering your memory and radiantly illumined by your miracles. It summons all lands to cry out: "Blessed . . ."

Through the deception of the most evil one, the land was once turned red by a fratricidal hand. Bloodstained now, it brings a fragrant sacrifice to Christ, crying out: "Blessed . . ."

(To the Mother of God)

Through You, O Virgin, a light shines forth through the darkness, for You have given birth to the Creator of all, and God. Beseech Him, O Immaculate One, always to bestow His great mercy upon us, the faithful.

Canticle Eight

First Verse: For the saints from the flames . . .

Through the goodness of joy and the gracious auras from on high, you, O most glorious one, shone in the land of Bohemia[24] more than the sun, extolling Christ forever.[25]

Receiving your holy body today, O blessed one, Prague, your most glorious city, proclaims your most wondrous miracles to the world, extolling . . .

Adorned with humility and illuminated by a knowledge of the true faith, O most wondrous one, you have revealed yourself as a true preacher of the Holy Trinity, extolling . . .

(To the Mother of God)

From the light of the Giver of Light the Word was conceived, and mysteriously You gave birth to the Supernatural One; for the Divine Spirit, O Virgin, took up His abode in You. Therefore, O Immaculate One, we laud You through all the ages.

Canticle Nine

First Verse: Receiving . . .

You have been deemed worthy, O glorious one, of great grace, and have illumined the entire universe, granting abundant healing to all.

Receiving angelic joy, O saint, and standing before your Creator, intercede for us who magnify you.

Receiving blessed peace now, cease not to pray, most glorious one, that we who magnify you may always share in your holy bliss.

(To the Mother of God)

O Mother of God, who through the Word gave birth beyond the Word to Your Creator, beseech Him, O Virgin, that our souls be saved.

Exaposteilarion[26]
Melody of: "Translated from the earth . . ."

From the earth you have departed to the Lord, O most blessed Wenceslas; now come spiritually and visit your grace upon us who laud your venerable feast today.

✝ Prologue Life of Saint Ludmila

Princess Ludmila, seventeenth-century fresco. Cathedral of the Exaltation of the Cross, Tutaev (formerly Romaovo-Borisoglebsk), Russia.

✝

On the Same Day.[1] The Holy Martyr Ludmila, Grandmother of Saint Wenceslas

B LESSED LUDMILA WAS from the land of the Serbs and the daughter of a Serbian prince.[2] And she was given in marriage to a Czech prince called Bořivoj.[3] However, all were not as yet baptized then. Thus, when they were joined in marriage, the eyes of their hearts were illuminated, and they were baptized in the name of the Father and of the Son and of the Holy Ghost.[4] And they built churches and assembled priests.[5]

And they begot three sons and a daughter.[6] Then, in his thirty-sixth year, Bořivoj departed from this life.[7]

And Blessed Ludmila committed all her cares to God,[8] and all her possessions she distributed to the poor as alms. And her son Vratislav[9] ascended his father's throne. After ruling for thirty years, he now reposed in the Lord. And Wenceslas,[10] Ludmila's grandson, assumed power.

Then Wenceslas's mother[11] began to plot evil against her mother-in-law and sought every way to destroy her. Realizing this, Ludmila left for another town, one called Tetín.[12] But her daughter-in-law conspired with two boyars[13] and sent them to Tetín to destroy her mother-in-law, Ludmila.

And when these brigands arrived, they assembled a host of evildoers of the same ilk. And as evening fell they surrounded the courtyard with arms. Then they broke down the doors and entered the house. And they seized Ludmila, threw a rope around her neck, and strangled her.

And thus she came to the end of her life on the day of the Sabbath, in the first hour of the night. She had lived for sixty-one years, was pleasing to God and received the martyr's crown. For through her God revealed signs and miracles at the place where she was buried. She was not laid to rest in the church but under a wall of the castle, where burning candles appeared each night. And a certain blind man gained sight upon touching the earth where Ludmila lay. And from thenceforth many miracles occurred.

Her grandson, Wenceslas, heard of this and hastened to translate his grandmother to the glorious city of Prague.[14] And he placed her relics in the Church of Saint George,[15] where even now many signs and miracles occur.

✝ Prologue Life of Saint Wenceslas

✝

On the Same Day.[1] The Passion
of Saint Wenceslas, Prince of the Czechs

FIRST AND FOREMOST it is fitting to know the lineage and dominion of the Holy Martyr Wenceslas. He was the son of Vratislav,[2] prince of the Czechs, and had two brothers, Spytihněv and Boleslav,[3] who were under him. And when their father died, Wenceslas assumed his father's throne.

Then evil people began to incite the brothers. First they persuaded Wenceslas to banish his mother, saying, "Together with your brothers she wishes to murder you; for previously she murdered your grandmother Ludmila."[4] And he banished his mother to Budeč.[5] But soon he repented and brought her back.

And the boyars summoned his brother, saying: "If you do not heed us and do not forestall your brother in the murder, he will murder you. We prefer you over him." And Boleslav took counsel with them. And he prevailed on his brother Wenceslas to come to him for the consecration of a church.[6] And when Wenceslas arrived, they spent the day of consecration amicably. Wenceslas now wished to leave the castle, but Boleslav prevailed on him to make merry until morning. For he was flattering in speech, saying that he loved him more than his life,[7] but in his heart he plotted murder.

Since Wenceslas decided to stay, that night in the castle Boleslav confirmed with his boyars the plot to murder his brother. And in the morning, while going to church for matins, Boleslav, together with his boyars, overtook him and struck him on the head with his sword. And Wenceslas ran to the church.[8] And Tira and Tista[9] overtook him and cut him down at the doors of the church. Then Hněvysa pierced his ribs with a sword.

And as Monday dawned, Saint Wenceslas commended his blessed spirit[10] into the hands of God. But for three days his blood could not be removed from the walls of the church,[11] for it cried out to God against Boleslav, like the blood of Abel.[12]

After several years, his relics were translated to the glorious city of Prague and placed in the Church of Saint Vitus.[13]

✝ Prologue Translation of Saint Wenceslas

✝

On the Same Day.[1] The Translation of Saint Wenceslas

THERE WAS A RIGHTEOUS PRINCE among the Czechs named Wenceslas, who was born of Christian parents, Vratislav, his father, and Dorogomil,[2] his mother.

But at the Devil's exhortation Boleslav[3] murdered his brother Wenceslas. Then a miracle took place over the body of Saint Wenceslas, for his blood did not soak into the ground for three days. And in the evening of the third day a church rose over him[4] so that all who saw this marveled.

Upon seeing this, Boleslav turned his heart of stone to repentence and bent his neck of steel in prayer.[5] He understood his sin, for he murdered not only his brother Wenceslas, but because of him he destroyed others. And he called the Lord to mind, and the number of sins he committed, and without ceasing he prayed to God and all the saints, and to his brother, Saint Wenceslas.

Then, having dispatched priests and his servants, he brought the body of his brother Wenceslas from Boleslav's castle to Prague, saying: "I have sinned and my sin and my transgressions I acknowledge."[6] And he placed him in the Church of Saint Vitus, on the right side of the altar of the Twelve Apostles, where he himself had said he should be buried when he built the church.[7]

Prince Wenceslas was translated in the month of March on the fourth day. May his soul repose in the bosoms of Abraham, Isaac, and Jacob, wherein all the righteous repose, awaiting the resurrection from Our Lord Jesus Christ.[8]

✝ Other Church Slavonic Works

✝ Life of Saint Vitus

The Golden Gates (Southern Portal) of St. Vitus Cathedral, Prague, fourteenth century.

✝

The Month of June on the Fifteenth Day
The Passion of the Blessed Martyrs
Vitus, Modestus, and Crescentia

Bless us Lord, Our Father

I N THE LAND OF LUCANIA,[1] during the time of the impious emperors
Diocletian and Antonius,[2] blessed Vitus performed many miracles
during his childhood.[3] Fearing the God of heaven and earth, he besought God day and night, he converted the souls of the faithless, and
he took care of widows and the sick.[4] Now the child was of a good
lineage and great wealth, yet he recited his prayers clad in a hair shirt.[5]
And he besought Christ, saying, "Deal with thy servant according
unto thy mercy [Psalms 119:124], and let me not wander from thy
commandments [Psalms 119:10], and separate me not from the assembly of the upright."[6]

Now his father was a pagan, a shameless man who would not
abandon the worship of idols. And a voice came from heaven saying:[7]
"Your prayer, O Vitus, has been heard. Behold, I shall deal with you
according to your request." His father, Hylas,[8] admonished him that
he might incline him toward the worship of idols. But Blessed Vitus
answered him and said: "I know no other God save the One God, who
is from eternity, whose spirit moved over the waters, who divided the
light from the darkness, and who summoned the light and there was
light, and summoned the darkness and there was darkness.[9] Him do I
serve, and the Holy Christ, King of the angels. To Him do I pray, who
created heaven and earth, the sea, and all that in them is.[10] Him will I
profess all the days of my life."

Hearing this, his father ordered the child beaten with rods, saying
to him: "Who taught you to profess that one? Do you not know that
you will perish if the rulers learn of this?" But Blessed Vitus said,
"You hear me speak what Christ has taught me; and I am His
servant."

Then his father[11] summoned Modestus, his tutor, and said, "See
that he never utters these words again." But in reply Saint Vitus said:

"This is fine nectar for me, as it was for the prophet who said, 'The law of thy mouth is better than thousands of gold and silver. Thy hands have made me and fashioned me: give me understanding, that I may learn thy commandments' " [Psalms 119:72-73]. And an angel of the Lord appeared to the child, saying, "I have been sent to you as a guardian, to protect you to your end; and whatever you shall ask, it shall be given to you."

And the father wept over his son, for he was his only son, and with kindly words he admonished him, that he might incline him toward the worship of demons. But Saint Vitus said to him, "Which gods do you bid me to serve?" And his father, Hylas, answered him and said, "Do you not know the true gods, Juno, Mars, Vesta, Hercules, and Minerva,[12] whom our rulers worship?" And Saint Vitus answered him: "You call them gods: they are idols, made by hands. They have mouths, but they speak not: eyes have they, but they see not [Psalms 115:5]. But I know the One God, Father, Son, and Holy Spirit; and I profess the one Son of God: He was sacrificed for our sins, and by His blood have we been redeemed. But you, father, know Him not. If you desired to submit to Him, you would know that Christ is the Son of God, the Lamb which takes away the sins of the whole world."[13] But in answer his father said: "I know the Christ of whom you speak was the son of a man, crucified on a cross. And he was scourged by Pilate and turned over for crucifixion. And you profess him, son!" And Saint Vitus said: "His betrayal and crucifixion were redemption for our sins, and no one can separate Him from me. For many of those possessed professed Him, and He gave sight to many of the blind and made the ailing well."

Upon hearing this, the emperor Valerian[14] summoned his father to him and said to him: "I hear that your son professes the Christ, whom the Jews crucified, but he reviles our gods. Therefore, command him to be brought here." And when the boy was brought, the emperor, sitting in judgment, questioned him saying: "Why do you not make sacrifice to the gods whom the rulers obey?[15] They have decreed that anyone found honoring this Christ shall die from terrible torture." But Blessed Vitus, being pure and filled[16] with the Holy Ghost,[17] made the sign of Christ, the Son of God, and without trembling or fear opened his mouth and said, "I will never obey an empty stone; but I have God, whom my soul will serve." Having witnessed this, his father cried out in a loud voice, exhorting his kin and saying, "Weep with me, for I see my only begotten son perishing." And Saint Vitus said,[18] "I shall not perish if I enter into the assembly of the upright."[19] Valerian said: "Because you are of high birth and your father's friendship restrains me, I now decree that you be beaten with sticks only. Obey and make sacrifice to the gods." And Saint Vitus answered, "Emperor, I have already told you: I worship Christ, the Son of God."

And the emperor was greatly wroth and ordered the lad whipped. But when he extended his hand toward the lad, it immediately withered.[20] And the emperor cried out, saying, "I have lost my hand and am in torment." He then summoned the lad's[21] father, Hylas, and said to him, "You do not have a son, for I see that he is a sorcerer." And replying, Saint Vitus said: "My sorcery is Christ, He who teaches me His commandments for all times; He for whose sake I am fulfilled; He who raises the dead and who walked upon the sea;[22] He who commanded the sea, and it was calmed from its wrath:[23] To Him am I a servant. If your gods can do these things, let them heal your hand." And Valerian said, "You do it." And Saint Vitus said, "I shall do it in the name of Jesus Christ." And immediately he healed this man's hand.

Then the emperor entrusted him to his father, saying, "Go and instruct your son, that he might obey the gods, make sacrifice, and not perish." Then his father took him and brought him to his home. And he tried to sway him with much wealth and flattering words, and to soothe him with cymbals and harps. Adorning his maidservants, he commanded them to dance before him. But the youth[24] directed his eyes toward heaven, saying, "God will not despise a broken and contrite heart."[25] And his father[26] ordered his chamber ornamented with rare and precious stones. And when he entered his chamber, his father ordered it closed. Kneeling, Saint Vitus now prayed to God, saying: "O God of Abraham, God of Isaac, God of Jacob,[27] have mercy upon me, give Thy strength unto me;[28] let not the iniquitous dragon conquer me, Thy servant; nor let the heathen say, 'Where is his God?' "[29] And his chamber was illuminated, as if twelve lamps were burning; and there was a scent, as if from many censers full of fragrance. And his father and all the servants said, "Never have our elders encountered such a scent." Then his father said, "The gods have come to the house," and he began to laugh and looked into the chamber through a small window as it shone. And his eyes were opened and he saw seven angels[30] with wings like eagles standing around the child. And from fear of them the father was immediately blinded.

Then Blessed Vitus offered a prayer for his father, saying, "O God of Elijah, Christ, Son of God born of the Holy Spirit, separate me not from my father, but command him that he might come into Thy holy palace." Being greatly afflicted with pain, his father[31] cried out, saying, "Woe unto me, because of him I have lost the light of my eyes." And there was wailing, as the servants and maidservants were grieving for their master. And the entire town was in tumult. Then Valerian said, "Why is there this trouble among you?" And as he asked, he saw the blind man. Summoning him, he asked, "How did you come to this?" And Hylas answered: "While sitting in my son's chamber I was astonished: I saw fiery gods around him. Their eyes were like sparks and I could not bear the sight of them." And Valerian said, "Truly, those were the gods." Then Hylas ordered his servants to bring him to the Temple of Jupiter. Promising horned sacrifices, he said to him, "O Lord Jupiter, if you restore my health, I shall sacrifice to you a bullock with golden horns as well as vestal virgins."[32] But his gods slept and none offered him help. And he cried out in pain.

Kneeling, Blessed Vitus continuously besought the Lord, saying, "Thou who hast given sight unto Tobit[33] and healed Job of his sores,[34] have mercy also upon my father." And they brought the blind man to him, and he fell at his son's feet and said to him, "My son, heal me." And Saint Vitus answered him, "Do you wish to be healed?" His father answered, "I do." And Saint Vitus said to him, "Will you renounce devilish rituals and deeds?" Hylas said, "I will." And Saint Vitus said to him, "Will you renounce Jupiter and Artemis and Hercules, Juno and Minerva?"[35] But Hylas said, "How can I renounce them?" Saint Vitus said,[36] "If you renounce them now, you will see the light again." Hylas said, "I renounce them." And Saint Vitus said, "I know that your heart has hardened, but for the sake of the people standing here I will have mercy upon you." And he touched his eyes[37] and immediately scales fell from his eyes,[38] and he was cured. Realizing that he could see, he cried out in a loud voice, saying, "I shall lift up praise to my gods, who have cured me." Upon hearing this, Saint Vitus began to laugh, saying to him, "Christ healed you, not your gods." And so he now tried to find tortures by which he might kill his son.

But an angel of the Lord appeared to Modestus and said: "Take the child and go to the sea. There you will find a boat. And I will take you away to another land; whither I will make known to you." But Saint Modestus, his guardian, said, "I do not know the way." And the angel of the Lord said, "I will go with you." At that time Saint Vitus was seven years old.

And they departed. And the angel of the Lord accompanied them to the sea. And they found the small boat that Christ had prepared for them. Testing the lad, the boatman said, "To what land do you betake yourselves?" And Saint Vitus said, "Whither Christ our God leads us." And the boatman[39] said to him, "Where is your toll?" Answering, Saint Vitus said, "Christ, whose servant I am, will give you the toll." And they got into the boat. Then they discerned that they were in a place called Alectorium.[40] And immediately the boat that brought them disappeared. And they came upon a river called the Silar.[41] Resting there beneath a tree, Saint Vitus performed many miracles. And at night an eagle brought them food.

But demons cried out then, saying: "What have we to do with you, Vitus? Have you come to torment us before the time?[42] For we have never known such torment. Cruel are your torments, O Blessed Vitus." And many people came to them, for he converted many by baptism and taught the commandments of Christ, saying: "I believed, therefore have I spoken: I was greatly humbled."[43] And in another psalm he said, "As the hart panteth after the water brooks, so panteth my soul after Thee, O God" [Psalms 42:1].

Now the son of the emperor Diocletian was oppressed by an evil spirit. And it[44] said, "If Vitus of Lucania[45] does not journey here, I will not come out." And Emperor Diocletian said, "Where can we find this man?" And the demon answered, "In the land of Tanagritano,[46] there you will find him." Then Diocletian commanded his armed servants to go and bring Saint Vitus. Going there, his servants found him at the river and said to him, "Are you not Vitus?" And Blessed Vitus answered, "You say that I am." The servants said to him, "The emperor has need of you." And Blessed Vitus answered and said, "I am only a poor person; what need does the emperor have of me?" The servants said to him, "His son is possessed by a devil." And he answered them, "I know that I must come to the land of the Romans."[47]

And they related this to Emperor Diocletian. Upon taking his place at the council, he commanded the youth[48] brought. Now Blessed Vitus was ruddy in appearance, like a fire, and very handsome; and his eyes were like the rays of the sun. He was suffused with the glory of Christ Himself. Diocletian said to him, "Are you Vitus?" But he did not answer him. And he asked Modestus, his guardian. But Modestus was old and by nature meek, and he did not want to answer the emperor, because the emperor had confused the old man. And Blessed Vitus said, "Emperor, why do you question an old man like[49] a young one? The man is gray and should be respected." Diocletian said, "Why are you wroth with us, and angry?" And Vitus answered, "We are not angry but meek as doves. For our teacher who taught us is good." But the demon cried out, "O Vitus, why do you trouble me before the time?"[50] And Emperor Diocletian said to Vitus,[51] "Can you heal my son?" Vitus answered him, "Not I but Christ, the Son of God, whose servant I am." And he approached the son, and placing his hand on his head, said, "Come out of God's creation, O unclean spirit."[52] And it soon came out. But the demon put many to death. Saddened now, Emperor Diocletian also became frightened and afraid. And the emperor said, "For I say to you, Vitus, obey me and make sacrifices to my gods, and I will give you as much as half my kingdom. I will also give you gold, and silver, and priceless robes." But Saint Vitus answered: "I have no need of your kingdom or your robes. I have God and walk always with Him. He will array me in a radiant and immortal robe, that darkness shall not gird me round." And Diocletian said to him, "Set your heart at ease, Vitus, and sacrifice to my gods, lest you perish in great torment."[53] And Saint Vitus answered, "I long to come to His hand, as the Lord has promised His chosen."[54]

And the emperor told them to take him to prison and to place one hundred and forty measures of iron weights upon him.[55] And with his ring he placed a seal upon the prison[56] so that no one would give him water. And when they brought him to the prison, at that moment a great light filled the prison.[57] And the guards were astonished. Then Blessed Vitus cried out in a loud voice, saying, "Hasten to succor us, O Lord,[58] behold[59] our misfortune and deliver us from torment as Thou didst deliver the three young Jews from the burning fiery furnace,[60] and Susanna from false witness."[61]

Then a light from on high lit the prison, and there was a great earthquake, for the Lord God Himself descended unto His servants and said to them, "Rise: lo, I am with you."[62] And, verily, the irons became as ashes, and there was a single voice of chanting, proclaiming: "Blessed be the Lord God of Israel; for He hath visited and redeemed His people, and hath raised up a horn of salvation for us in the house of His servant David" [Luke 1:68-69]. Hearing this, the guards ran to the palace and cried out in a loud voice, "Emperor, the city is doomed!" But Emperor Diocletian was in confusion and answered, saying: "What is this? And what are you saying?" And the guards said: "Vitus, the one you ordered taken to prison. . . . There is a great light in the prison and a strange fragrance, and a man is there whose very sight no human can endure."

Then the emperor commanded that an arena be prepared, saying, "Let me give their souls to wild beasts and see whether their God can deliver them out of my hands."[63] And when they were led into the arena, Saint Vitus strengthened his guardian Modestus, that he should not be afraid, and said to him, "Be brave; do not fear the Devil's weapons. Behold, our crown is now at hand!"[64] And an innumerable number of people were watching this spectacle, four thousand men and women, and an innumerable multitude of children. Then Emperor Diocletian said to Saint Vitus, "Vitus, where do you find yourself?" But he lifted up his eyes and looked toward heaven. And again he said to him, "Where do you find yourself?" And Saint Vitus said: "I find myself in an arena. If you are going to do something, do it quickly."[65] But Emperor Diocletian said, "Be mindful of your soul and make sacrifice to the great gods." But Saint Vitus said: "May you never be at peace, you devil, you wolf and plunderer, you torturer of innocent souls.[66] I am astonished by your mind, Emperor, because if a dog is told, 'Get out!' it goes, ashamed. Are you not ashamed? But I have Christ and Him do I serve."

Then Emperor Diocletian was filled with anger, and he ordered his servants to prepare a cauldron and to throw lead and pitch into it.[67] And the servants did as they were told. And the emperor said, "Can their God deliver them out of my hands?"[68] And Saint Vitus was cast into the middle of the cauldron after he made the sign of Christ. And the cauldron boiled like the sea. But an angel of the Lord calmed the boiling cauldron, and from its midst Saint Vitus offered thanks to God: "Thou, who delivered the sons of Israel from the land of Egypt and from the bonds of slavery through Thy servants Moses and Aaron,[69] hast shewed mercy upon us for Thy name's sake." And looking about, Saint Vitus said: "What is it, Diocletian? Where are your threats? I offer you my thanks for providing us with a bath. You should have prepared soap also!"[70] And all the people cried out, saying: "Never have we seen such a miracle. Verily, his God is great!" And he emerged from the cauldron unharmed, without a single wound on his body. Indeed, his body shone like the snow. And he said, "Shame be upon you, Emperor, and upon your father, the Devil."

And the emperor was filled with wrath. He commanded that he be attacked by a savage lion, whose charge no human could withstand. The emperor said to him, "Can your sorcery surmount this?" And Saint Vitus said: "O witless fool, Christ is with me together with His angels. He will deliver me out of your hands." And they set a lion upon him. Making the sign of the cross, Saint Vitus overpowered the lion's fury. Running up to him, the lion fell at his feet and with its tongue licked the sweat from his face. And in answer Saint Vitus said to the emperor: "Behold, emperor, a beast honors God, yet you cannot recognize Him. Were you to recognize Him and believe in Christ, you would be saved." But the emperor said, "You and your generation believe!" And, smiling, Saint Vitus said, "You answer well, Emperor, for my entire generation hopes for eternal life and is established in paradise." Witnessing this, many people, up to one thousand, instantly believed. And the emperor said to him, "Vitus, how is it that you can command the fire and beasts?" And in answer Saint Vitus said, "The beast honors the Lord, and not me, for it recognizes its Creator."

Then the emperor ordered his servants to prepare racks of iron. And on them[71] they stretched God's valiant servants,[72] Saint Vitus together with Crescentia, his nurse, and Saint Modestus. And Saint Vitus said to the emperor: "Be ashamed of yourself and be appeased! Of what concern is this woman to you? Yet you also torture her at the trial." Then Saint Vitus said to Diocletian, "Brazen torturer, of what concern is this woman to you?" And the emperor was greatly wroth and ordered them tortured until their innards were torn asunder. Then, raising his eyes toward heaven, Saint Vitus cried out, saying, "O

Lord God, deliver us!" And immediately there was a great earthquake, and lightning, and thunder. And the pagan temples fell down, and a third of the people perished.[73] And the emperor fled, striking his forehead with the palm of his hand and saying, "Woe is me, for I have been overpowered[74] by such a child." And an angel of the Lord descended and delivered them from the rack.

And immediately they found themselves near the river called the Silar,[75] and they rested beneath a tree. And Blessed Vitus invoked Christ, saying: "O Lord God, Jesus Christ, Son of the living God, receive our souls unto Thyself! Yea, I beseech Thee that no fly appear on this spot for four days after my birth into heaven."[76] And a voice came to him from heaven, saying, "Vitus, what you ask has been given you." And they rested in peace. And their souls appeared white as doves, indeed more than seven times whiter than snow. And a choir of angels sang in heaven and on earth. And for three days eagles guarded their bodies.[77]

When the horses drawing her as she sat in a carriage suddenly bolted, Florentia,[78] a noblewoman, found herself in need, as she was being carried toward the river. And Saint Vitus appeared to her, walking over the water. When the woman saw him, she cried out and said, "If you are an angel of God, deliver me!" And Saint Vitus said: "I am Vitus. If you will perform a service and bury our bodies, what you ask of the Lord He will give to you, and you will receive it."[79] And being delivered from the dangers of the water, she gathered up their holy bodies, wound them with spices,[80] and buried them at the place where they rested, which is called Marian.

Thus the Blessed Martyrs Vitus, Modestus, and Crescentia were martyred on the fifteenth day of the month of June, during the reign of Diocletian and Antonius, when the Lord God and Our Saviour Jesus Christ reigned over us in heaven and on earth. And unto Him be honor and glory now and always and forevermore. Amen.

✝ Office in Honor of Saint Vitus (Glagolitic Fragment)

Saint Vitus. Illumination, ca. 1410.

✝

The Month of June on the Fifteenth Day
Vitus and His Companions

For Vespers

Chapter

Brethren, through faith the saints subdued kingdoms, wrought righteousness, obtained promises [Hebrews 11:33].

Responsory

Blessed Vitus . . .

Versicle

Rejoice . . .

Antiphon

I will give my saints an honorable place in the kingdom of my Father, saith the Lord. Hallelujah.

Prayer

O Lord, we beseech Thee, help us through the intercession of Thy Blessed Martyrs Vitus and his companions; for we honor their glorious birth unto heaven[1] in this office.

For Matins

Invitatory

O King of martyrs . . .

Antiphon, Psalm, and Responsory

See the lection in the office of martyrs.

Lection

The blessed youth Vitus was born of venerable parents. His father, named Hylas, was a high official[2] for Emperor Diocletian. He was a pagan. When Vitus[3] was seven years old, an angel of the Lord appeared to him and said: "For all the days of your life I am given to you as a servant. And for you the Lord will fulfill all your requests."

Lection

And Vitus[4] always glorified Christ. And his father was annoyed that he glorified Christ and required him to serve idols and false gods.[5] And Blessed Vitus said to his father, "Which gods do you bid me to serve?" And the father said to him, "Do you not know the merciful gods, Hercules and Jupiter,[6] whom the emperors serve?" And Saint Vitus said to his father: "I know no other gods save the One God, the Father and Son and Holy Spirit, which is the divine Trinity. I believe in Christ,[7] who suffered for the sake of our sins, and through whose blood we have been delivered from death.[8] But you, father, neither know nor have knowledge of Him. For if you knew Him, you would not call mute idols gods." Indeed, by telling him about the Christian God, Vitus condemned his father and his gods. Hearing this, his father reprimanded him and ordered the child beaten with rods. Thus, he disputed much with his father. But his father was unable to induce him to worship idols. And when Emperor Valerian[9] heard this, he seized his father and said to him: "Your son professes Christ and blasphemes the faith of our gods. Therefore, order him brought forth so that we may question him before you." And when he was brought forth, the emperor questioned him, saying: "Sacrifice to our gods, Vitus. If not, you will die through many torments."

Lection

But Blessed Vitus was filled with the Holy Spirit. He made the sign of the cross without fear or trembling, opened his mouth, and said, "I never worship an empty stone, but I have a living God whom my soul will serve." Then his father cried out in a loud voice, saying, "Weep with me, my friends, for I see my only begotten son perishing before my eyes." And Vitus said, "I shall not perish if I may enter into the assembly of the upright."[10]

Lection from the Holy Gospel According to Mark

At that time the Saviour said to His disciples: "For whosoever will come after me, let him deny himself, and take up his cross, and follow me" [Mark 8:34], etc.

The Blessed Pope Gregory's Homily

The words of the Lord, O most worthy brethren, can arouse inner reflections, and one should perceive the thoughts so as to understand what good is found in them.

Responsory

We honor forever the memory of Christ's blessed martyrs. The Lord, God of Israel, is blessed in their accomplishments and miracles.

Versicle

The bodies of the saints are buried in peace, but their names live on.

✝ Prayer Against the Devil

ꙗкотъінесиб҃ллоин
токѣславоунаалⷮ
коувъіллаюеъѡ҃цмь
исѣстъіллъдꙑмь инъі
наиприсн҃овъвⷰкъ
поклонн꙼ ꙗ г҃ шдꙑ доло
иꙗ глⷶⷩ ѿг҃непⷩ҃пⷩдшю
скърбаноуѿнапасти
нгрѣха нкꙗкоꙗпе
чали꙼ г҃иполлилоун по
г҃шдⷣеови азлоуллⷡꙗша
ꙗхⷤꙁови мⷪ надꙑиво
ла инлꙗеунⷭтꙑижд҃ꙑ кⷪ
в꙼жлⷤⷩстъіль какоподо
влетⷮⷳорити нилл꙼вож
мал꙼цⷩ

ЗѿкапенъінрабЪ
бж҃ни нарⷣꙗ приⷣⷰꙁа
даюкъвсⷮꙗллстꙑ

Prayer Against the Devil.

✝

Prayer against the Devil and against unclean spirits, and to all the saints, characterizing your name, as is fitting to do

I, WRETCHED SERVANT OF GOD (name),[1] approach all the saints, praying to them, who pleased God with their great struggle from the creation of the whole world, and with their many toils vanquished the Devil, the Enemy of mankind, and trampled his creation to nought along with his demons. Receive me, a sinner, unto yourselves and remove me from my Enemy, from the one who terrifies my soul and torments my body. Save me now from it all by delivering me from him. For you can do this with the grace and help of the Holy Spirit residing in you by virtue of your holiness.

O Enoch, virtuous man of God, you who are still alive and will be kept so until the last days to reveal the Devil, reveal him now and drive him away from me; help me, a wretched one.[2]

O benefactor Noah, righteous man of God and preacher, together with your children save me through your righteousness, drive the great sin away from me and destroy it by flood like the ancient sin; preserve me as you preserved the races of old.[3]

O father Abraham, you who are called a true friend of God,[4] just as you asked for salvation from the Lord not for many people but for a few righteous ones from among many, gain salvation for me too, and receive me on your bosom.

O Isaac, joyful one,[5] as you are an image of Christ, mark me with the sign of Christ so that my enemies will run far away from me.

O beloved Jacob, chosen from your mother's womb; O pure mind that sees God, sever the evil serpent from me with your heel,[6] and mark me with the sign of the cross just as you blessed and marked your decendents with this sign. Illuminate me, forbid it[7] from approaching me with its deceitfulness.

O Job, you who loved your Lord God in true faith and thus called God-loving, pray for me as you would for your friends, that I be saved through you from the inexhaustible serpent wishing to devour me, just as He saved you from all the calamities that hindered you, like many and great troubles, and a wall of stone.[8]

O great and gentle Moses, as you saved[9] the Israelites from the evil Satan nesting in Egypt with your staff that symbolized the sign of the cross, as you drowned him in the depths of the sea, and the Pharaoh in the Red Sea along with his Egyptian hordes,[10] and smote the proud Amalekite in the desert, defend me with the power of the cross.

O Joshua, redeemed commander and victor,[11] as you brought[12] the people of another tribe to salvation, for my sake, a servant of Christ (name), help me with your sword by cutting down the Lord's enemies warring against me; take me across the Jordan on dry land to God's promised land together with His new people.[13]

O Samuel, you who call to the Lord for universal help, and to whom He listens because of your grace,[14] when you call to Him, call to Him for me (name), an injured servant of God, and upon blessing me, anoint me with the oil of the Holy Spirit just as He anointed the shepherd David and sent him against the evil spirits to drive them out with his psalms.

O you twelve holy prophets, Hosea, Amos, Micah, Joel, Jonah, Obadiah, Nahum, Habakkuk, Zephaniah, Haggai, Zechariah, and Malachi, and you four other great pillars, Isaiah, Jeremiah, Samuel,[15] and Daniel, who appeared in the image of the four evangelists, all of you together beseech the Lord, whom you proclaim, for me; save me from the visible and invisible enemies fighting against me with all their cunning in thought and action instead of speech, and with unclean spirits. Fill my entire essence with the most pure spirit residing in you. You foretold about Him, and what you were saying was fulfilled in that which has taken place, in that which is not occurring now, and in that which will be. You foresaw the distant like the near: the first coming of Our Lord Jesus Christ, Immanuel; the second serene revelation from the heavens of His coming again, of all the majesty of His Divinity, and of the final end when He will throw the haughty into endless torment, and the Evil One, the Devil, together with all the apostates and fiendish spirits into eternal suffering.

O prophet Elijah, holy servant of God, as you destroyed the vile servants of the Devil together with all his creation, having driven him out of Israel with the fervor of the Lord,[16] and thus were translated to paradise where you are even now and shall be preserved until the last days to reveal his wickedness, so now drive him away from me into eternal perdition.

O holy prophet Elisha, twofold miracle-worker, having saved me from the evil infirmity, undoing the barrenness,[17] heal me as you healed the waters so that I, being well, could make God's truth fruitful.

O holy disciples of the Lord, Peter, Paul, James, John, Andrew, Philip, Thomas, Bartholomew, Matthew, James of Alphaeus, Simon Zelotes, and Judas of James, you twelve apostles of Christ whose names are written in the heavens, since you sit on both sides of Christ on Judgment Day, judging all nations, having received power from God's most eternal Son, trample the serpent and the scorpion and all inimical force, and heal every infirmity and every disease among the people and in the lands through which you pass. Drive them out of me. Drive the evil force of the Devil and all his cunning away from me, and having doctored me, heal me, filling me through your prayers with the body and spirit of the Holy Spirit.

O holy passion sufferers for Christ, all of you who proclaimed[18] His Divinity, Stephen the first deacon, the martyr Gregory, Theodore, Demetrius, Nestor, Mercurius, Samonas, Abibus, the holy Forty Martyrs, pious Vitus, Laurence, Florian Chrysogonus, Zoilus, Boniface, and the holy innocents killed for Christ's sake, and all you others, you other countless martyrs, who through your torments drove the Devil out of the whole world, uprooted the deceit of idolatry, and purified the earth with your blood, having washed it, cleanse me, a captive of my sins. And through your poignant torments and holy forbearance save me from the darkness of captivity and from him.

O holy doctors of the Lord, divine miracle-workers, Cosmas and Damian, Hermolaus, Pantaleon, and Habakkuk, Cyriacus, and John, you who through the grace of the Lord received the gift of healing, heal without reward not only man, but also beast; and heal my body and soul of all my evil temptations.

O holy confessors, all you brilliant ones who did not turn away from God through the temptations but with real daring confessed the faith of Our Lord Jesus Christ before numerous tormentors and corrupters, free me of all my evil.

O Saint Clement, Saint Dionysius the Areopagite, Gregory Thaumaturgus, Silvester, Ambrose, Jerome, Martin, Jeremy, Cyprian, Basil, Nicholas, John Chrysostom, and all you other innumerable saints, martyr-saints, who in your weakness defeated him with your stout forbearance, and with your prayers you had the strength to smite the vain, many-headed, and many-tailed serpent appearing in you and in others, now remove me, who has torn himself from him.

O Saint Thecla, first martyr among women, Saint Anastasia, deliverer from poison,[19] Euphemia, Eugenia, Barbara, Juliana, Febronia, Agatha, Lucy, Felicitas, Walburga, Marina, Margaret,[20] and you other holy martyrs, our holy fathers defeated our visible and invisible enemies through your incessant prayers, psalms, and fasts, and upon revealing their weakness, they trampled it to nought like dust and replaced it with your prayers, now take my weak soul away from them and preserve all of me.

O Saint Anthony, Paul the first hermit, Euthymius the venerable, and Sabbas the sanctified, father Hilarion and Theodosius, who was given by God, Simeon Stylites, Benedict the blessed, and Ephraim the glorious, together with all the holy and venerable fathers and others who are without number; O Saint John, percursor and Baptist, twofold preacher, you who are greater than all born of woman, and unto whom grace was given by God to pray for all, pray also for me, a wretched and sinful servant of God (name), and protect me from all my evil.

O all you heavenly and incorporeal powers, holy angels and archangels, leaders of the commander and ruling forces, seraphim and cherubim, dominions, protect me everywhere with your holy, fiery wings from Satan and Beelzebub, who fell from you through pride; may he not come near me for all the days of my life.

O holy Mary, Mother of God, of whom He chose to be born in the flesh of man for the sake of our salvation, Jesus Christ, the Son of the living God, save me, who am humbled and burdened by my sins and discouraged by the many temptations, from that compulsion of mine; protect me from my enemies with the shield of Your guardianship and by Your intervention with Your Son Jesus Christ, Our God, whom everything visible and invisible obeys and fears, and to whom everything inimical and not inimical yields. For unto Him be the glory and praise together with the Father and Holy Spirit now and always and forevermore. Amen.

✝ Prayer to the Holy Trinity

✝

O LORD, SAVE ME in the hour of my departure, receive my soul in peace, number me among the chosen flock of Thy sheep, and pasture me in a cool, peaceful place. For all the righteous ones rest by Abraham, Isaac, and Jacob. For there is no grief on their bosom, no sickness nor sighing but life eternal. But Thou, O merciful Lord, have mercy on me and save me. For I have sinned against Thee in soul and body—whether by word or deed or thought, whether knowingly or unknowingly, whether willfully or unwillfully—forgive me, O Lord, Thy sinful and unworthy servant (name).[1] And You, O Lady, Most Holy Sovereign, Virgin and Most Gracious Mother of God who prays incessantly for the entire Christian world, pray for me, Your sinful and unworthy servant (name). And together with Michael and Gabriel and Uriel and Raphael, and with all the angels and archangels, with the cherubim and the seraphim, and with all the heavenly powers, with John the Baptist and the apostles, with the four evangelists and the prophets, with the martyrs and most venerable fathers and patriarchs, with the unrewarded, the seven youths and three confessors, with the children and the fools for Christ and myrrh-bearing women, and with all the saints standing at the throne of the Lord with venerable arms stretched to merciful God, O Lady, pray for me too, Your sinful and unworthy servant (name). O Most Holy Lady, Sovereign and Most Gracious Virgin, beseech God, all the heavenly powers, and the holy angels and archangels for me, a sinner. Implore God for me, a sinner.

O Saint John, prophet of the Word and baptizer of the Lord, beseech God for me, a sinner. O Holy Apostles Peter, Paul, Andrew, John the Divine, James, Mark, Matthew, Luke, Philip, Thomas, Bartholomew, James of Alphaeus, and Judas of James, all you Holy Apostles, embodiers of the Holy Spirit, beseech God for me, a sinner. O holy

138

assembly of Popes Clement, Silvester, and Leo, Pope Stephen, Gregory, and all you holy martyrs, Zenobius, Blasius, and Vojtěch, beseech
God. O great Saints Nicholas, Basil, John Chrysostom, John the Theologian, Stephen, George of Mytilene, Gregory Thaumaturgus,
Amphilochius, Alpherius, Capiton,[2] Martin, Polyeuctus, and all you
holy teachers and priests beseech God for me, a sinner. O holy first
martyr for Christ, Stephen, O George, Theodore, Demetrios, the holy
Forty Martyrs, Pantaleon, Florus, Lorus, Procopius, Mercurius, Andrew, Eustratius, Nicetas, Mina, Christopher, Vitus, Wenceslas, Ma-
nuel, Sabiel, Benedict, Ismael, Olaf,[3] Botulph, Sozon, Romanus,
Anthimus, Maximus, Boris and Gleb, Pancratius, all you martyrs be-
seech God for me, a sinner. O Saints Joachim, Zachariah, Simon God-
Receiver, Paul of Theben, Antonius, Macarius, Ephraim, Sabbas, Hilarion, Euthymius, Pachomius, Arsenius, Simon Stylites, Andrew the
Fool for Christ, Simeon the Fool for Christ, Acacius, Xenophon, Cyril,
Methodius, Benedict, all you saints of God and venerable fathers be-
seech God for me, a sinner. O holy prophet Elias, Isaiah, Jeremiah,
Daniel, John, Moses, Aaron, Malachi, Solomon, Jonas, Abraham,
Isaac, Jacob, Enoch, Ezekiel, Gideon, Ammon, Habakkuk, David, O
great father George,[4] all you holy prophets, fasters, and hermits be-
seech God also for me, a sinner. Assembly of holy women, O Ann,
Elizabeth, Mary. . . .

✝ Latin Works about Wenceslas and Ludmila

✝ Life and Martyrdom of Saint Wenceslas (*Crescente fide*)

su inlonginqua regione. sed te cōmen
do scis cosme & damiano. In domo tua
reside. & erit tibi signū hoc. cū uoluer
ris .si mittas & accersiā te. Post hoc pfec
tus est frer suū. uxor aur ei dōm resedit.
Interieceris aut paucis dieb; serens dia
bolus signū qd maritus ei dederat trans
figurauit se inhomine. & dix uxori ei.
Ecce maritus tuus abilla ciuitate direx
me. ut adducā te aderū. Cui illa nolens
ire respondit. Signū quide agnosco.
Sed ñ possū hoc tacere: quia scii cosmi
& damiano cōmendauit me. Sed si
uis ut ueniā receu accede & tene cornu
altaris & uinge nihil mali facturu mihi.
& credā tibi. Tune uinuit diabolus
dicens. P uirture sciq̄ cosmq damia
nu nihil mali facia tibi. Si me tome
marito tuo repsentabo. Hsdicens. secu
ra e eū. Et reū ueniste inquendā
locū secretū. uoluit eā de uiuro pci
pitare. ut eā ītficeret. Illa ø eleuans
ad ceelū oculis magna uoce clamauit.
Ds scq̄ cosme & damiani adiuua me.
..olus credidi. & secuta sū eū. festina
... meus liberet me amanu
iniquissimi diaboli. Statim apparueri
ei sci inhabitu equitu & multitudine
albarorū. Princeps aut iniquitatis hoc
uiso se pcipitat dedit. & tusqui cōpa
ruit. F impleta e scriptura dicens.
Lacū aperuit & effodit eū & incidit
infoueā quā oparis est. Conuertetur
dolor ei & incipit ei. & inuertice ip
sius iniquitas ei descendit. Serui aut
xpi cosmas & damianus apphenden
tes eum. pduxerr indomū suā & dixer
ei. Hos sumus cosmas & damianus quq̄
sacramro credidisti. ido q̄ festinauim
uenire adauxiliandū tibi. Sed & alia
multa mirabilia quq̄ enarrare longū
e peos dñs ad laude nominis sui pre
star fieri. usq inhodiernū die. qui

& pomia secula seclōrū amon. Explicit
passio scq̄. mart. cosme &
Damiani.
Incipit passio scī
Venezlai martyris.
In diebus illis
CRESCENTE FIDE XPIANA
di nuru sponte dux boemie.
nomine borwiu. unā
eū exercitu neeū & omi
pplo suo sordes idolorū
abiecerit baptismu est
eusq̄ filius hp magnen
inurbe praga condidit
euclm scē di genitricis
marię. & alia quo q inho
nore scī petri apostolorū principis. Insb;
di grā largiente plurima opariū bene
neficia. Cunq̄ psatus uir uenerabilis mi
lister de hoc seclo omis ppli qui ei fuerar
congregari elegerr frem eiū militorem
nomine wratislaum ducē & prepe
inloco eius. Qui etiā inreligione xpia
na magnopere pseuerabat. Qui constru
xit ecclsam innomine scī georgiu mar
tyris xpi. Cui filius maior beatus uenlt
laus instinctu di abm euntr etare sem
desiderabat discere litteras. Cuius pat de
siderū animi eius cupiens implere.
misit eū inurbē nuncupata bundlin.
ut ibi discere psalteriū a quodā sacer
ui. rem pbro nomine uento. Tunc beatus
uenelhaus capi lici mente gentant cepit
discere. dedit in diē melius meliusq̄
pficeret. Postea aut abiit pat ei nomine
urratihlaus de hoc mundo. Interea
uenerunt omis ppli regnus illius &
elegerūt beatū uenehlaū ducē inloco
patris sui. & sedere eū fecerr in throno
ipsius. Tē pd ice puerulus p maiens in
principatu. minime discessit adisciphs
fidelis nāq̄ erat & sapiens & uerax in
sermone. & iustus inindicio. Cūq̄ ur

Crescente fide (Bohemian Recension). Stuttgart Passionale.

✝

1

As the Christian faith was spreading, a Bohemian sovereign by the name of Bořivoj repudiated abominable idolatry by the will and behest of God, and was baptized together with his retinue and all his people. And his son Spytihněv[1] founded the Church of the Blessed Mary Mother of God in Prague, and another one in honor of Saint Peter, Prince of the Apostles,[2] in which, by the ample grace of God, many miracles take place.

But when the above-mentioned venerable man departed from this world, all the magnates of that land assembled and elected in his place his younger brother, Vratislav, as their sovereign and prince. He, too, was very zealous in the Christian faith and built the Church of Saint George, Christ's martyr.

From his tender youth his older son, Blessed Wenceslas, constantly yearned for learning through divine inspiration. Thus, his father, wishing to grant his heart's yearning, sent him to the town called Budeč[3] so that he could study the Psalter with a venerable priest by the name of Učen.[4] And here Blessed Wenceslas joyfully began to study with a receptive mind, improving by the day. But at that time his father, named Vratislav,[5] departed from this world. And then all the men of that land assembled and elected in his father's place Blessed Wenceslas as their sovereign, and installed him on his throne.

2

And after that, the above-mentioned noble lad, despite having to cope with his princely office, did not stray from his pious way of life. For he was faithful, wise and truthful in speech, and just in judgment. And when his judges wished to condemn someone to death, the youth named above, if he could not free him in any way, would immediately find a pretext to leave, bearing in mind the Gospel precept which says: "Judge not, that ye be not judged" [Matthew 7:1]. He also razed the prisons and struck down all the gallows. And he was merciful to orphans, was a father to those who wept and to widows, and a kindly consoler of the wounded. He sated the hungry, gave drink to the thirsty, and clothed the naked with his own garments. He visited the sick, buried the dead, and joyfully received strangers and wayfarers like his own relatives.[6] He respectfully served priests and clerics, and showed the way of truth to those who had gone astray. Moreover, he practiced humility, patience, moderation, and, most important of all, charity. He did not deprive anyone of anything by force or deceit. And he provided his retinue not only with arms but also with the best apparel.

Conducting himself in this manner and similar ones from the tenderest years of his youth, he piously pursued a contemplative, ecclesiastic life. And during the time of the forty-day fast, he would make his way from castle to castle, walking barefoot over frigid and impassable trails, visiting churches. Thus, blood that had gushed forth could be seen in his footprints. And on the outside he was wrapped in a royal robe, but beneath he was clad in a rough hair shirt. He was content with modest nourishment. And during the night, persevering untiringly in prayers, he continually gave untold thanks to the One God.

And thus, during harvesttime as well, rising during the night, he would secretly walk to the fields, reap wheat, and carry it home on his own shoulders. Then he would thresh the wheat, grind it in a small mill and sift the flour. Also, in the dead of night he would take a pail, along with one of the members of his retinue, and hasten for water. And while drawing the water he would say, "In the name of the Father and of the Son and of the Holy Ghost." After he brought it home and mixed it with the flour, he baked wafers. Also, during the quiet of the night, he would hasten to his vineyard along with a faithful companion. Gathering grapes, they would put them in baskets and carry them secretly to his chambers. And there they would squeeze the wine out on a press and pour it into pitchers. He did that without anyone knowing, so that from this the priests could bring a sacrifice to the Lord.

3

From trustworthy people we also learned about the following matter, which would not be fitting to pass over in silence: through divine inspiration he foresaw the future. And from the many of his other prophecies, I shall make note of one: once, in the course of the year, he ascended to the uppermost part of the palace and, upon looking out of the window, he said to one of the members of his retinue, "It appears to me that the home of the elder priest Paul is forsaken."[7] In the meantime, his mother, who came from a tribe of godless pagans, was taking counsel with most treacherous men.[8] And they said, "What should we do when he who is to be prince has been ruined by priests and is like a monk?" And she sent wretched and pernicious men to kill her mother-in-law, a most blessed lady by the name of Ludmila.[9] And they did as they were commanded. Indeed, her soul, freed from her body and delivered from the suffering of this world with the palm of martyrdom, undoubtedly hastened to the Lord on High. And many priests and clerics were driven out of the land, after being stripped of their property. Then the prophecy which he had made known shortly before that was fulfilled.

4

Consequently, from that time on they importuned Most Blessed Wenceslas with grave threats, wanting him to abandon his faith and pious way of life. And they posted reserves at the byways to determine whether any cleric approached him, so that they could sentence him to death immediately. However, he, together with his faithful ones, made an opening in the back part of the house, and after the sun set and everything became quiet, the one who taught him would come to him and at dawn would leave secretly. And at all times Blessed Wenceslas carried a small book on his person, hiding it beneath his cloak. And he read it diligently whenever he found a suitable place. Sighing heavily, he was grievously saddened beyond measure over the blindness of their hearts.

Finally, while all these evildoers went to sacrifice lambs and piglets to the idols so as to partake of these shameful offerings, he shunned them, seizing upon an appropriate pretext, and he never defiled himself by partaking of their feasts. And thus he never tasted any of the drinks with which they offered a libation.[10]

5

Afterward, when he came of age, he summoned all his men and his mother and reproached them for their lack of faith and hardness of heart, saying: "Why were you opposed to my studying the law of my Lord God and to my serving Him alone? However, if hitherto I have been in your power, henceforward I will not obey you, for I wish to serve God!" And he recalled from exile the priests and clerics, to their great joy. And the churches were opened. The Christian faith began to rejoice and great harm was inflicted upon the Devil.

Thus, hearing reports about him at this time, many priests from the land of Bavaria and Swabia[11] flocked to him with relics of saints and with books. And he joyfully gave much gold and silver, furs, slaves, and garments to them all, according to their needs. For he could be compared to the Psalmist who said with pride, "I have more understanding than all my teachers: for thy testimonies are my meditation" [Psalms119:99]. For in his mind only the radiance of the rare pearl shone.[12] And the Lord deigned to grant him such abundant grace that he was also victorious in battle.[13] He had an air of distinction about him, and he was so pure in body that he voluntarily chose to remain chaste all his life.

He conversed kindly with the moderate, but if he learned of certain immoderate people, loitering in taverns, drinking and abandoning the faith, and indulging in revelry without cause, he immediately had them put in irons and severely flogged with many blows.

And he did not cease to offer prayers during both day and night. He always took hold of the shield of faith and the invisible sword of the Holy Ghost, which is the Word of God, against the inveterate enemy. Indeed, he was without a blemish, a true servant of God, according to the Apostle's precepts, reproving, exhorting, and rebuking many.[14] He invited them to the Lord's banquet. And when he tore them out of the Devil's throat, he brought them to the bosom of the Mother Church and nurtured them constantly with divine nourishments.

6

But then his younger brother Boleslav, deceived by the Devil's guile, devised an evil scheme together with other godless ones against the aforementioned man, Blessed Wenceslas, whom they wanted to destroy.[15] He knew about this but, like a man who reaps in the heat of the day thirsts for water, he undoubtedly yearned to attain martyrdom. But not from the hand of his own brother, for he loved him very much and knew that he would not escape the eternal fire of hell if he did this.

At that time he resolved to build a church for the Lord. And he inquired through emissaries of the bishop of Regensburg, named Tuto, saying, "My father built a church for the Lord God and, likewise, I, too, want to found a church for the Lord God in honor of Saint Vitus."[16] Then Bishop Tuto, giving thanks, extended his arms to the Lord and, rejoicing, said, "Go and tell my son Blessed Wenceslas, saying, 'Your church is already standing before the Lord, most beautifully built.'" And when they told him this, in accordance with the bishop's command, he rejoiced greatly. And upon convening all the people, after having made a beginning himself with God's help, he founded the church in honor of Saint Vitus with wondrous efficiency.

At that time he wished to go Rome so that the pope could invest him in monastic habit, and he could give up his princedom out of love for God and cede it to his brother.[17] But he was unable to do this because of the aforementioned church, for it was not as yet completed.

7

Then his aforementioned brother, in keeping with his arrangement with the godless ones, cunningly sent a messenger to invite him to his home, ostensibly to a banquet but actually to kill him. But he greeted all his relatives for the last time, and when the time came to set off, he departed at once, though he knew this.

And on that day he feasted together with those insensitive murderers. Here a man, leaning over to his ear, said to him in a whisper, "See here, I will bring you a horse in secret, mount it and flee from these people, my lord, as swiftly as you can, for, you see, they really want to kill you." But he did not wish to do so. And he stepped into the banquet hall again. And taking up a goblet, he said in a raised voice before all without fear, "In the name of the Blessed Archangel Michael, let us drink this goblet with a prayer that he bring our souls into the peace of eternal joy, amen!"

8

And as was often his habit, that night, before the next day dawned, he set off for matins. But into his way stepped his brother, to whom he said: "You served us well yesterday. May you receive ample reward from the Lord." However, he drew a sword from his scabbard and, upon striking the holy man on the head, said, "And this is how I wish to serve you today!" But blood scarcely appeared, for he was weak because of his horrible fear. Now the Blessed Wenceslas could have easily overcome him, but he did not wish to defile himself. But that villain called in a loud voice, saying: "Hey, where are you, my men? Help me!" Then all those scoundrels came running from their hiding-place with swords and spears and, inflicting many blows upon him, killed him. And his soul, liberated at that battleground from the prison of this world and glorified by blood, departed to the Lord on the twenty-eighth day of September.[18]

9

Taking his lifeless body and simply laying it in a grave, they covered it with earth. And with water they washed away and wiped off his innocent blood which spurted on the ground and on the planks. And when they arose the next morning, they saw blood spilled on the same spot, and once again they washed it away with water and wiped it off. And when they arose on the third day, again they saw blood spilled on the aforementioned spot, and for the third time they washed it off with water.

Then those murderers, riding swiftly, hastened to the castle of Prague. And they slaughtered all his relatives, and thrust their children alive into the depths of the river. But although we unworthy ones do not know their count or names, because of their great numbers, nevertheless we believe that God knows them.

And they even persecuted his priests,[19] so that what the prophet said long ago about the Lord, we, who trust in His gracious mercy, also dare to say about His warrior: "Smite the shepherd, and the sheep shall be scattered" [Zechariah 13:7]. However, harried by evil spirits, those murderers fled and showed themselves no more. But some of them, having withered and become deaf, remained that way until death. And the others died off, barking with their mouths like dogs and gnashing their teeth. Verily, the Lord is mindful of His words, which He spoke through the Apostle Paul: "Vengeance is mine; I will repay" [Romans 12:19].

*

And his body reposed in that same place for three years. And some people had a revelation in their dreams, to translate the body to the church he had built. Thus, having arisen in the middle of the night, they took his body from the grave and placed it upon a carriage. And they came with it to a river[20] whose stream had overflowed its banks and flooded the meadows, and they were unable to cross. They were stricken with great sorrow. And while looking for wood to make a bridge, they saw, upon their return, that the carriage with the holy body stood on the other side of the river and was not wet. Well, what else are we to conclude other than that the power of Almighty God translated it? Seeing this miracle, the coachmen were absolutely astonished. And thus they arrived with him at the aforementioned church. When they were inside and had lit a candle, they saw that his body was intact and all the wounds were healed. Only one wound was bloody, the one his brother first made.[21] And the memory of his translation is celebrated on the fourth day of March.[22]

Thus, when crowds of the faithful had gathered, they laid the body in a coffin to the accompaniment of hymns and songs, and buried it next to the altar, where with the assistance of the Lord at his intercession, many miracles take place even unto this day. Verily, it is fitting that we say something about them.

Shortly afterward a great number of people were imprisoned, locked in stocks, with an iron collar placed around each of their necks. And in their anguish all these people in unison beseeched the Almighty Lord, saying, "O Lord God, help us for the sake of Blessed Wenceslas's merits and prayers!" And the following night, it was as if a bell began to ring in their ears, and a light began to shine in the prison. And suddenly the stocks bent like a bow and they pulled their legs out of the stocks. Then they all cried out in unison, saying, "O Lord God, have mercy upon us!" Immediately Christ's power manifested itself, and the collars shattered and fell off each of their necks to the ground. Upon their release from prison, they went around the country and told of the Lord's great miracle, which they beheld before their own eyes.[23]

Seeing this miracle, one pagan, who was also confined in that prison, made a vow to the Lord, saying, "If the Lord will help me for the sake of Blessed Wenceslas's merits, I shall believe in Christ and offer my son to His service." And immediately all the fetters fell off of him. Again and again they shackled him more firmly, but once more, as before, the chains fell off from him. Thus he was released immediately. And he allowed himself to be instructed in the holy faith and baptized, and he lived for many more years.

Another man was cast into prison in the same way, by decree, and, similarly, all the irons shattered and fell from him. But this one they seized immediately, not believing him, and sold him to pagans who had come from afar.[24] And as they were taking him away, the chains fell from his hands and the collar from his neck, for the sake of Blessed Wenceslas's merits, as frequently happened. And now, having seen God's miracle, these people released him, although they were pagans. At that time the prince ordered yet another man locked in prison. And he, sighing, frequently invoked the Lord, saying, "O Lord God, help me for the sake of Blessed Wenceslas's merits." And after he had fallen asleep, he awoke suddenly standing outside the prison. And there were neither chains on his feet, nor fetters on his hands, nor a collar on his neck. And upon returning to the guard, he told him how he was miraculously plucked from the prison, and they released him.

In that same city there was a certain very poor woman who was blind and crippled. Entering the church, she fell to the ground before the tomb of Blessed Wenceslas and prayed for a long time. And she regained her eyesight, and her hands were relaxed. On another occasion a man was bound by people to whom he owed something. And it happened that they left him, chained, by the same church. And as he extended his bound hands toward the inner doors of the church, he said, "O God, help me at the intercession of Blessed Wenceslas." Immediately his hands were unbound, and they released him.

There was a crippled man in the land of the Franks to whom a man dressed in white appeared in his dreams and admonished him, saying, "Arise and go to the city of Prague, to the Church of Saint Vitus, where the body of Blessed Wenceslas reposes, and there you will regain your health." But not having heeded this, the same man, dressed in the same clothing, the one who had appeared to him before, came to him again in his dreams, and said to him, "Why have you not fulfilled my command, and why have you not gone to the place where you will regain the ability to walk?" Now he said, "Lord, I am going," and upon rising, he went limping to the merchants and paid them. They now took him along in a carriage and came with him right to the aforementioned church. Thus, he began to pray here, and immediately cast himself down on the pavement in the presence of the people. And through God's mercy his knees and his heels and soles were strengthened. And rising up, he gave thanks to God and Blessed Wenceslas, for the sake of whose merits the Lord God deigned to help him.

*

Therefore, we beseech you, O most blessed lord Wenceslas—since in days of yore the Lord, for the sake of your most holy intercession, freed many people from prison and from fetters—that now, considering our innumerable vices, you be our trustworthy intercessor with that same merciful Father; and, appeased by your gracious intercession, that He may deign to shelter us in this earthly life and strengthen us continually in His holy service; that He may shield us steadily from all the visible and invisible snares of the Enemy; that He may turn sickness away from us; that He may deliver us from menacing dangers; that He may mercifully remove us from worldly passions, sorrows, and fears, and endow us with spiritual virtues; that He may not let our days end before He forgives us our past, present, and future sins; that He may turn the attacks of evil spirits away from us, and not lead us into temptation; but that He may grant us a peaceful life in which we may glorify the Lord Father Almighty. And when the Lord Jesus Christ comes as Judge at the end of time, may He separate us from the goats, place us among the sheep at His right hand,[25] and permit us, upon coming, to hear the desirable voice in which He will say to His just ones: "Come, ye blessed of my Father, inherit the kingdom prepared for you from the foundation of the world" [Matthew 25:34]. May Jesus Christ deign to grant us this, the Son of the living God, who with the eternal Father and with the Consoler the Holy Spirit lives and reigns forevermore. Amen.

✝ Passion
of the Martyr Ludmila
(*Fuit in provincia Boemorum*)

†

1

IN THE LAND OF BOHEMIA there was a prince by the name of Bořivoj,[1] who at that time still lived according to pagan customs. And he took a wife for himself from another tribe, the daughter of Prince Slavibor, by the name of Ludmila.[2] When she was very young she made offerings to idols and devoted herself to their veneration with great enthusiasm. But as they lived together, they were brought to sorrow by God's direction and desire, and they accepted the purification of holy baptism together with their subjects.

2

Afterward, three sons and three daughters were born to them.[3] And from the day they accepted the grace of baptism their entire kingdom flourished.[4] Then Prince Bořivoj, who had completed thirty-six years of life, departed from this world. After him his firstborn son, who was called Spytihněv, assumed reign.[5] He lived, reconciled to Christ's faith, and assembled priests and clerics. And upon completing forty years of life, he parted from this world. After his death, Vratislav, his brother, took the helm of government.[6]

3

After her conversion from pagan error, their mother, the venerable lady Ludmila, wept and lamented bitterly every day that previously she had venerated idols. However, she herself turned it to the better—that is, she became a mother to the poor, a foot to the lame, an eye to the blind, and a benevolent consoler to orphans and widows.[7] Now, when Prince Vratislav had completed thirty-three years of life, he relinquished the oppressing fetters of this world, and his son Wenceslas, who at that time was still a boy, assumed his father's power and reign. The boy's mother, who was called Drahomira, remained a widow.[8]

4

Then the enemy of mankind, the Devil, became envious that God's pious handmaid Ludmila excelled in many virtues. And the prince's mother began to hate her mother-in-law and took counsel with her unjust counselors. And she said: "Why should she be, as it were, my mistress? I will destroy her, inherit everything that she has, and I will rule freely." Her son Wenceslas, to wit, was still a juvenile. As soon as Ludmila, God's venerable and devoted handmaid, discerned this scheme, she said to her daughter-in-law: "I do not long to rule nor do I yearn for even the smallest share of your power. I ask that you permit me to serve God uninterruptedly to the end of my days."

5

With these words Ludmila left the castle of Prague and went to a small town called Tetín.[9] There the aforementioned handmaid of God, anticipating her coming martyrdom, strengthened herself vigorously in the knowledge of sacred things. And she performed good deeds for the poor with increasing fervor but was unable to fulfill her yearning entirely. After her departure, the young prince's mother, upon taking counsel with her villainous counselors, sent men to destroy her. They took along a large force and marched on the small town of Tetín.

6

Then the aforementioned handmaid of God, in anticipation of the coming events, summoned a pious priest by the name of Paul and exhorted him to offer a holy, solemn mass.[10] Afterward, she confessed sincerely in the presence of the Most High Judge, and strengthened herself by receiving the body and blood of the Lord. Being aware of her imminent death, she began to array herself in the armor of faith, and persevered in prayer so that she might commend her soul to God, adorned with good deeds.

7

After it grew dark, these cruel men headed for her residence. They smashed the gate and ran to the doors of the house where the handmaid of God was, broke them open, and went inside. And she said to them: "Brethren, why have you come in such a frenzy? Have I not nurtured you like sons? I gave you all my gold, silver, and valuable garments. And if I have committed some faults against you, tell me!" But, disregarding her peace-loving words, they pulled her out of bed and cast her to the floor. Now she said to them in tears, "Brethren, wait just a moment, at least until I finish my prayers!" And with arms outstretched she prayed to the Lord. Having completed her prayers, she said to them, "I implore you, brethren, decapitate me!" She said this so that she might be worthy of receiving the crown of martyrdom by shedding her blood. However, they did not consent, but they put a rope around her neck and strangled her. Thus, she departed to the Lord, having completed sixty-one years of life in great faith and devotion. For Christ's devoted handmaid Ludmila was martyred on Saturday, the fifteenth day of the month of September, during the early evening hours.[11]

Her entire clergy and all her domestics, both male and female, dispersed to hiding-places here and there in an effort to save their lives, which were threatened after the loss of their shepherdess.

8

But after these most cruel murderers left, they assembled again apprehensively in order to serve at the burial. They prepared everything that was necessary with great respect and committed her most holy body to the earth's sod. And those most cruel murderers, having ravished all the spoils, returned to their mistress with immense joy and brought tidings to her of the death of an innocent being, believing that they would forever be richly rewarded.

Then, after seizing all the property of her mother-in-law, the aforesaid mistress of these treacherous men began to rule together with these cruel men, having enriched them and their families and servants with a remarkable quantity of gold, silver, and valuable garments. And they ruled over the entire land of Bohemia like grand dukes, but not with God's grace.

9

While they rejoiced immoderately, the vengeance of God's retribution came upon the wicked ones, who were not afraid to commit such a cruel crime, and it caught them unawares. For their father, the

Devil, incited discord among them, and they began to hold all their companions in contempt. And hatred grew between the wicked ones, Tunna and Gummon,[12] and their mistress, so that all their mistress's thoughts and words were preoccupied with their destruction. When Tunna saw this, he fled together with all his relatives, and lived now here, now there. However, Gummon was seized while looking for a suitable refuge for his brother, and he lost his life on earth as well as in the hereafter, along with his brother. Seeing them on the run, their mistress now turned her fury against their descendents—from the oldest to the youngest—and with a like verdict destroyed them all in one day.

10

Then, at the grave of the Blessed Martyr Ludmila, the merits of her virtues began to shine forth through the workings of divine grace. For a wondrous aroma emanated from her tomb, surpassing the fragrance of all aromatic substances. Moreover, three, four times during the deepest silence of night there appeared, in the presence of onlookers, numerous bright illuminations and lights burning with a heavenly glow. All this was not kept secret from the murderess. Upon learning of this, she was struck with great fear and did not know what to do. Finally, after resuming deliberations with her malicious counselors, she sent her servants to Tetín, where the venerable body lay buried, and charged them to rebuild Blessed Ludmila's house over her grave in the form of a basilica.[13] And she, it seems, conferred the name in honor of the Blessed Archangel Michael so that miraculous signs, if any were to appear in the future, would not be added to the merits of the blessed martyr but rather to the merits of the saints whose relics were kept there. When the basilica was erected, sacred awe seized all who entered so that they dared not step inside without the greatest respect. Since that time, many glorious miracles have occurred at this place.

11   The Translation of Saint Ludmila

Calling to mind his grandmother and the saintliness by which she distinguished herself in this life and the preeminent renown she earned from the Almighty, Blessed Wenceslas shed a torrent of tears. And upon consulting with priests and some pious men, he sent them to the town of Tetín with orders to bring him the bones or dust of the decomposed body in a befitting manner. Thus, carrying out their lord's command, the messengers went to the basilica, and having scraped away the earth, uncovered the grave. However, seeing that the tomb's slab, which covered the venerable relics, was partially deteriorated with decay, they hesitated to raise it, saying: "If the wood is rotted, would not that which was covered beneath it be all the more decomposed?" And they wanted to close the grave again very carefully.

But a priest named Paul, who had always served the deceased faithfully while she was still on earth, was against their plan. He said: "It is not at all as you say, but do as the prince ordered! If I find only the dust of her decomposed body, I will raise her." The others agreed with him unanimously and lifted the slab. But as they were lifting it, the slab broke, and Paul, mentioned above, along with the earth fell onto the body of the deceased. Then, getting up at once and removing the earth, he found the holy body preserved from all corruption, save for what had stuck to it after the cover broke as they removed it.

Thus, they rendered thanks to God with great joy. Raising the most holy relics and wrapping them in fine cloths, as was fitting, they placed them before the altar. Having done all this with solemnity, they laid the relics on a litter, loaded them onto the backs of two horses, and that very night set off for the city of Prague with sustained haste.

And the body of the blessed and devoted handmaid of God, Ludmila, was found on Wednesday, the nineteenth day of the month of October, during the ninth hour. It was then brought to Prague on Friday, the twenty-first day of that same month, with infinite exultation, during which everyone extolled Christ.[14]

12

Before reaching the city, those who were carrying the relics sent heralds to the prince. These servants found him asleep when they arrived. They awakened him so as to announce their joyful tidings to him. He rose immediately, betook himself to church, and there rendered ardent thanks to Christ for such a great act of kindness.[15]

Then, as day was breaking, he summoned the clergy and a multitude of the faithful, and hurriedly set off to meet them with an immense procession. On the way they met with those who were faithfully carrying the holy relics. Now, after immediately placing the relics on their shoulders, the priests and Levites carried them to the castle, praising God by singing psalms and hymns. Upon entering the church, they placed the relics before the altar so that all believers and unbelievers could see that the body of the saint was preserved without a blemish by Christ. Everyone saw that her body, hair, and clothing were as though she had been buried that very day. And thus they came to the general conclusion that she was worthy of all praise and honor.

However, when they wanted to dig a grave, water unexpectedly appeared in the hole that was dug. Now everyone concluded that this place was unsuitable for Christ's handmaid. After filling the hole again, they placed the reliquary with the extraordinary remains over it, and awaited God's help. Thus, they returned to their homes.

13

And after a short time, the aforementioned prince dispatched messengers to the bishop of Regensburg in order to get advice on this matter. He answered them in words according to the Scriptures: "Earth thou art, and unto earth shalt thou return, dust thou art, and unto dust shalt thou return,"[16] that is, they should deliver the body to the earth from which it originated from the beginning with the first-created man until they behold the glory of Christ.

Then the prince appealed humbly to the bishop with an urgent request: that he might vouchsafe to come to him, bury the body himself, and consecrate the basilica, which had not as yet been consecrated by the bishop.[17]

And the bishop arrived and first dedicated the church to the Lord. Then, after six days, he committed the holy body to the ground in the same place that was previously flooded with water. Here a wondrous thing has to be made known publicly in praise of Christ's handmaid: whereas before, when the priests wanted to bury her in an unconsecrated place, water began to appear, now, after the bishop's arrival and the consecration of the basilica, the water disappeared entirely. Verily, this was exceptionally fitting testimony that she, who spent her life in blessed communion, had to be buried with the highest blessing, since her place was to be among the saints at the right hand of Christ.

And thus, after this was properly completed, the bishop received gifts from the prince, as was fitting, and set off for home.

14

On the day of the first anniversary of the translation of the holy relics,[18] Christ deigned to work a special miracle in order to make known the merits of His handmaid. On that day, in accordance with the Christian custom of celebrating the memory of such persons, the clergy assembled. The prayers had been concluded already, and everyone had sat down together to refresh their bodies with food. Now, before entering the basilica in which the body of the extraordinary lady reposed, a small boy—afflicted and crippled by a disease of the body, and not even able to raise his head— invoked her and the power of Christ. He was righted and completely restored to health. Seeing this, the huge assembly sang praises to God, through whose venerable handmaid He deigned to reveal His power. And unto Him be the honor and glory forevermore. Amen.

✝ Life and Martyrdom of Saint Wenceslas and His Grandmother, Saint Ludmila (*Legenda Christiani*)

Legenda Christiani.

$$+$$

Prologue[1]

TO THE MOST BLESSED LORD Vojtěch,[2] the second bishop of God's holy church of Prague: a most humble brother, one unworthy of being called the last of all monks and a Christian only in his name, Christian,[3] wishes in Christ Jesus to attain ample and successful fulfillment of his prayers.

Discovering that the martyrdom of Blessed Wenceslas and his grandmother Ludmila[4] of blessed memory—who, like new stars, illuminated the land of Bohemia and all their people with the light of their virtues—has been described incompletely and in diverse compositions, I deem it proper to turn to Your Holiness, who descends from the same lineage, so that at Your behest and with Your consent I may in part correct this description, or should something be missing from it, I may complete it by asking some of the elders or monks, while such are still alive, who have seen the deeds of these saints before their own eyes or have heard others tell about them.[5] I have not dedicated myself to this work out of yearning for glory, for I am quite ignorant of rhetoric, and all verbal eloquence is alien to me. Nevertheless, even if I were copiously accomplished in this, yet the weight of my sins would inhibit me when praising the merits of such great saints. And though my incompetence and inability are great, and though my education—if compared to the education of learned persons—ceases to be an education, I will still attempt, as far as my powers suffice, to write in detail about events as they in fact took place, not losing hope for forgiveness, my immeasurable faults notwithstanding, and trusting directly in the help of these saints.

But first I must say this: if in the lands of the Lothairians or Carolingians,[6] or in that of other Christian nations they possessed the relics of such eminent saints and worthy witnesses of Christ, who abound in wonders of famous miracles, they would have described these events long ago and, if I may say so, in letters of gold. And they would have sounded their praises in the chant of responsories and antiphons, and in eloquent sermons, and in building many monasteries, although they themselves are able to rejoice, since they possess the venerable relics of martyrs, confessors, virgins, and other saints similar to these. Whereas we, who on the whole are destitute of saints and have only these two, if I may confess, next to God, conduct ourselves somewhat unworthily toward them. And though we see wonders worked by them day after day, we seem to persist in disbelief and we forget to serve them. Let only this be said about our apathy.

Now I earnestly beseech You, o esteemed bishop and dearest nephew, since You have prevailed upon me, an unworthy one, for this work, that You support me with prayers to our mutual protector, and that he, through whose merits You attained the episcopal dignity, deign to obtain for me at least forgiveness for my sins, and for You deign to gain from Christ the Lord a crown of glory in the next life as profit, transferred from the sheep charged to you. Furthermore, I urgently beseech You, with Your superior wisdom to smooth over anything unwise in my work , which foolishness alone allowed, and to embellish it with Your knowledge. Also deign to provide it with Your approval so that it might be copied and read at least in Your diocese.

Let this suffice for the brief preface. Sustained by the merits of the blessed martyr and by Your prayers, let us proceed to the commemoration of those deeds with the help of Our Lord and Saviour Jesus Christ.

1

It is believed and acknowledged, according to oral tradition, that Moravia, a Slavic land, received Christ's faith in ancient times, in the time, as is said, of the renowned teacher Augustine. However, the Bulgars, or Bulgarians, it is said, attained this grace long before that. For after the Bulgarians received the faith, Cyril, a Greek by birth, who was educated in Latin letters, and in Greek as well, also began to preach the faith of Our Lord Jesus Christ in the name of the Holy Trinity and Indivisible Unity to the above-mentioned people residing in Moravia. And when he had won them for Christ, he, with the aid of God's grace, also invented new signs or letters, and translated the Old and New Testament, and other books from Greek and Latin into the

Slavonic language.[7] In addition to that, he resolved that in church the mass and other canonical hours be sung in the common language, as is commonly done even to this day in Slavic lands, mainly in Bulgaria. Thus many souls are won for Christ the Lord.

And once, when the above-named Cyril came to Rome because of his devotional practice, the pope and other authorities and heads of the church accused him of daring to resolve contrary to canonical regulations that the liturgies be sung in the Slavonic language. After he had humbly justified himself before them, he was nevertheless not able to mollify them in any way. He seized the Psalter and read publicly before all the verse of the Psalmist, in which he says, "Let every thing that hath breath praise the Lord" [Psalms 150:6]. And pointing to this verse, he said: "If every thing that has breath is to praise the Lord, why, O chosen fathers, do you prohibit singing the divine service in Slavonic, or the translation of other texts from Latin or Greek wording into this language? For if I had been able in some way to help those people, like other peoples, with Latin or Greek, I certainly would not have dared to do this. But seeing that these people were stiff of neck, and that they were uneducated and ignorant of God's ways, I found only this means, which Almighty God instilled in my heart and by which I have won many of them for Him. Therefore, O fathers and lords, do not take this amiss. For even the Blessed Apostle Paul, the teacher of the pagans, says: 'forbid not to speak with tongues'" [1 Corinthians 14:39]. Hearing this and marveling at the faith of this great man, they resolved in a decree and confirmed in writing that in those lands the rites of the mass and other canonical hours be permitted to be sung in the aforementioned language.

Blessed Cyril then remained in Rome. Attiring himself in monk's habit, he completed the last days of his life, having left in the above-mentioned lands his brother, named Methodius, a zealous man adorned with all manner of sanctity. And when he had gathered many sheaves into the barn of Christ the Lord, he was appointed archbishop by the ruler himself, who at that time reigned in that region, and ruled all his lands like a noble emperor. And he had seven bishops under him of equal sanctity. But since the Enemy of mankind from the very beginning of the world—from the moment the first man tasted the bitterness of the forbidden apple—has not ceased to sow the seed of discord between humility and pride, between love and hate, and between the fragrance of virtue and the stench of vice, so now he could hardly bear being deprived of a people who had always submitted to his bondage but who were now being won for the true King, Christ the Lord. And arraying himself in all the weapons of malice, he acquired new and unknown helpers in his infamous battle, and he sowed the poisonous seed of strife among the rulers and chieftains, and prepared fiery projectiles of pride and avarice. And now Svatopluk, the nephew of that illustrious ruler or king,[8] who was the gracious founder and leader of all Christianity and religion, traitorously attacked his uncle, dethroned him, and blinded him, and he attempted to take his life with poison. However, though he drank the death-dealing drink, he suffered no harm, for he was protected by God's grace.

After he seized power by force, Svatopluk, in a fit of pride and arrogance, together with his courtiers spurned Bishop Methodius's teachings, which flowed like honey. And he disregarded completely his most holy admonitions but permitted his members—that is, his people and nation—in part to serve Christ, in part the Devil. Therefore, his region and land, together with the people inhabiting it, were anathematized by the above-mentioned bishop of blessed memory and overwhelmed by various calamities in the fields and in the crops, and even to this day they groan for that reason. Thus it was ceded to plunder and captivity, to exploitation and ridicule, and to demoralization and disgrace before everyone who passed through it, for light has no communion with darkness, nor is there concord between Christ and Belial.[9] And these examples evidently also apply to us who venture to walk in the same footsteps. For he who sees his neighbor's house on fire must be concerned about his own house.[10]

2

But the Slavs of Bohemia, who settled under Arcturus[11] and venerated idols, lived like horses unrestrained by a bridle, without law, without a prince or ruler, and without a city. Roaming about sporadically like reckless animals, they inhabited only the open country. Finally, after being overtaken by a disastrous plague, they, as the story goes, turned to a prophetess to request good advice and a prophetic pronouncement. And having received it, they founded a city and named it Prague.[12] Afterward, they found a very discerning and prudent man named Přemysl, who merely spent his time ploughing,[13] and in keeping with the pronouncement of the prophetess, they appointed him prince or ruler, giving him the above-mentioned prophetess for a wife.

And after the above-mentioned prince, when they were finally delivered from the various sores of the plague, they appointed for themselves rulers or commanders from among his descendents. They served idols and pagan gods, and wantonly made offerings according to pagan customs until dominion over this land at last fell to a man from the line of these princes by the name of Bořivoj.[14]

Sparkling with the bloom of remarkable handsomeness and youthful vigor, he once called on his prince or king in Moravia, Svatopluk, about a personal matter and one concerning the people entrusted to him. And he was received well by him and was invited along with the others to a banquet. However, he was not permitted to sit among the Christians but was asked to take his place on the floor in front of the table in the manner of pagans.[15] And now, they say, Bishop Methodius was distressed by his humiliation and said to him: "What a pity, such a remarkable man! Although you also have princely power and rank, you are not ashamed of being banished from princely seats and would rather sit on the ground with swineherders for the sake of shameful idolatry." Then he said: "To what danger will I expose myself for this matter? What good will the Christian religion bring me?" "If you renounce idols and the evil spirits residing in them," said Bishop Methodius, "you will become the lord of your lords, and all your enemies will be subject to your power, and your descendents will grow daily like a great river into which the flow of various streams pour." And Bořivoj said, "If that is so, what prevents me from being baptized?" "Nothing," said the bishop, "only be prepared to believe wholeheartedly in God the Father Almighty, and in His only-begotten Son, Our Lord Jesus Christ, and in the Spirit, the Consoler, the Enlightener of all the faithful, not only for the sake of worldly happiness but also for the sake of salvation of your soul. In this way you may gain the glorious palm of eternity and may become a partaker of ineffable joy in the community of the saints." By this and similar stimulation, which flowed like honey, the youth's mind was inspired and he yearned to receive the grace of baptism. Throwing himself, together with his entire retinue, to the ground at the bishop's feet, he entreated him most earnestly that this take place without delay.

What need was there for more words? On the following day he instructed the commander in the principles of the faith along with thirty of the courtiers who were with him. And after they observed the customary ritual of the fast, he regenerated them in the holy fountains of baptism. And after he instructed him thoroughly in Christ's faith, he allowed him to return home, having enriched him with many gifts.[16] And he gave him a priest of the venerable life named Kaich. Returning home, they established the aforesaid priest at the small town called Hradec, and there they founded a church in honor of the Blessed Pope and Martyr Clement, gaining people for Christ the Lord and causing Satan much harm.

When that perfidious serpent became aware of this, he took up arms and attempted to renew the old battle. He provoked a revolt against the prince among all the people of Bohemia, because, it was said, he had abandoned his paternal customs and accepted the new and unknown Christian law of sanctity. They rose against him as one and in unison, and strove to banish him from the land. They even attempted to take his life. When the prince realized this, he left them and took refuge again with King Svatopluk and Bishop Methodius. And they received him with great honor. Remaining with them for a time, as was fitting, he became more thoroughly acquainted with Christ's science. But the aforesaid people, persisting in their iniquity, brought home again Prince Strojmir, whose name can be translated into Latin as *rex pacatus*, who, having fled from his land, lived like an exile among the Germans. Upon dispatching a message to him, they appointed him as their prince. However, since Truth can not be deluded, as it says in the Gospels, "Every plant that my heavenly father hath not planted will be pulled up by the root" [Matthew 15:13], with its aid the scheme of the villains was quickly frustrated. For the prince whom they elected, though he descended from them, had forgotten how to speak his native language during his long exile. Thus he was rejected by his own electors, who primarily blamed themselves for having chosen a man whose voice or speech they were not able to understand, and whose ears, ignorant of their language, their calls could not reach. By the direction of divine providence the aforementioned Prince Bořivoj, after departing, had left many friends behind. They took counsel as to how to calm the feelings of the people who were raging against this benevolent ruler, and how to turn them and all their might against the perfidious intruder and destroy him. But because the great majority of traitors favored the tyrant, both sides agreed to leave the metropolis, that is, Prague, and go to an open field where they would decide what to do. But the perfidious side of traitors, acting wrongfully, secretly took weapons and armor to this open field. And they arranged a secret signal among themselves for attacking the side of the just. That is, if any of Bořivoj's followers did not agree with them, a secret watchword would be cried out loudly in public, saying, "Let us change, let us change," and now, dressed in the armor and helmets that were brought in secret, they would kill all their opponents with their swords.

But their dastardly scheme did not remain hidden from Bořivoj's side. And they left for the open field where the appointment of the prince would be decided, having also put on armor under their clothes. Now, when Strojmir's side did not like the counsel of Bořivoj's side, one of them raised his voice and cried out, "Ah, my people, let us change!" And when Bořivoj's party, which arrived wearing armor under their clothes, heard and recognized the voice, they shouted: "Good, good you said that. Now you will be changed into loud colors." And putting him to the sword, they routed his comrades and drove their false prince out of the land. Afterward they hastened to Moravia and brought back the former commander, and they installed him again in his place.

While residing in Moravia, the prince had made a vow to God Almighty: if the Lord would bring him back to his country with honor, he would erect a basilica in honor of the Blessed Mother of God and Ever-Immaculate Virgin Mary. Thus, when he returned, he saw to the fulfillment of his vow without delay. He is considered the first builder of holy places, the assembler of priests, and the founder of the Christian faith, which at that time was certainly insignificantly disseminated.

3

He also had a wife by the name of Ludmila,[17] the daughter of Prince Slavibor from the Slavic region which formerly was called Pšov, but which the people of today now named after the newly constructed castle of Mělník. And as she was like him in pagan error, so also did she emulate him in Christian faith, even surpassing in virtue the virtues of her husband. Indeed, she became a handmaid of Christ. The aforementioned prince had three sons with her, and as many daughters. And as Blessed Methodius had predicted with prophetic lips, every day he gained more power, along with all his people and his princedom. Finishing the course of his life and filling his days with good deeds, he concluded the last day, having completed the thirty-fifth year of life.[18] And after him his first born son, Spytihněv,[19] assumed power, a man who sparkled with diverse virtues, a good character, and a reputation for sanctity beyond measure. Emulating his father by being perfect in the faith of Christ, he founded churches of God and gathered priests and clerics around him. And he departed this world for the stars, having completed forty years of life. After his death, as is well known, his brother Vratislav[20] assumed control of the princedom. He had a wife named Drahomira, from the Stodorane, a land of pagan Slavs.[21] She should be compared to Jezebel, who in her wickedness murdered prophets; or to Eve, the wife of the first man, who gave birth to Cain and Abel.[22] For Drahomira bore the prince two sons, one named Wenceslas, the other, Boleslav.[23] But enough will be said about that in the appropriate place.

Thus, after becoming a widow and losing her eldest son, the pious lady Ludmila stayed at home, recalling her former ignorance and errors, and tearfully she lamented her past sins daily. And as she had previously yielded her members to serve uncleanliness and iniquity unto iniquity, so now she brought them into the service of righteousness unto holiness, saying with the Apostle, "What fruit had I then in those things whereof I am now ashamed?"[24]

Testifying to this is the manner in which she frequently eased the misery of the poor whom she helped in their want, she nourished the hungry, refreshed the thirsty, and clothed strangers and the needy. Priests can also testify to this, for she looked after them as devotedly as she did her own sons. And if all these people should remain silent, it is attested to by Christ's dwellings, which she enriched with stores of gold and silver from the property entrusted to her by God, and not, as some do, from theft or from the property of the needy. She was pious and moderate in all things, and filled with all the fruits of kindness. She was generous with alms, persevering in nocturnal devotions, devout in prayers, and perfect in charity and humble among the unknowing. She was so willing in her care for God's servants that to those to whom she was unable to offer help during the light of day, she would send urgent help through her servants during the dark of night. She fulfilled the precept of the Gospel, according to which we are to bestow alms in such a manner that our left hand will not know what our right hand is doing. However, if we would wish to recount with our pen all the manifestations of her saintliness, we would run out of daylight before we would pages of a book. For day and night the doors of her home were open to all who passed by. Hence she could cry out with Blessed Job, "I opened my doors to the traveler; I was eyes to the blind and feet was I to the lame."[25] This mother to orphans, consoler to widows, and indefatigable visitor of the fettered and imprisoned was perfect in all good deeds.

Therefore, as we already noted, after his brother died, the aforementioned Vratislav seized power. And upon strengthening his domain, he founded a basilica in honor of the Blessed Martyr George. But he was overtaken by death and did not witness its consecration, which he had yearned to do for a long time. He had sent his older son, Wenceslas, a fervent-minded lad, for an education in the law of God and the Scriptures to the town called Budeč,[26] where there was and still is a church dedicated by his brother and predecessor, Spytihněv, in honor of the Prince of Apostles, Blessed Peter. Being intellectually astute with the aid of the Holy Spirit, he impressed deep into his memory everything that his teacher explained. And when in the meantime his father departed from this world in about the thirty-third year of his life, he was recalled to the capital city, Prague, and elevated by all the people to his father's throne. But because he had not yet matured from boyhood or adolescence, all the magnates, having conceived a wise plan, entrusted the young prince, together with his brother Boleslav, to Ludmila of blessed memory, a handmaid of Christ, to raise until they attained the vigor of a mature age with the help of God.[27]

However, through the instigation of the Devil, the mother of the aforesaid lads, a widow exercising her husband's power as ruler, took note of this and was gripped by evil suspicion. And she flared up against God's handmaid Ludmila with all the anger of a venomous heart. For she thought she would be deprived of her rule and of her property through the youths' upbringing which the entire nation had entrusted to her mother-in-law, who would gain all the power of a ruler. And she came to an agreement with the sons of Belial on a most infamous plan, and with all her might she sought to destroy her. But the venerable and pious handmaid of Christ, Ludmila, grasped this. Clutching the weapons of humility and patience against the thorn of pride, she sent word to her daughter-in-law through intermediaries, saying: "My soul is not allured by evil greed and does not yearn for any part of your rule; nor does it wish to reign over you. Take your sons and rule with them as you like. However, allow me the freedom to serve Almighty Christ in whatever place you wish."

But as always happens, the more humility humbles itself in keeping with God's will, the more pride vaunts itself through the Devil's agitation. Thus her daughter-in-law, the princess, not only refused scornfully to fulfill Saint Ludmila's very friendly and kind request, but she disregarded it entirely. When Christ's handmaid saw this, she departed from the capital city with her people and betook herself to a nearby small town called Tetín,[28] remembering the words of the Apostle: "Avenge not yourselves, but give place unto wrath,"[29] and the words of the Gospel: "When they persecute you in this city, flee ye into another."[30] The more certain she was that the persecutor would soon overtake her and that she would earn the victorious palm of martyrdom, the more she adorned herself with jewels of virtue. And she persisted very devoutly in prayer, zealously observed vigils, fasted, and offered alms to all with a generous hand.

Although Blessed Wenceslas was still of a tender age and living with his mother, he was famous already in those days for his spirit of prophecy, and he discerned everything that was to come, for Christ the Lord revealed this to him in a clear vision. Once in the still of night it seemed to Wenceslas, a saintly youth filled with the spirit of God, that he saw quite clearly the home of the priest Paul, who was frequently mentioned above and who faithfully stuck by the side of Ludmila of blessed memory and served her very devotedly, whose home, which was surrounded on all sides by lovely and spacious porticoes, lacked all its beautiful buildings and was completely deserted.[31] And now, casting off the weight of bodily sleep and roused to vigilant contemplation, he informed several people about his dream in a wise discourse. And at once he explained with prophetic lips the true meaning which the revelation already described would have in the future. Thus he addressed those whom he had summoned: "My dear friends and you, my courtiers, after I went to bed in the evening an important and meaningful vision awakened me in the still of night. For I saw that the home of the priest Paul lacked all its splendor, and was completely abandoned by the people. I am dejected with sorrow over this vision, and grievously anxious with concern for God's faithful. Nevertheless, because the immeasurable mercy of the Judge of the universe leads me to hope that a man who believes can accomplish all things, as was promised, I shall attempt to interpret the correct meaning of this dream, which soon will be manifest in actual events, with a clear commentary that aims for a reliable explanation of the matter. Therefore, the ruined house I saw portends the felicitous death of the saintly and venerable lady Ludmila, my grandmother. Indeed, at not too distant a time she will be attacked by armed scoundrels. They will come in secret to her in an insane conspiracy that my mother, a pagan by descent and also by her despicable deeds, is planning with several helpers who are equally predisposed to crime. And she will be subjected to cruel bodily torment for the confession of the name and faith of Christ. And, as in the vision, the splendid home deserted by the people signifies, sadly, that the clergy entrusted to our protection will be banished from the land and undeservedly lose all their property. For my mother of accursed memory has an evil hatred for the living faith—which I do not and will not ever hereafter cease to confess and honor with all my strength, and to follow and love with all my heart— and will do her utmost to deprive these priests of various rank of their earthly estates, and drive them mercilessly out of the principality because they share my sentiments."

Thus, knowing the truth, his spirit was not mistaken in this astute prediction. Indeed, it was entirely in agreement with his prophetic interpretation concerning the destruction of the aforementioned lady, and concerning the merciless banishment of the clergy who willingly submitted to his rule, or rather to his magnificent generosity, in the broad territories of the adjacent districts. Soon after, as is known, all this was fulfilled, unchanged in order.

4

For after the handmaid of Christ was out of sight of the traitors, as we already said, she was overtaken by her enemies at the very castle where she took refuge. Indeed, the aforementioned princess sent some

of her magnates, Tunna and Gommon,[32] the sons of iniquity, to Tetín
with a mighty host to destroy her daughter-in-law. However, foreseeing the future, the handmaid of Christ summoned the above-mentioned priest Paul, and asked him to offer Holy Mass. Making a sincere confession in the presence of the Tester of Hearts, and certain
that she would receive a reward from the Most High, she armed herself fully with the weapons of faith. Then she knelt in prayer and sent
pleas to God that He might deign to receive in peace the soul which
He Himself had created. After mass was finished, she began to chant
psalms zealously, having strengthened herself with the reception of
the body and blood of the Lord. And when evening came, the aforementioned brutes attacked her home. Upon forcing the gate, they
stationed their other associates outside, armed with swords and
shields. And only the leaders of the murderers, Tunna and Gommon,
along with a few other men, broke open the door, and with wild
shrieks entered the bedroom where the handmaid of God was resting.
Now Blessed Ludmila said to them in a humble voice: "What manner
of sudden insanity has set you off? Are you not ashamed and do you
not remember how I nurtured you like my own sons, and how I gave
you gifts of gold, silver, and fine clothes? But if you know of some
wrong that I have committed against you, I beseech you, tell me what
it is."

But being more immovable than rocks in their frenzy, they refused to listen to her words and made bold to lay hands on her. Pulling
her out of bed, they cast her to the ground. And she said to them, "Let
me pray a little." And when they permitted this, she prayed to the
Lord with outstretched arms. Then she said, "if you have come to kill
me, I earnestly beseech you to behead me with a sword." That is, she
longed to bear witness for Christ by shedding her blood in the manner
of martyrs, and to receive with them the palm of martyrdom for eternity. And we, too, do not doubt that she deserved it, as the Holy
Scriptures affirm by saying, "But though the righteous one be prevented with death, yet shall his soul be refreshed."[33] Now the deadly
henchmen disregarded her pleading words, threw a rope around her
throat, and strangled her. They deprived her of earthly life that she
might live forever with the Lord Jesus Christ whom she always loved.
Thus, the devoted-to-God and fortunate handmaid of Christ Ludmila
was martyred on the seventh day, on Saturday, the sixteenth day of

September, during the first vigil of the night (in the sixty-first year of life).[34]

But when the shepherd was killed, her entire clergy and all her household servants, both men and women, dispersed here and there. They hid themselves in various hiding-places and thus preserved their earthly life. After these cruel henchmen departed, they assembled with great fear and lamentation for her funeral. And they entrusted her most holy body to the earth, having done everything that seemed necessary for her burial with the utmost respect. And the bloodthirsty henchmen returned to their mistress after they plundered the spoils, and brought her a most joyful account of the murder of the innocent one, presuming they would be enriched for all time and would live forever. However, punishment by the terrible and unquenchable fire of hell soon awaited them. Having appropriated all the property of her mother-in-law, the treacherous mistress of traitors began to rule together with the aforementioned brutes. And she gave them and their relatives and servants gifts of unusual quantities of gold and silver, and extraordinary and expensive clothes. And they ruled the entire land of Bohemia like mighty lords, but not with the grace of God.

While they were living in splendor and made merry and rejoiced in excess, the just vengeance of divine punishment suddenly overtook these wicked people, who were not afraid to commit such a great and cruel sin—to lay their most vile hands on Christ's most illustrious handmaid without cause. Being instigated by their father the Devil, the prince of discord, they began to hold all their peers and contemporaries in contempt. This led to dissention and great hatred between the aforementioned magnates, Tunna and Gommon, and their mistress. Hence day and night all her words and thoughts were preoccupied with their destruction. When the aforementioned brute Tunna saw this, he was overcome by terrible fear and fled this land with all his relatives. Hated by everyone, he wandered here and there like an outcast, and not one of his descendents ever returned to the country. At that time Gommon was seized when he, together with his brother, sought deliverance in flight. And he was condemned to death, and together with his brother lost his earthly and eternal life. Seeing them flee, their mistress vented all the fury of her venomous heart on their descendents, and in one day with a single verdict she slaughtered them all, from the oldest down to the youngest. And the first sign of

Ludmila's sanctity was clearly manifested in this: for not one of her murderers remained alive, by the dispensation of Divine Providence. Others who left their homes and scattered in various directions incurred the hatred of all the people and were overtaken by God's vengeance. And they exhaled their souls, and their children died the most ungodly deaths. However, most of them were put to the sword. Thus was fulfilled the word of the Lord, who says in the Gospel: "All they that take the sword shall perish with the sword" [Matthew 26:52].

Now in those very days, through the aid of divine grace, the most glorious merits of her virtues manifested themselves at the grave of the Most Blessed and frequently mentioned Venerable Lady and Martyr Ludmila. For from her tomb such a profusion of wondrous and very sweet fragrances emanated that it surpassed the aroma of all fragrant substances and flowers. Here also, in the still of somber night, many repeatedly saw before their very eyes illuminations and lights, burning with a divine glow. And all this did not in any way remain hidden from the ruler, her murderess. When she learned of this, she was struck by unspeakable fear and knew not what to do. Finally, she again conceived a malicious scheme, and sent her servants to Tetín, where the venerable body reposed, and had them rebuild Ludmila's home over her grave in the form of a basilica. And she commanded that it be named in honor of the Blessed Archangel Michael, so that miracles which might possibly manifest themselves there in the future would not be attributed to the merits of the blessed martyr but rather to the merits of saints whose relics would be preserved there. But when this took place, such sacred awe filled all the people entering the basilica that they ventured to enter only with the utmost reverence. And since that time, the most glorious and splendid miracles have been wrought at this place.

5

In the meantime Blessed Wenceslas, who had been elected as ruler through the inspiration of Christ, outgrew his adolescence, and was radiant with the bloom of most graceful youth. Moreover, deep in his memory he retained the instruction of his teacher of Scripture and fervently yearned to fulfill in deed what he had become acquainted with through hearing. Therefore his perfidious mother, together with several sons of Belial who shared her thoughts and hated him because of his deeds and most holy thoughts, took counsel among themselves and said: "Ah, alas, what are we to do and where can we turn! For our prince, whom we elevated to the throne, has been corrupted by priests and does not permit us to pursue the bold and usual ways of our depravity, having become, so to say, a monk. And if this is how he acts now as a boy or youth, what will he do as a young man or in his old age?" Thus from then on they began to treat him with enmity; they threatened him and otherwise caused him much injury.

But being beloved of God, this man bore it with a pure mind. He warded all this off with the weapon of faith, and protected himself with the shield of patience. For these wicked men even tried to kill his priests and some monks, with whose instruction he strengthened himself. Constantly plotting against them, they sought to frighten them with grave threats so that none of them would have the courage to go to him. But he knew about all this. And together with men who were loyal to him, he forced an opening in the rear, and when the sun set, he secretly sent for some priests. After he learned all that was useful to him during the night, at the break of dawn he let the teacher or priest dear to him depart in secret. And he carried a booklet hidden beneath his clothes and read it diligently whenever he found a quiet place. Deeply lamenting inwardly, he grieved over the callousness of his people and over their blindness and disbelief. Finally, having girded himself with virtue, and strengthened by God, he sent for his mother and all the magnates. And, as was fitting, he rebuked them, as the Book of Wisdom says: "The words of the wise are as goads, and as nails deeply fastened."[35] Then Blessed Wenceslas spoke thus: "O sons of criminals, seed of lies and unjust men, why were you opposed to my studying the law of our Lord Jesus Christ and heeding His command? If you do not wish to serve Christ, why do you not at least allow others to do so? However, if until now I have lived under your guardianship and control, henceforth I will reject it. I wish to serve Almighty God wholeheartedly."

For this reason and for various others, great differences arose then between the magnates who remained on the side of the pious ruler, and the ones who supported the contemptible side of the wicked regent. And the counselors and foremost men of the land were divided, and the thorns of discord grew between them and led to bloodshed. Although very small, the side of the righteous nevertheless gained the upper hand over the side of the unrighteous which, as always, was disunited. For Prince Wenceslas, who has been mentioned repeatedly, was inspired by the Holy Spirit, and while striving to obtain peace, he planned to banish his mother, the cause of all the malice, from the country. By driving her out, and all her wicked followers, the fury of the rebellion would abate and peace would thrive in Christ's church, and all would become thoroughly familiar with the true teaching of Christ, having one and the same ruler. And he would call his mother back again to the country with honor after banishing and driving out the sons of discord, and when everything that appeared to serve harmony and the principality was arranged and peace was established. And he in fact accomplished all this with the help of God the Creator, for he exiled his mother in utmost disgrace from the land. Thus Almighty God afflicted her with deserved punishment for shedding the innocent blood of Blessed Ludmila, and for shedding it without cause. However, since he was filled with proper fear that lasts forever, and since he was mindful of God's commandment to honor father and mother, he brought her back again after a time; but she was deprived of her former dignity as regent until the day she died. But let us remain silent about how all this happened because of the grimness of these events, and let us continue the exposition with which we began. After many misfortunes and sorrows, she lived to see one of her sons murdered by her other, younger offspring.

Remembering his grandmother and the sanctity in which she lived on this earth, and the glory she earned in return from the Almighty, Blessed Wenceslas shed torrents of tears. And together with priests and some pious men he conceived a most solemn plan: He sent them to the aforementioned town of Tetín and commissioned them to bring him at least the bones and dust of her decayed body in a dignified translation.

But through the inspiration of the Holy Spirit he himself was certain, and he made mention of this to several of his loyal friends, that with the help of God's grace the aforesaid messengers would find some signs there. The messengers fulfilled their lord's command. And when they entered the basilica and scraped away the earth, they uncovered the grave. Observing now that the tomb's slab, which covered the venerable body, was partially decayed, they were afraid to raise it. Thus they said among themselves, "If the wood is rotted, would not that which is inside be all the more decayed?" And they wanted to close the grave again very carefully. But one of them, the priest Paul, about whom mention has been made already and who was closely associated with her as a friend while she lived on this earth, and always supported her in everything with his services, was opposed to their plan and said: "It is not at all as you say, but do as the prince ordered! If I find only the dust of a decayed body, I will take it with me." And the others agreed with him and together they lifted the slab. But as they were lifting it, the slab broke and Paul, mentioned above, and some earth fell onto the body of the deceased. Rising at once and quickly scraping away the earth, he, together with his companions, found the holy body entirely incorrupt. Only the face was covered with much dust because the cover slab, as I noted above, broke as they were removing it. Thus aglow with immense joy and expressing untold gratitude to Almighty God, they raised her most holy body from the ground and wrapped it in fine linen, as was fitting. And they placed it before the altar and offered untold thanks to God's grace.

And after all the rites were performed in an orderly fashion, they laid the body on a litter and then loaded it on the backs of two horses. And that very night they set off for the capital city, that is, Prague, with sustained haste. Thus the body of the blessed and devoted handmaid of God, Ludmila, was found on Wednesday, the nineteenth day of the month of October, during the twelfth hour. And they brought it to Prague on the third day, on Friday, the twenty-first day of that same month[36] with infinite joy. And everyone rejoiced and extolled Christ. Before they reached the castle, those who were carrying her sent messengers ahead to the prince with the good news. But they found him asleep when they arrived. Awakening him joyfully, they announced their comforting tidings to him, that with the help of Almighty God the body of this most admirable lady, that is, his grandmother, was found incorrupt.

He rose immediately, hastened to church with utmost joy, and offered untold thanks to Christ the Lord. When the sun lit up the earth with its rays and its glow dispersed the darkness, he summoned the clergy and a multitude of the faithful, and hurriedly set off to meet her with an immense procession. Then they met the faithful bearers who were carrying the body of Saint Ludmila, which has been mentioned frequently. And immediately the priests and deacons joyfully placed it on their shoulders and carried it to the castle, praising God and singing psalms and verses of praise. Entering the church, they placed it on the floor before the altar and began to sing in a powerful voice. And believers and unbelievers flocked to this place, and with a curiosity that is inherent to man, they moved toward the doors of the church, seeking to learn what happened. Having taken counsel with the priests, the prince together with them uncovered the body in the presence of all the people so that all might believe that Christ the Lord preserved her incorrupt. And, seeing this, all untiringly glorified Christ's miracles and no one could deny the truth, for it was obvious to all that her body was incorrupt and her hair resilient, and her face shone as though she were alive. Moreover, her garments gleamed with such beauty and soundness it seemed they had been woven that day. And now everyone who saw this glorified her with loud rejoicing and declared that she was worthy beyond measure of all honor and praise. Having dug out the earth and prepared the grave, they tried to bury her in the basilica. But water suddenly flooded the unearthed grave. And many who saw this concluded that this grave site displeased the handmaid of Christ. Refilling the grave, they placed the coffin with her holy relics over it, and awaited God's help. Then they joyfully hastened to their homes.

And after a short time the aforementioned prince dispatched messengers to Regensburg and asked the bishop of that city, named Tuto,[37] for at the time the Bohemians belonged to his diocese, for advice on how to deal with the aforesaid body. Examining the prescriptions of God's law as given to him according to God's wisdom, he sent word to him in answer: that the body, which originates in the first man, should be placed in a grave until the time the glory of Christ is revealed. For to him it was said: "Earth thou art, and unto earth thou shalt go, dust thou art, and unto dust shalt thou return."[38] And now the prince was enkindled with limitless divine fervor, and he appealed very humbly to the aforementioned bishop, that he deign to come to him and bury the body himself, and that he dedicate the basilica, which had not yet been consecrated by the bishop. However, he excused himself for being unable to come on account of weakness and old age, and sent his coadjutor bishop with several priests as assistants to dedicate the church. And when he arrived, he first consecrated the church to the Lord. Then, after six days had passed, he buried the aforesaid body in the same place the water had flooded previously. This is remarkable and sufficient evidence of the merits of Christ's handmaid: for when the priests wished to bury her in an unconsecrated place, water appeared there; whereas after the coadjutor bishop arrived and consecrated the basilica, the water disappeared entirely. Verily, it is fitting that she, who blessedly spent her life in blessed communion, should be buried with the highest blessing, for she was to be seated with the saints at the right hand of Christ. After the coadjutor bishop duly performed this, he was properly rewarded and returned again to his country.

On the anniversary of the translation of her holy body, Christ the Lord deigned to work a special miracle so as to glorify His name and make known the merits of His handmaid. For when they sat down together after prayers to refresh their bodies—in accordance with the custom celebrated in the Christian faith, that is, that the clergy assembles and celebrates the memory of such events—a boy, debilitated and deformed by a disease of the body and not even able to raise his head, invoked the power of Christ before the doors of the basilica, where the body of this remarkable lady reposed, and appealed to the merits of this saint. He was righted at once and regained his former strength. Seeing this, the multitudes sang praise to Christ Almighty, that He deigned to reveal His power through His handmaid. Unto Him be the glory forevermore, amen.

6

Thus, after Blessed Prince Wenceslas pacified and consolidated his princedom with the help of Christ, how he proved himself before Christ, and what a vessel, a chosen one he became! Neither my spirit, nor language and speech, nor a book would be sufficient to describe this. And because I am burdened by a multitude of sins, I would be unable to explain how much harm he caused the Devil, fighting for the Lord as a warrior of Christ, and how many sheaves he gathered into Christ's barn as His faithful servant. But I can at least tell a little about many things. Even as a boy he did not deviate from divine teachings. He was truthful in speech, just in judgment, honorable and worthy of trust, and merciful beyond the usual measure of human nature. For whenever someone stood accused before an assembly of judges and was condemned to death in his presence by a judge, he withdrew under some pretext and hid, as best he could, mindful of Christ's threat in the Gospel: "Judge not and ye shall not be judged: condemn not, and ye shall not be condemned" [Luke 6:37]. He razed prisons and gallows built during earlier times that still remained. Untiringly he comforted orphans, widows, the poor, the sorrowing, and the wounded. He sated the hungry, gave drink to the thirsty, clothed the naked, visited the sick, buried the dead, and received strangers and wayfarers like his closest relatives. He honored priests, clerics, and monks like the Lord. He showed the way of truth to those who had gone astray, and he practiced humility, patience, moderation, and charity, which stands out above all. He did not deprive anyone of anything by force or deceit. And he provided his retinue not only with the best arms but also with apparel.

Even from tenderest youth he distinguished himself by these and similar virtues. Putting the cross of Christ on his limbs, he was mindful of God's commandment, which says: "If any man will come after me, let him deny himself, and take up his cross, and follow me" [Matthew 16:24]. For during Lent and in winter he walked barefoot from town to town over frigid and impassable trails, visiting Christ's churches on foot. Thus his footprints could be seen wet with blood. And he wore a very rough hair shirt to keep himself chaste and pure. This shirt is preserved like new to this very day out of respect for him. He always wore a woolen garment on his naked body like a monk, but on the outside he was wrapped in a most beautiful robe. He shone before God and before man. He strengthened his limbs with moderate nourishment, and during the night, persevering untiringly in prayers, he did not cease to give untold thanks to the One God. And if it happened on occasion that he, as prince, feasted in such company that he drank more than usual during the evening, as soon as he awoke early the following morning he hastened as quickly as possible to church, took off the beautiful robe that he wore, and gave it to any priest or cleric that he found there. Falling to his feet, he earnestly beseeched him to offer especially devout prayers for him to Christ the Lord, that He might mercifully forgive him the sin he had committed the previous night.

Moreover, he took part in divine services with such zeal that every day he provided sacrificial bread which he had prepared with his own hands. For during harvesttime, in the deep still of night, he would go to his field together with his most faithful companion, about whom I shall later relate a special miracle that beautifully demonstrates both their merits. And having reaped the wheat, he would carry it home on his own shoulders and grind it in a hand-mill. Being both baker and prince, he would sift the flour, and then, also during the night, he would go for water, drawing it with the words, "In the name of the Father and of the Son and of the Holy Spirit." And when he brought it home, he would mix it with fine flour and make wafers from it. And he would hasten to the vineyard, pick grapes, press them with his own hands, pour the wine into pitchers, and save it for use at the holy sacrifice. Since at that time superstitious pagan practices were not yet thoroughly uprooted, a multitude of others would zealously bring shameful offerings to the idols and defile themselves by eating and drinking of them. But he was never guilty of taking part in this, for he always shunned them by finding some excuse. In his mercy he demolished prisons, and he razed to their foundation gallows and racks, which until that time had been used to execute people. And he leveled pagan shrines to the ground.

When Christians heard tell of this, priests, deacons, and a multitude of servants of God from the land of Bavaria and Swabia and other regions flocked to him, much like bees to the hive, with the relics of saints and with many books. And he received them all with untold respect. He treated them kindly and supported them as was fitting, distributing much gold and silver among them, and readily bestowing upon them gifts of fur, slaves, and garments. And to all he rendered services according to their needs. And all these teachers marveled at his wisdom so that he could clearly declare with the Psalmist, "I have more understanding than all my teachers: for thy testimonies are my meditation" [Psalms 119:99]. For in his mind only the radiance of the precious pearl sparkled.[39] And for his piety the Lord also deigned to grant him abundant grace so that he was victorious in a great number of battles.

His face had a distinguished appearance. And he was soberly chaste, though this is a rare virtue among married men, and he yearned to end his earthly life with a martyr's death. He always spoke kindly with the meek. However, under the pretext of dining together—if he was unable to reach them in another way—he summoned the dissolute, loafers, and people given to gluttony and drunkenness, or those who wished to break away from the true faith and right path, and in divine indignation he flogged them soundly with reproofs. Against the eternal Enemy he always seized the shield of faith and the sword of the Holy Spirit, which is the Word of God. Untiringly he combated the earthly powers of this world.

Thus he was without blemish, a true devotee of Christ, and, according to the Apostle's precepts, he reproved, exhorted, and rebuked untiringly.[40] He invited them all to the banquet of the true Master, and he continually invigorated with divine nourishment those whom he snatched from the Devil's throat and led to the bosom of the Holy Mother Church. Later, when God's grace inspired his heart with the idea to build a church for the Lord in honor of the Blessed Martyr Vitus, he dispatched messengers to the bishop of Regensburg—to whose diocese, as we said above, Bohemia belonged at that time—in order to receive his permission, according to canonical rules, to build a basilica. And he conveyed this to him: "My father once built a church for the Lord in honor of Blessed George. In accordance with that custom, I, too, long to build a church, with your permission, in honor of Christ's Blessed Martyr Vitus." When the venerable bishop heard this, he extended his arms in thanksgiving to Christ the Lord and said: "When you return convey this message to my son, the Most Blessed Wenceslas: 'Your church is standing already before the Lord, most beautifully built.'" When the prince heard this, he rejoiced in his heart. Soon he laid the foundation of the church and built its walls exceedingly well.

But he was still not satisfied with this, for he wished to journey to Rome, to the thresholds of the Blessed Apostles Peter and Paul, to ask the pope of that time to invest him in monastic habit and to ordain him a priest. Afterward, out of love for God, he would give up his princedom and cede it to his brother, who, alas, was much too attached to worldly interests. And while living in peace he would seek to win some new sheep for the fold of Christ the Lord. And he in fact would have done this had the construction of the basilica, of which mention was made already, not kept him from it. However, since the Enemy of mankind, who from the very beginning of the world has attacked multitudes of the faithful, could not conquer, even with all his might, the unconquerable servant of Christ, he resorted to an old weapon and strove to destroy the Christian faith. For his younger brother, whom we compared to Cain in the preceding narrative, and for whose benefit he intended to give up everything, as we mentioned before, and to lay aside all worldly splendor, was deceived by much advice from evil people, who resented having to forsake their customs and not being allowed to do forbidden things. And they incited him against his most holy brother with the fatal weapon of hatred. However, although he foresaw all this through the inspiration of the Holy Spirit, nevertheless, just as the hart pants after the water brooks,[41] so he longed to attain the palm of a martyr's glory—but not at the hands of his brother, for he feared for his eternal damnation—and always trusted in Christ.

7

Then these things came to pass during the time of Henry, king of the Saxons, who, with the grace of Christ, was the first of his line to place a crown on his head, and with whom this blessed man was associated in a lasting friendship.[42] But let us continue further. Thus Boleslav, who had his own home or court at the castle which bears his name, was now being prodded on all sides by the Devil's arrows and aroused by his longing to rule. Considering that the feast of the Blessed Martyrs Cosmas and Damian was coming[43]—the one celebrated two days before the feast of the Blessed Archangel Michael—they presumed this was now a suitable occasion to invite cunningly his aforementioned, blessed brother as though to a banquet, for a church was there consecrated in honor of these saints, but actually, as the deed demonstrated, to his death. However, although all this was well known to him, nevertheless he maintained a gallant spirit and took leave of all his friends and relatives with a kiss. Having said his last farewells, he set off, protected by the weapons of faith.

When he arrived there, he saw that everything was doubly prepared for him, that is, a banquet had been arranged with great splendor, as well as a powerful band of secretly armed enemies. He then betook himself to the church. After he had properly participated in the divine service, he commended himself to God and Saints Cosmas and Damian, whose anniversary commemoration was being observed that day, and cheerfully entered the banquet hall. And when the hearts of the banqueting villains, which had long been saturated with the venom of murder, were warmed by food and drink, gradually they began to show their hidden weapons. Thinking constantly about the attack, they rose three times, and three times they sat down again, for God through His power prevented them from carrying out that deed, perhaps because He wished to sanctify the following day, since hitherto no feast day fell upon it. Thus, when the saint observed how wild they had become, he indeed maintained his fearless composure but nevertheless hastened to rise from the table as soon as he could. And as he was leaving, one of his friends approached him from a place near the banquet and said, "Look here, I have secretly prepared a horse for you; mount it, my lord, and be sure to ride away from here as quickly as possible, for death threatens you." However, not paying any attention to his words, he returned again to the banquet hall, seized a goblet, and pronouncing a toast in the presence of all, exclaimed in a raised voice, "In the name of the Blessed Archangel Michael, let us drink with the supplication and prayer that he might now deign to lead our souls to the peace of eternal joy." And when some of those faithful to him answered "amen," he drained his cup, kissed all of them, and returned to his guest dwellings. Allowing his most extraordinary limbs some rest after he prayed to God for a long time and sang psalms, tired, he finally fell asleep.

And the hour to celebrate vigils approached. As always, the blessed man devoutly participated. For, verily, his holy soul was so attached to the customs of the Christian faith and the regulations of the church that on vigils he would have his people read aloud the entire narrative of the Old Testament during the prescribed time, which we consider the mark of the most perfect monks. And if on the most important feasts no children appeared at the time of baptismal examinations—on Holy Saturday and the Saturday before Pentecost when mass baptism is performed in God's holy church—he would send to the marketplace and purchase, only out of love for God, all the young slaves, which the merchants brought to sell,[44] so that nothing which belongs to God would be missing. And thus, supporting the work of God through his own work, this blessed spirit never allowed something to be missing from divine usage.

You read this narrative, O gracious Bishop, and are extremely surprised how that which the very priests of the church, by the grace of the Most High God, could hardly accomplish, as you know, a layman did very conscientiously; moreover, one who stands at the head of an entire nation which, according to its natural disposition, is considered an especially wild nation. I beseech you, O most blessed father, to draw from your innate source of wisdom and together with me to glorify with deserving praise these events about which I have written, and about which I am yet to write. For, as you commanded me, I do not intend to touch upon anything with my pen other than that which I heard from your lips, or that which you together with me learned as true from people filled with faith and sanctity. But let us continue with the narrative that was begun.

The blessed martyr, who would soon be adorned with the crown of glory and honor for perseverence in his work, as we have said, made ready to depart for the tabernacle of the Mother of the Church so as to render praise to God in the morning prayer. Now the man of eternal remembrance was so renowned for this grace that no one doubted that he would come to the portals of sanctity before dawn to perform his prayers. And the second Cain awaited this hour, considering it opportune for carrying out a murder. Verily, I see that everything will be fulfilled down to the last letter as foretold by the book of Sacred Scriptures, which also mentions evildoers, saying: "Every one that doeth evil hateth the light" [John 3:20]. For before nightfall the martyr's brother, in reality no longer a brother but a perverse fratricide, ordered the priests of the church of Saints Cosmas and Damian to stop him, should he come, from even entering the church, perhaps lest he be freed by his faithful courtiers and servants, who would still be in bed, or by people who would come running; or lest it be necessary to defile and desecrate the church with criminal bloodshed.

Lo, at the time of this writing a recollection comes to my mind of an unjust assembly of Jews, who were indeed afraid of being defiled if they entered Pilate's judgment hall[45] but who were not afraid to kill the Lord. And so was this wretched butcher of his own brother afraid to defile the walls of the church, but he did not stay his hands from fratricide. You, O cruelest of all murderers, are condemned and defeated by your own verdict for fearing that a holy place would be soiled by the blood which you were shedding. But it came to pass as Thou commanded. For as the dear martyr hastened to church before morning devotion, yearning to pray to God the Father as solitarily as possible in the chamber of his most holy heart and undisturbed by the hum of the crowd, a plot was being arranged against him by his brother's faction, and the sword was being sharpened so that an offering would be prepared for Christ. But why the pain in my heart, why do the tears in my eyes multiply twofold when I force myself to narrate at length about the death of the just one and the end of the innocent one? Verily, immeasurable pain has many words, but I dare not tarry long with the description of the suffering of the holy martyr before those who longingly yearn to hear about it.

Blessed Wenceslas, who was soon to become an offering to Christ, arose. He longed to hasten to church, according to his holy custom, and to kneel in prolonged prayer as solitarily as possible before the crowd of people assembled. And while he yearned to hear and to sing the morning praises with them like a good shepherd with his flock, he was soon caught in the snares of the plot. For as soon as he saw the man of God coming, the priest of that church, one of those from whom the iniquity of Babylon proceeds, shut the doors of the church, as commanded by the criminals. The assassins, that is, his brother with his entire armed band, stood ready. Seeing his brother, God's chosen warrior wished to thank him. And he embraced him with both arms around the neck, kissed him, and greeted him with the words, "May you always be healthy, my brother, may you have an abundance of the goods of earthly life as well as of the future one, and may Christ receive you at His eternal banquet with the same generosity you extended to me and my retinue yesterday."

But with a malicious look he unsheathed the sword which he had hidden beneath his cloak and replied arrogantly to this, "Indeed I feasted you yesterday as the moment demanded, but now this is how a brother serves a brother!" And swinging the sword, he struck him on the head. However, since the power of the Lord was shielding him, he scarcely drew blood. For that wretch was so paralyzed by dread over the cruelty of his deed that even when he struck a second time, he saw to his amazement that he was unable to do anything worthy of a strong man. Now, upon seizing the bared sword with his hand, Blessed Wenceslas said, "How badly you behave hurts me!" But when he perceived that his brother would in no wise dispense with the deed he had begun, he finally took hold of him, as some say, knocked him to his feet, and said: "Do you see how you have destroyed yourself by your own decision? I could crush you in my hand like a little whelp, but far be it from the hand of a servant of God to be stained with a

The murder of Saint Wenceslas. From the Wolfenbüttel Manuscript (eleventh century) of Gumpold's *Vita*. The scene follows Christian's account of the murder, and it has been used as an argument for the tenth-century origins of *Legenda Christiani*.

brother's blood." And to his brother he returned the sword which he had taken from him, his hands already smeared with blood from it, and he quickly hurried toward the church. However, that wretch ran after him and cried out in a loud voice: "Comrades, my comrades, where are you? You are helping your lord very badly and backing him up poorly though he is in such distress!" And then a whole crowd of villains ran out from their hiding-places. Pouncing on him with many swords and spears, they mangled him with severe blows and destroyed him before the doors of the church. And then, on the twenty-eighth day of September, in the nine hundred and twenty-ninth year from God's incarnation,[46] while heaven rejoiced and the earth wept, his holy soul departed victoriously to the Lord, liberated on this battleground from the prison of this world and glorified in blood.

And his mother—whom he had recently driven away for her sins and then called back again in peace for the love of Christ—and some of the faithful took his lifeless body and simply put it into a grave. And they covered it with earth, not as befitted a martyr but as is done with an ordinary man who is not party to honor and bliss. But this blessed warrior would rise from suffering and humiliation to a richer glory. For the more ignominiously the sons of the Devil and those of his loin treated the extraordinary martyr, the more was his arrival esteemed by the Lord and His fellow inhabitants of heaven. He became a friend of the angels, a companion of the apostles, and a fellow heir of the martyrs. He partook of the peace of the confessors and the innocence of the virgins, and he received the crown of eternal youth and the beauty of everlasting grace. And thus, scorning earthly distinction in the principality where he was once prominent by virtue of his power, he entered the kingdom of heaven as a true prince and martyr. However, since we have such a dry style and are so uneducated, let us leave this material to wiser people and turn our pen to a simple account of his miracles!

8

The blessed martyr's blood, shed impiously by impious men and spattered on the ground and on the walls, was washed away with water and wiped off. But on the second day, when those who had previously washed it away returned, they found the walls and the ground stained with blood as though they had never washed them with water. They now hastened to clean them again. Only after they had done this again a third time did they see that it was to no avail, and they departed. But even after his death the murderers of the holy martyr did not intend to spare the one whom they had persecuted to death. Riding swiftly, they hastened to the city of Prague and by various means cruelly destroyed all his friends and threw their children alive into the depths of the Moldau River. And we believe these were good people who were loyal to a good man. And since they were partakers of martyrdom, we believe that they also became partakers of glory. And although we unworthy ones do not know their count or names because of their great number, nevertheless we truely believe that God knows them and chose them. While he was still alive the blessed man gathered around him a considerable number of clerics and servants of God, whom the persecutors of the holy martyr pursued to such an extent that nearly none of them remained in the country. Thus, we now indeed see fulfilled that which was foretold about the Lord as we read, "Smite the shepherd, and the sheep shall be scattered" [Zechariah 13:7; Matthew 26:31].

But now, as my pen describes how severely the wrath and vengeance of the Lord were inflamed against the enemies, lo, I must praise the miracle-working power of God, who always shows Himself to be the most just Avenger,[47] which fulfills what He once promised as the true Guarantor, saying: "Vengeance is mine; I will repay" [Romans 12:19]. For some of those who rose against their holy lord with cruel thoughts, or those driven by evil spirits into becoming accomplices in such a crime by their consent, fled to desolate places and were punished by a wretched and deserved death, and they never showed themselves again. And some remained paralyzed and sterile until death; others among them died barking with their mouths like dogs and gnashing their teeth. And their entire line was, so to say, removed by the root. However, if, nevertheless, some of them have remained alive, they are seeking a livelihood with their own hands.

The body of the blessed martyr lay buried in the church of Saints Cosmas and Damian for three years. And then it was revealed to some of God's servants that they should translate this servant of God from the place where he was buried to the basilica of Saint Vitus the Martyr, which he built from its foundation in the metropolis of Prague through God's influence and adorned admirably with church ornaments. There, they say, he once had uttered the verse of the Psalmist as he walked through it while it was being built, "This is my rest for ever" [Psalms 132:14].

And the merciful Lord deigned to bring this about for the honor and glory of His name and as proof of the merits of this blessed man. Thus it would appear brighter than the sun to all nations that Almighty God in His condescension to the Bohemian nation, which had only recently turned to Him, had prepared a great defender, according to the words of the Scriptures that "in every nation he that feareth him, and worketh righteousness, is accepted with him" [Acts 10:35], and "where sin abounded grace did much more abound" [Romans 5:20].

This was made known to the fratricide. And since he was hiding under the cloak of a Christian warrior, he could not resist God's miracle, and, though belatedly, he began to recollect his sin. And he sent people and instructed them to translate the holy body during the night, warning that if before daybreak the holy limbs were not brought to the place where they were to be buried, all those to whom this was charged, to the last man, would be put to the sword. Therefore, they came at night, took the most holy body and placed it on a carriage, and brought it to a river called the Rokytnica.[48] And lo, the water rose, overflowed its banks, and flooded all the meadows. And thus those bringing the body could only expect death. And when they found themselves in this difficulty, it occurred to them that through prayer to Blessed Wenceslas they could obtain compassion from him, for that martyr had deigned to indicate through numerous revelations that he should be translated. And they said, "O blessed martyr, because we sought to fulfill your command devoutly, we all are now to be punished by a death-dealing sword." Nevertheless they labored to make some kind of bridge. While working, they suddenly looked up and saw that they as well as the carriage with the body of the extraordinary martyr were standing on the side of the river to which they wanted to cross.

And seeing this, the servants of the holy martyr praised God and His saint in a loud voice and with all their hearts, that through such miraculous help He freed His servants who had been placed in such danger. Thus the Lord's graciousness and the merits of His servants were shown through such a wonder. Thus God's glory and the martyr's power were proven when even his body was honored with a worthy translation, and the bearers of his relics were freed by such a miracle. Hastening on to the Moldau River, they found the bridge damaged. And they started to complain and, moreover, they began to feel fatigue and were unable even to lift the saint's body. Again they began to pray that he should help them, according to his customary mercy, so that they would not lose their earthly life, since the time limit set by the prince, morning cockcrow, had already passed. And soon they discerned that they were heard. They lifted him up on their shoulders as though he had no weight, and they crossed the broken bridge without difficulty, rendering thanks to God.

Without further impediments and delays, they then came to the place which the saint had once prepared for himself. When they lit a lamp and looked at him, they saw that his body was incorrupt, and that all his wounds were healed save the one wound which his most cruel brother had inflicted on his head. Indeed, though this place was also healed, it nevertheless differed from the others—as if it were covered by some kind of white membrane. This, too, they then tried to wash off, but it became evident that it was the same as the others.

At that time, they say, there was among the people who took care of the burial a certain clergyman of a venerable life, who had been associated in a most faithful friendship with the saint while he lived in this world. And as this man was stroking each limb of the most holy body, he took the saint's hand into his own hand—his eyes flooded with a torrent of tears—and, as he gently touched his fingernails, he saw that one of them was loose. And in a sorrowful voice he said to his companions: "Woe to us sinners, it seems the most holy body is very close to decomposing. For, behold, the fingernails are obviously loose." But the others rebuked him and said: "Why do you speak thus, brother? Does your mind not grasp that he wishes to present you with a piece of the relics from his body for the devotion that attached you to him?" And now he beat himself on the breast with his fist and said, "Truly, truly, I also think that is so." But upon taking hold of the most holy hand again, he touched the fingernail once more but found it so firmly fixed in the flesh as if there had been no sign of loosening before this.

Also his ear, which had been cut off completely by a blow from the sword and which his sister found when guided by his revelation, was now completely sound and grown back in its place. For the afore-mentioned venerable lady, that is, the sister of the blessed martyr named Přibyslava,[49] was instructed from the very cradle to serve Christ the Lord without blame, according to the commandment of the Gospel.[50] Thus, after the Lord freed her from the yoke of matrimony, she devoted herself completely to the service of God, longing fervently to clothe herself in a holy garment and to spend day and night constantly in prayers, in vigils, and in fasts. Blessed Wenceslas appeared to her in a vision and said, "My persecutors have cut off my ear which from the time it was cut off till now lies between the tree standing by the church and the walls of the church itself." Receiving this revelation, the venerable lady roused herself from sleep. And she sought out the place by the church and found the treasure, the most holy ear, where it indeed lay. She picked it up with reverence and great joy, and rendering thanks to Almighty God, she went to the grave of her brother and lord and martyr along with some of those who were most faithful. She opened it with the utmost reverence, placed the ear there, and with great care she closed it again. After the translation of his venerable body, this ear was then found incorrupt and grown back to the body, as we first stated, as if the sword had never touched it.

Thus priests and crowds of as many as could come gathered. And while singing hymns and songs, they laid the body in a coffin and buried it in the basilica of Saint Vitus the Martyr, where with the assistance of the Lord many, innumerable miracles are wrought for the merits of Saint Wenceslas the Martyr and for the praise and glory of the name of Christ Our Lord. Moreover, the memory of his translation is celebrated on the fourth of March, through the grace of Our Lord Jesus Christ, who with the Father and the Holy Spirit lives and reigns forevermore, amen.

9

With the help of God I shall now relate new miracles to those who sincerely wish to be informed about a new martyr.

After the martyrdom and victory of Christ's glorious warrior, and after the star which irradiated the entire land with its merit fell, when those who had been devotedly attached to him, as I have said, and whom he had gathered around him to serve Christ were either put to the sword by the impious ones or buried in the river at the hands of the unjust, and others dispersed over the entire world, one member of his retinue, Podiven by name—who, we said, was a partaker and companion in all the deeds which the martyr first performed, and about whom we promised to report and are now preparing to do so—fled to the Germans after his lord departed from this world to Christ, and lived there in exile for a long time. But later, when he thought that peace had been restored in the country, he returned again, and for some time stayed at home, hiding himself. And about him I would say with what love and inviolable loyalty he loved his lord while he was still alive, if the event about which I intend to write would not in itself suffice as proof of this.

One day, feeling more acutely than usual the sorrow which he had borne in his heart from the time he lost his lord, he seized a sword and quickly hurried to the home of the man whom he knew to be the head of the conspiracy that had striven to murder Saint Wenceslas and, moreover, the one at whose hands the blessed one had been put to death. And when he arrived there, he found him lying in a steam bath, which in common speech is called "the room." Seeing him coming, he greeted him in the popular manner, "Health to you, my friend, health to you." But since his heart was stirred with sorrow, Podiven answered, "God will take care of my health and salvation; but you lost all health and salvation long ago and therefore you will die in sin and perish forever." And he attacked him and put him to death. Hoping he could save himself through flight, he departed hastily and took refuge in a forest. But as he was moving about there carelessly, the death of the courtier and the murderous deed were reported to the fratricide, and he had the forest quickly surrounded by his servants, and they caught him immediately and hanged him.

Now as I prepare to relate a great wonder, I admit that I considered whether I should not remain silent about it because of its greatness. However, since the lips of so many are constantly proclaiming it and are convinced of it more clearly than the sun, I consider it unworthy of myself to remain silent about it. He was hanging there for three years; neither a bird, nor beast of prey, nor even the natural decomposition and putrefaction of the human body touched him. Instead, his fingernails and whiskers grew as if he were alive,[51] and his hair turned gray and even became completely white. Finally, out of annoyance over the talk everywhere of the Lord's miracle, that fratricide ordered that he be buried in the ground at that very place. But neither in this way could the acts of God be hidden; indeed, on the contrary: in order to reveal the merits of His servant to the people, those that passed this way would very frequently see a heavenly light over his grave. This continued for a long time until people came from everywhere. They began to bring sacrificial gifts, placed them on the grave as evidence of their pious veneration, and in the anxieties of their lives they appealed to God and this murdered man for help. After a short time the body of this man was raised from this place, translated by a pious procession of priests and devout men and women, and buried in the graveyard of the church of Saint Vitus. Thus, Saint Wenceslas, who is buried inside the church, and that courtier, who is buried outside of it, are separated from each other only by a wall.

And the sincere loyalty with which he served his lord reliably during his entire life won this glory for him. For when he was steward for all who lived in Saint Wenceslas's home, he educated nearly all the domestics, down to the last cook, in such a way that among the court servants there were hardly any who did not know how to sing the hymns of the Psalmist and how to write[52] or who did not learn something useful about church ceremonies. He loved them all like his own sons and was respected by them all like a father. And if at times he was commissioned to distribute ten coins in alms, he himself would add five more out of loyalty to his lord. And when he received an order to divide food among thirty or more of the poor, he himself added another fifteen. Therefore he deserved to hear the words of the Gospel from God, according to His promise, "Well done, good servant, because thou hast been faithful over a few things, I will make thee ruler over many things."[53] And together with his corporeal lord he deserved to enter the joy of Christ Almighty, which continues without end. Burning lights would be seen at night in the basilica where both saints reposed, and there many frequently heard the voices of angels singing psalms.

10

Although in his mercy and goodness our venerable patron, Wenceslas, a saint and one worthy of frequent remembrance, offers help to all who beseech him; nevertheless, he does not cease to help especially those who are imprisoned and put in jail. Indeed, in this way his mercy manifested itself there through the first miracle after the venerable translation of his body. For when some accused persons were shackled in iron fetters, condemned to severe punishment, and, according to the custom of their country, detained in large numbers in a public prison without any hope of something other than death, one night it occurred to those who had been put through these agonies, as we believe, through God's influence, to beseech Blessed Wenceslas to take pity on them. They said, "O Lord God, for the sake of the merits and prayers of our lord Wenceslas, Thy most holy witness, deign to help us in this, our agony, through Thy proven power." The following night, while everyone in this world reposed in peaceful slumber—and only these poor wretches did not know what repose was—God's power, which frequently helps the tormented graciously, also came to their assistance. At first there was ringing in their ears like the sound of a bell, and then a strange light began to shine for all of them in the prison. And suddenly the wood in which all their feet were enclosed bent like a bow, and soon all of them drew their feet out of the stocks. And seeing that the Lord's miraculous power was helping them for the sake of Saint Wenceslas's merits, they now gained hope of salvation, and being strengthened by it, they cried out incessantly, "O God, Father of Our Lord Jesus Christ, help us, Thy servants who trust in Thee, for the sake of the merits and prayers of Saint Wenceslas, who was murdered by impious men out of love for Thee." Immediately Christ's miraculous power manifested itself, and the collars broke asunder and fell off their necks to the ground. And upon being released from prison, they went around the country and told about God's great wonder, which they had seen before their own eyes.

After the account of this miracle had spread everywhere because of his greatness and glory, it came to pass that an imprisoned pagan heard that Saint Wenceslas is greatly concerned that people detained in prison be set free. Since he was oppressed by untold hardship, he made a promise upon hearing this, saying, "If through His goodness the God of Saint Wenceslas and the God of the Christians will extricate me from this misfortune and return me to my former dignity, I will believe in Christ the Son of God, I will receive the baptism of salvation, and with all my mind I will devote myself to religion and Christian charity and consign my son to the everlasting service of this martyr." Scarcely had he finished speaking, and lo, all the fetters fell off him. And they seized him a second and a third time and cast him into prison, perpetrating a new wrong. But as before, the fetters and shackles fell off him. And his lords became filled with pious respect because of the repeated miracle, and rendering thanks to God, they permitted him to leave freely. Thus, upon being released, he immediately had himself instructed in the holy faith and baptized. And after he had consigned to the martyr the son whom he promised to him, he lived for many more years.

Yet another accused man was, on orders, also cast into prison in the same way. And when he invoked Saint Wenceslas aloud and with many sighs to take pity on him as he had on the preceding ones, all the shackles also fell off his hands and feet. But since they did not believe him, they seized him and sold him for foreign money to a distant land, not knowing that God is Ruler of the whole world, and that the earth is the Lord's, and the fulness thereof [Psalms 24:1]. They also supposed that the blessed martyr cannot hear the prayers of people who are far away. But when they were leading him away, suddenly, for the sake of Blessed Wenceslas's merits, the shackles fell off his hands, as did the iron collar off his neck. And though those who bought him were pagans, they let him depart freely, having beheld such a great wonder from God.

After a short time the prince ordered another man put into prison. And after this man prayed to the Lord with many sighs and said, "O Lord God, for the sake of Blessed Wenceslas's merits, help me," it came to pass one night that he fell asleep with his agonies. And when he awoke suddenly, as happens to tormented people, he saw that he was standing outside of the castle in an open place, and that there were no shackles on his feet, nor a collar around his neck, nor any fetters on his hands. Returning to the jailer, he told him how he was miraculously freed by the power of God. Then the jailer, discerning God's miraculous power and the influence of the blessed martyr in this wonder, gave the accused man his freedom.

Once again I, the one who stands here out of love for such an extraordinary man, wish to relate old miracles to you about a new martyr.[54]

There was a woman in the city of Prague who was blind and crippled over her entire body. Coming to the church of Saint Vitus, she fell to the ground before the tomb of Saint Wenceslas. Filled with faith, she prayed until she regained her eyesight and the health of her entire body, according to her merit.

It came to pass another time that a man was taken by his creditors and shackled in iron fetters because he could not pay the lenders. And by chance those people who shackled him placed him next to the church where the body of Blessed Wenceslas is buried. Being in such agony here, he extended his hands laden with fetters toward heaven, turned his eyes toward the church, and prayed thus, "O God, help me for the sake of Saint Wenceslas's merits and intercession." As soon as he said this, immediately his hands were unshackled and they released him.

There was a lame man in the land of the Franks to whom, in his dreams, a man dressed in white appeared and admonished him, saying: "Arise and go to the city of Prague, to the church of Saint Vitus. There reposes the body of Blessed Wenceslas the martyr, and there you will regain your health." But when he did not heed this, that same man, dressed in the same clothing, the one who had appeared to him before, came to him again and said to him, "Why have you not fulfilled my command, and why have you not gone to the place where you will regain the ability to walk?" Now he awoke as if in a trance and said, "I am going, Lord." And upon rising and supporting himself with a cane, he went to the merchants who were making ready to go there, paid them, and managed with their help to come to the aforementioned place. Having entered the church of the saints, he cast himself down on the pavement in the presence of all the people, and in a long prayer he besought the Lord in tears to have mercy upon him for the sake of Saint Wenceslas's merits. And when he arose from his prayers, his knees became firm through God's mercy. And he gave thanks to God and Blessed Wenceslas for the sake of whose merits the Lord deigned to cure him.

When the glorious report about these and similar miracles of the blessed martyr had spread everywhere, some people were tempted to possess the relics of the blessed body and to keep them for themselves or distribute them to their relatives. To be sure, some of them attempted this in good faith and with good intentions, so that the martyr's name would spread everywhere. But indeed, some ventured this with bad intentions or out of greed for profit, and as a consequence vengeance overtook them. Thus, his sister, Přibyslava, who, as far as the human eye can judge, led a most saintly life in the sacred garb of a nun, took part in such a deed, having the priest of that very church, Stephen, as a helper in her undertaking. But a hermit, an immured recluse, to whom some were attached as to a very saintly man, took up residence near the church. And following his bad advice, they did this. In a word, they came on a predetermined night, and having dragged him out, made him an accomplice in their deed. Upon exhuming the venerable body, they began their wickedness. For the son of that priest very disrespectfully seized hold of the saintly man's jaw and pulled it out. And they wrapped it in a veil and reburied the rest of the body in the ground. Then each of them kept a part of the relics for himself, according to his pleasure, and a part they distributed to their relatives. But soon God's vengeance unexpectedly overtook them all. Since this happened in recent times, as is well known, and a great number of people are aware of it, I considered it superfluous to include a report of it in this work. I will only note that they were surprised by a sudden and unexpected death, and departed from this world.

Now I wish to tell about one miracle which Christ, God Almighty, deigned to manifest through His warrior in recent times.

When a considerable number of divers people were being held in prison—some because of their guilt, but others because of the slander of accusers—and they had already been imprisoned for a long time, they raised their prayers to the Lord to be freed for the sake of Saint Wenceslas's merits and managed to be set free. However, because some people, unbelievers, recommended that they be prevented from going free, for, it was said, they were not freed by the miraculous power of God and the saints, but because a corrupt prison guard released them and many others from their shackles, it was decided that he be tried in God's court.[55] And thus, while a large crowd of divers people gathered, an iron was placed in the fire and heated until white-hot. And when the guard was brought, they ordered him to carry it in his bare hand up to a place marked out in the field. Not hesitating at all but trusting in the saint's merits, he took the iron from the fire and carried it far beyond that point and would have run three times as far with it, had others not prevented him from it. Thereby every doubt, even the slightest one, was banished from the hearts of all; and they praised and glorified God that He delivered prisoners from jail only because of His mercy and at the intercession of His martyr, Wenceslas.

Thus, if I were to attempt to detail with my pen all the miracles of the blessed martyr which the Lord deigned to manifest through him, I would run short of daylight before I would pages of a book. For the Almighty Lord frees some from prison and many from shackles; others He saves from disasters and all kinds of illnesses, delivering them from various afflictions and difficulties, and visible and invisible enemies for the praise and glory of His name and upon the intercession of His warrior and martyr, Saint Wenceslas.

Also at the supplication of this saint, God often aids those fighting in a war with miracles and glorious deeds. And He helps all who invoke Wenceslas, just as He frequently came to the saint's assistance with living and clear signs while he was alive.

For a castle, called Kouřim, which at that time was still powerful with a number of people, rebelled and attempted to oppose this saint with the prince who was living there.[56] But after a sufficient number of people were slaughtered on both sides, everyone agreed that only the two princes should fight each other, and whichever of them was victorious, that one would rule. Then, when the princes were advancing toward one another, ready to confront each other, the God of heaven showed the Kouřim prince a heavenly sign, that is, Saint Wenceslas had a blazing image of the holy cross on his forehead.[57] As soon as he saw this he threw his weapon far away, cast himself down at his feet and declared that no one could vanquish the one to whom God brings aid with such a sign. When he said this, the saintly prince raised him up so as to give him the kiss of peace. And he confirmed his sovereignty over him and his castle peacefully, granting him the power to govern that region for as long as he lived. In truth, he did see a cross, for Wenceslas followed Christ and most felicitously attained the kingdom where Christ reigns together with the Father and the Holy Spirit forevermore. Amen.

✝ Homily for the Feast of Saint Ludmila (*Factum est*)

Saint Ludmila. Detail of tombstone, ca. 1380.

✝

Homily for the Feast of Saint Ludmila, Patroness of the Bohemians[1]

1

IT CAME TO PASS that after the death of her worthy husband, Blessed Ludmila, a follower of Christ, subdued her body through vigils, fasts, and divers mortifications, persevering in the purity of both natures to the end of her life.[2] She subjugated it to the spirit, proving herself saintly and immaculate, irreproachable, and unswervingly confident in the Gospel which she observed. Indeed, she was a true widow, for she was bereft of a husband as well as love for this world.

2

Verily, she was like the blessed Jael, who lulled Sisera to sleep with the milk of the Gospel inside him, and pierced and smote him with the nail of penance.[3] Thus, following the example of this renowned woman, whoever mortifies his earthly members—avariciousness, fornication, and the like[4]—it will be as though he smote Sisera in his bedroom. And because she was worthy among the wicked, she could say with the Psalmist, "I was like a bottle in the frost."[5] For what is meant here by frost? Is it not her wicked contemporaries who were not aflame with love but chilled by disbelief? Therefore, were she to say, "I was like a bottle in the frost," the meaning of this is: I have kept myself pure among the wicked, as I was commanded, for I have not forgotten the Lord's instruction. Or, since a bottle is made from the stretched skin of a dead animal, what this blessed woman understands by it is that, after racking her body, she nailed it to the cross along with its depravities and appetites, and, consequently, like the skin of a dead animal, she no longer felt the chill of sin. For she mortified her bodily desires in such a way that she no longer felt them, as if she herself were already dead. And she was not wearied by disappointments, because she willingly obeyed the dictates of her soul.

3

Thus, she could in truth say to the Lord, "I have not forgotten Thy instruction."[6] Also, she zealously performed acts of charity, being hospitable to strangers, offering comfort to the discouraged, willingly distributing alms, and dutifully providing for the Lord's priests and for all the clergy. And like a true mother to the faithful, she exerted every effort to extend Christ's faith. She was like the widow Judith, greatly esteemed by all, for she feared God greatly.[7] And there was no one who would say a bad word about her. Fasting often and praying incessantly, because she certainly always turned her piously inspired mind to God, she performed good deeds zealously, as we said above. She saw to the salvation of the faithful, and, remaining without blemish of sin, she vanquished Holofernes, that is, the Devil, the prince of confusion. I say, being joined to God through firm faith, intense hope, and deep love, through a peaceful and pleasant disposition, and through the bond of achievable perfection, she was not separated from Him even in death.

4

She rose in Bohemia like a morning star which, like a harbinger of the sun of justice, that is, Christ, drove away the darkness of error with the light of faith. She was the primrose of true spring, that is, of God's grace, for she, as is known, was the first to be proclaimed a saint among the saints of the aforementioned land. Verily, she can also be called the fiery spirit of dawn, for she introduced the day of venerating God with the light of her sanctity. She was the first of the vine branches that Pharaoh's chief butler saw—the second was blessed Prince Wenceslas, and the third, holy Bishop Vojtěch[8]—all of whom fortunately flowed through the press of martyrdom into the King's goblet at the heavenly banquet. And with divine succor, the vineyard of the Lord, the God of Hosts, was propagated by them in a land of coarseness and uncivilized desolation. And even to this day it is irrigated by the dew of their prayers so as not to be parched by disbelief. Thus, not only was Blessed Ludmila the first mother to the faithful in the land mentioned frequently, but she also became their first intercessor in heaven. Indeed, her merits require that proper deference be granted her by the faithful.

Therefore, it is for us to cultivate and zealously honor this vine branch so that on behalf of her merits the cup of salvation might be filled for us. For the more firmly the press of martyrdom squeezed her, the more fruitfully she clung to the true vine, Christ.[9] However, let us hear how through her elevation she reached the heavens when her fruit ripened.

5

For when the prince of darkness, who is the Devil, perceived that the darkness of disbelief among the people was diminishing on account of the light of Christ's handmaid, he inclined the heart of her daughter-in-law,[10] who hitherto maintained pagan customs, to yearn for her death. Thus, aflame with the spirit of Jezebel,[11] she summoned two of the most contemptible members of her retinue, Tunna and Gommon,[12] and commissioned them to carry out carefully the scheme that she designed in her heart, that is, to murder her mother-in-law. She did this so that after her murder the blessed youth Wenceslas, who was placed in her custody, more easily could be turned away from Christ's teaching and the Christian faith, and later, during her reign, it could be completely destroyed in the land. And after her death, she attempted to do this mercilessly. For having deprived the priests of their property, she expelled them from the land, and, under pain of death, prohibited them from appearing again in the land or from conversing with the holy prince. And now, after blocking the doors of the churches, she made offerings with impunity to idols and not to God, according to pagan manners.

6

Foreseeing her death, Saint Ludmila sought refuge at Tetín.[13] She thus followed the example of the Lord, who slipped away from those who wished to stone Him and left the temple.[14] For through this flight the Lord gave a sign to His beloved that they should flee from the bow, and that His beloved should save themselves thus.[15] Indeed, I believe confidently, it was for the sake of the faithful, whose mother she was then in Bohemia, that she sought shelter in flight so that they would not lose their consoler in her. For though she yearned to die and to be with Christ, nevertheless she would still gladly remain in this world so as to protect and support the faithful.[16]

But because her soul pleased God, He decided to take her away as quickly as possible from an ignoble and foolish people.[17] And now, filled with the spirit of God, that pious lady made ready for her departure. Continually singing David's verses of praise in her heart and with her lips, she commended her struggle to the Lord so that He would deign to receive her soul in peace. Nevertheless, she strengthened herself, having also confessed and received the food of salvation for the journey, that is, the body and blood of Our Lord Jesus Christ.

7

And thus the time came upon which the executioners of the most criminal command agreed. Insolently, maliciously, sharp of tongue, and filled with death-dealing venom, they broke down the doors of the house where the handmaid of Christ was resting, and having altogether cast aside their shame, they were not frightened to drag their mistress down to their feet. But reminding them in a dove-like manner of the favors she had amply granted them, she strove to divert them from the crime they were about to commit, and she was distressed over their depravity rather than over herself. But like enraged dogs utterly devoid of compassion, they proceeded with the utmost savagery to do what they had begun, and drew a rope around her neck. Then she said, "I earnestly beseech you to take my head with the sword so that I may lie in my blood; and permit me to depart to heaven in the manner of the holy martyrs, shedding blood for Christ's sake." But having stopped their ears to all her pleas, they tightened the rope until it began to cut her throat, and they squeezed the soul out of her body like a serpent.[18] Verily, this came to pass through the providence of the Lord so that the crueler the death to befall her, the greater the grace she would attain.

8

Thus, by means of a rope she was pulled from the mire of this world, and by means of a rope she gained a golden chain for her neck. Thus, like Esther, she walked into the King's palace, having become a partaker in the dominion and radiant in glory.[19] And through her prayers she shelters Christ's people so that they are not destroyed by their enemies. And as a wholly reliable sign that she was received in glory, this was what the follower of Christ was granted after her death: the very moment her blessed soul returned to God who created her, after it was drawn out from her contracted throat, rejoicing and triumphant, she gained a latitude not restricted by any limits. And, verily, all the saints, from the greatest to the least, came to meet her along with the Most-High Priest, Christ Jesus. And these spiritual luminaries surrounded her as if with kindled torches and congratulated the new arrival.

9

O Bohemia, if you were aware of how precious a gift you were given, of how bright a light bathes you with its rays, of how powerful a protectress assists you with her intercession, you would realize that you have been given a reason for infinite joy and gladness! O if you reflected on how glorious a treasure has been given to you, you would greatly esteem and glorify the gift entrusted to you by God! Thus beware, lest your ingratitude shackle the hands of the donor; for, verily, you would have greater success in your entreaties through the power of the treasure entrusted to you if you were to guard it more carefully! Remember that a mother of the faithful and supporter of the Christian faith who was crowned with laurel departed for heaven from your midst; a mother, I say, who has already attained honor on high, and who has joined God so as to intercede for you if you show yourself worthy of it! Commemorate the day she began to rejoice in heaven so that you may merit a share of her joy! Consider yourself fortunate that you may celebrate the good fortune of the one who was received in heaven from your midst! Let this day be holy for you, and let work not be permitted on this day so that you may thus merit to celebrate an eternal feast day with Saint Ludmila in heaven! Let all your churches solemnly observe this great feast day; let your lips sound in harmonious accord; let your voice not grow silent in a pious melody; let the organ resound in a triumphant ring; let your heart be filled with holy exultation; let your priests and laymen, the young with the old, the men with the women, and also the rich with the poor, rejoice in this festive splendor. For a propagator of the faith and an esteemed mother and intercessor graciously intercedes for all of those whom she sees devoutly participating in her commemoration.

O fortunate land of Bohemia, sheltered by fortunate patronage! O, how many lands are there that are deprived of such support and that would surely exult most joyfully if they had it! Thus, let the lips of your preachers reverberate in glory and praise of such a great feast day about which God's miracles from heaven have instructed us!

10

But I do not consider that one holy who mockingly scorns the glory of the saints or who, out of indolence, neither praises them himself nor listens attentively to or respects their eulogist. Thus, O Bohemia, be cognizant of what a precious thing you have! Be not silent but proclaim what glory, what honor, and what privilege you have; what a treasure has been entrusted to you, a treasure that is equally gratifying and wondrous! Celebrate the memory of her sanctity, be aware of whom you venerate and venerate her fervently, whose importance you are thus cognizant of! Consider her your patroness, and you will venerate her with joy!

You, too, take heed, O assembly of Christ's holy ladies, by whom such a rare treasure has been placed,[20] lest you be chastised when the Lord comes, like the wicked servant who hid his master's money. Consider that it profited him not to have it hidden in a napkin while he did not labor to increase it.[21] Thus, it would not be sufficient for you either to preserve in a reliquary these most holy relics, covered with gold and wrapped in rare cloths, if you did not labor to increase their glory so that they themselves would enjoy glory not only among you, but also that the glory of her whose relics these are would spread far and wide. Indeed, neither did the glory of Jesus Christ Himself spread through the world by silence or hiding but by preaching. Therefore be watchful, lest on account of your negligence the veneration of so beloved a martyr of Christ, who is even glorified in heaven, decrease on earth; lest you cease to extol highly in songs of praise the gold, purified by the fire of martyrdom and set in the crown of the heavenly King.

For this gracious mother, a refuge for the poor and propagator of the Christian faith, who has already been brought into the assembly of celestial beings and with an uncovered face has already beheld the King in glory, must not remain without solemn veneration.

11

When she departed to the Lord, this first patroness of Christ's faithful in Bohemia, this mother to priests, consoler to the forlorn, this mirror and example of sanctity, left her body with you so that in time she could recover it again in the glory of resurrection.

She bequeathed to you the limbs of her body as a consolation for you, as a refuge for sinners and a commemoration for your dwelling place. I beseech you earnestly, let this reliquary diffuse the fragrance of the virtues of its contents; that is, untiringly imitate her, whose relics you protect so faithfully, those relics whose sanctity has been ascertained by splendid miracles.

12

For the murderers of Blessed Ludmila and the adversaries of Christ's faithful soon met their deaths in various ways. Also, not one of their kin remained alive. Verily, she obtained this from Christ, as Esther did from Ahasuerus,[22] as a consolation for those whom she left behind forsaken when she departed from this world.

Moreover, from the relics of her body there issued a marvelous fragrance which surpassed the fragrance of all aromatic substances and thus demonstrated the effect of her sanctity. Besides, fiery torches could be seen descending upon her grave repeatedly, thus indicating the radiance of faith with which she shone in life.

When her vile daughter-in-law heard about this, she was seized by great fear. And she ordered that the house in which the lady of Christ had lived during her lifetime be rebuilt over the grave of her venerable body in the form of a basilica as though in honor of Blessed Michael,[23] so that miracles which might take place there in the future would not be attributed to her but to Blessed Michael.

Thus an unsought opportunity presented itself to increase Christ's glory, one downright contrary to her will. And, verily, she did not know that by this means the joy of Christ's handmaid would grow whether Christ was preached unintentionally or intentionally. And she now began to shine in this place through many miracles so as to arouse the people and as proof of her sanctity, which she attained by the power of faith in Jesus Christ, who lives and reigns with God and the Holy Ghost. God forever and ever, amen.

✝ Legend of Saint Wenceslas
(*Oriente iam sole*)

Saint Wenceslas as sovereign, fourteenth-century Breviary. National Museum, Prague.

†

The Legend of Saint Wenceslas
the Martyr Begins

1

AFTER THE SUN of the Christian religion had already risen over the land of bleakness and uncultivated wastes, that is, over Bohemia, which was almost entirely covered by a cloud of blindness, lo, a most brilliant ray, one not overshadowed by even a small cloud of sin and error, that is, venerable Wenceslas[1]—who had innocent hands, a pure heart, and was filled with the gifts of heavenly grace—blazed the first trail along which light diffused until it broke into broad day and began to shine for those who were living in darkness and in the shadow of death.[2]

He was descended from noble, princely blood. However, his mother was given to pagan idolatry and was unworthy of such a son, and of the name mother.[3] His father, Vratislav,[4] was indeed a Christian prince, who saw to the education of the saintly youth in the Scriptures. Being zealous in his undertakings, he soon surpassed his elders and teachers in wisdom because above all else he sought the Lord's precepts[5] in the sciences he studied. Verily, he was a youth of genius, for his soul was so good that he inculcated everything he read into his heart with fervent devotion, and thus did he perfect himself.

When his father, Prince Vratislav of blessed memory, died, lo, the inhabitants of the land assembled and elected the blessed youth Wenceslas, despite his unwillingness and opposition, to succeed his father to the princely throne. Verily, he was elected because he was older than his brother Boleslav,[6] and also because of his virtuous life, through which he surpassed him and all others. However, since he was still of a tender age and was not yet capable of directing the government, the magnates of the land entrusted him to his grandmother, the Blessed Ludmila,[7] Christ's handmaid, to be educated by her until his maturity.

2

Then his mother, who was filled with cunning and envy, and was crueler than a rapacious beast, raged against the innocent woman and killed the noble lady. And upon seizing control of the saintly youth's upbringing, she separated him, under penalty of capital punishment, from the guardians and executors of grace, that is, the clergymen and priests of the Lord. Nevertheless, finding refuge at times in secret places, the youth prayed to the Father who is in heaven. Secretly, he sought out priests to converse with; he repeated to himself what he might forget and whatever new he was taught, and he strove for purity of heart, confessing what he neglected as well as what he committed. And with all his virtuous zeal he made certain that a pure stream of deeds issued from the spring of thoughts, and he shielded the sight of his heart most carefully against the harmful impurity of sin. Proceeding along this path, he never acted with boyish imprudence although he was only a youth. Finally, while all went to make offerings to the idols that his most contemptible mother venerated, he alone avoided their gatherings and hastened secretly to the churches that his father had built, and he prayed to the Lord Jesus, gaining more in virtue and in age day by day.

But the aforementioned reverer of idols, emulating Jezebel[8] and not wishing Christ's faith to be spread, strove with all her might to make the wondrous youth abandon his sacred rituals. She complained, for example, that he was corrupted by priests, and that he was like a monk, and she said: "If he is already opposed to our efforts now, what will he do when he outgrows his adolescence and attains power?" For already then a state that aroused respect and fear was concealed behind his youthful face. And from that time forth, together with her retinue of unbelieving followers, she began to act hostile toward him, threatening him and harassing him with slurs. And their often repeated abuses were like portents of the death being prepared for him. Besides this, she placed guards on the street and tried to kill the priests and monks whom she heard were visiting him. But the saintly youth bore all this with an even temper for the sake of the Lord, and kept peace in his soul.

When he had matured to manhood, he summoned all the magnates of the land and his mother. Shaking off their yoke, he reproached them for their want of faith and hardness of heart, saying to all who were unbelievers: "O unwise people and sons of villainy, the seed of Canaan and not of Judah![9] Who has charmed you into not heeding the truth? If you yourselves do not choose that which leads to salvation, at least allow those who choose that to seek it! I am a servant of Christ. I will not serve your idols, and henceforth I will not submit to the power of any one of you. Until now you have kept me from serving Christ, and have banished all the faithful from the land. No longer will it be so; for we shall serve our Lord freely."

3

And from that time, at his command, they began to smash idols and open churches of Christ, and the faithful, who were previously dispersed, reassembled. Praise to God, which previously had grown silent, began to resound, and the holy faith began to thrive more distinctly and to celebrate a magnificent victory under the crown of Jesus Christ, when priests who fulfilled God's law of sacrifices gathered around Him and proclaimed His works, exulting how great is the Lord and greatly to be praised.[10] Through this and similar struggles against the unbelievers, by proclaiming and witnessing the truth of the Christian religion, and by assembling preachers and Christ's other faithful, he himself unquestionably became a faithful and renowned proclaimer of Christian and heavenly truth. And in consequence thereof the saintly prince prospered, surrounded by a multitude of the faithful, protected by the helmet of salvation and the shield of faith, and girded by the armor of justice with the sword of the Spirit, which is the Word of God, while all rejoiced and praised God through His faithful servant.

At the same time his unbelieving mother, envious of Christ's glory, stirred up a riot between the pagans and the believers so that much blood was shed on both sides. The peace-loving prince found this hard to bear. And because she was also a blasphemer, and because she had had his grandmother Ludmila strangled, he banished her from the borders of his domain so that her bad example would not become the undoing of Christ's faithful, and so that she would be punished for the crime she perpetrated by such disgrace. Moreover, in this deed he emulated Asa, king of Judah, who cast out his mother, Maachah, so that she would not set an example in sacrificing to the most abominable idol.[11]

4

Conducting himself wisely in all things, he was humble in glory, obliging to all, and kind to poor people. He did not refuse anyone who wished to speak with him in good conscience, he lent an ear to every supplicant, he supported the poor in a particularly open-handed way, and thus he won the love of all the people. He visited the sick, clothed the naked, received wayfarers in his home, and fed the hungry. And, if I may say so briefly, this venerable prince performed many acts of mercy, not only publicly but also in private, and at the same time he mortified his body. For, rising during the night, he would carry wood on his shoulders and place it at the doors of the poor. He did not take anything by force from anyone, but, as was said, he would sooner give generously of his own.

He urged all to Christian honesty, now persuading them, now imploring them with all manner of patience and learning. But since the fool does not allow himself to be corrected by words, defiant people, especially the incorrigible ones, he sometimes brought to the good by thrashing. However, like a father, he did not think of killing any of them. Moreover, if sometimes he threatened the especially hardened unbelievers with the death sentence—not that he would have been willing to impose this sentence—he did so because they would be frightened by the threats and turn away from evil. For, if someone went too far in callous wickedness and could not be corrected otherwise, his goodness would have undoubtedly yielded to the rein of justice.[12] Verily, if the judges of the land had condemned such people, he could have borne it, but with sorrow in his heart. Nevertheless, being filled with compassion, he was unable to be present at judgment when someone's excessively grave offense required the death sentence.

Whereas the Bohemian nation at that time was very wild, and in its pagan frenzy was ready to torture and kill people, he, on the other hand, intended to govern his land with great moderation. As a disciple of mercy, he wished to give an account of excessive goodness rather than cruelty, knowing, according to the saying of the philosopher, that the human spirit is noble beyond measure and allows itself to be led rather than dragged by force, and that the king's throne is strengthened by forbearance.[13] And for that reason he razed prisons and gallows. Therefore, his most distinguished quality was goodness, which accomplishes all things.

In his personal dealings he was friendly. He had a kind expression on his face, and being of an honorable and modest disposition, he illuminated all the people with the rays of his exemplary life, one worthy of admiration and emulation. Therefore, one can imagine that by virtue of the merits and forbearance of such a good prince the land enjoyed more peace than it would have if ruled by cruel tyrants. For his soul was illuminated by divine wisdom, which rules the whole world mightily from one end to the other, and orders it sweetly.[14]

5

Furthermore, he had great success in his struggle against the unbelieving tribes, subjecting them to the Christian faith. And it was obvious through whose power he accomplished this when he fought against the prince of Kouřim.[15] That is, after a number of people were killed on both sides, everyone agreed that only the two princes should combat one another, and whichever of them was victorious would rule. And lo, when the armed princes confronted each other, the sign of divine power, which was sent down from heaven, did not elude the prince of Kouřim. For in the middle of the battle he saw that Saint Wenceslas had the image of the holy cross on his forehead, which had not been fixed there by any human hand but imprinted by divine power, blinding the eyes of the one who looked at it with an extraordinary light. When he saw this he threw himself at his feet and subjected himself to his power. Raising him up, the saint allowed him to return to his castle.

And while he was kind to everyone else, he was very severe with himself. For beneath his bright apparel he mortified his body with a hair shirt. And during the night he would persevere in vigils. Content with only one person to accompany him in order to pray, he would make the rounds of the churches barefoot, so that his tender soles would be lacerated and his footprints on the roads were stained red by the blood flowing from them. Thus, his sleep was sweet because there was not much of it, and his rest, relaxed and not like the body at burial of someone strangled. The pious zeal with which he provided for the Sacrifice of the Altar is very clearly evident from the fact that during harvesttime he would rise during the night and go to the field with his aforementioned companion, whose name was Podiven, and who was as loyal as he was devout, and whose merits and loyalty our pen will describe, should God grant it, in the appropriate place. Thus, the blessed prince would secretly leave his bedroom with him, and no one from the military retinue who slept with him knew either when he left or when he returned. And with his own hands he would reap the wheat, thresh it, grind it, and, mixing water with the flour, he made wafers. Similarly, when the grapes were gathered, he pressed them with his own hands and distributed the wine among the priests. And along with this gift he also offered his labor for the performance of divine services. Who is so devout now? We will praise him.[16] Furthermore, who with such joy ever gives something to the poor and to God's church that he received without any effort as he gave them gifts gained by the labor of his own hands? Or, which of the princes is so humble and zealous as to condescend to such work, rising in the middle of the night?

And I believe that I dare not pass over in silence yet another deed of this admirable supporter of the faithful and zealous propagator of the holy faith. Filled with the divine spirit, this good man himself purchased, especially on Holy Saturday, pagan servants who were brought to market so that on that day the church would have someone to regenerate in Christ, as is the custom. Thus, he devoted himself more to hunting souls than to hunting animals, which certain people are not in the habit of doing while roaming around the forests. He knew that no offering is more pleasing to God than zealousness of soul.

6

Now it came to pass during his days that the emperor held court after convening an assembly of princes in one city. But because God desired that His miracle be manifested through him, saintly Prince Wenceslas was the last to arrive, not coming until the third day of the solemnity. Angry with him over his tardiness, the emperor and all the princes agreed among themselves in the meantime that the one who would rise before him and offer him a place would pay for it with his head. Thus, when the saintly prince entered the assembly hall, the emperor was the first among them to rise before him. And he offered him his hand as he stepped out to meet him and seated him next to himself on the throne. Of course, the princes also stood up when the emperor did, astonished at what had happened. For, verily, it was not fitting for an emperor to break an agreement among such a distinguished assembly.

But when the emperor later summoned all the princes and they queried him in astonishment as to the reason for his behavior, he apologized to them, asserting that he distinctly saw angels escorting the saintly prince as he entered, and how his face began to glow with an extraordinary resplendence, and a brightly shining cross appeared on his forehead. And he added: "Thunderstruck in body and in soul, I dared not deny due honor to such glory. For obviously the power of the hand of the Lord God was with him." When the princes heard this, all of them treated God's saint with extraordinary respect, and those who had previously resolved to insult him, wishing to deny him a place, now rose before him as if before their superior, offering him a higher place so that he would sit with the sovereigns and receive a throne of glory.

Afterward, when the court meeting was over and the individual princes were making ready to return home, the emperor detained God's saint. Conversing with him in private, he invited him to ask for anything that he considered most beneficial for himself. But God's saint requested neither worldly honors, nor riches, nor the extension of his domain, nor the royal scepter but, being exhorted, as is believed, by a vision of Saint Vitus and being devoted to the spirit and not the body, he requested only the relics of Saint Vitus, and he received them.[17] Besides this, he was also honored by the emperor very generously with many other gifts, although he did not request them. And having gained freedom for his country, which previously was tributary, he returned home with glory.

Then, in connection with the receipt of the relics and through the inspiration of divine grace, he conceived the idea of building a church in honor of Saint Vitus the Martyr,[18] emulating his venerable father, Vratislav, who had built a monastery in honor of Saint George in Prague. And when the bishop of Regensburg, under whose jurisdiction Bohemia belonged at that time, consented to this, he built it as a very splendid work of art and adorned it with magnificient decorations. And it is that church to which the episcopal see is now attached. And while he was building that massive church, a plan arose in his holy

mind to build a perfect temple for the Lord from himself, according to
the words of the Gospel, "If thou wilt be perfect, go and sell that thou
hast, and give to the poor, and come and follow me" [Matthew 19:21],
that is, to be separated from worldly cares and clothed in monastic
garb by the pope, whom he intended to visit, so as to prepare within
himself a thoroughly peaceful dwelling for Jesus Christ. And he would
have done so, had he not been prevented by a pious solicitude for the
work that had begun, and had he not been held back by the voices of
orphans and widows, crying out in tears, "O father, why do you abandon us?"

And his renown, scented with the pleasant aroma of grace, spread
to all the neighboring lands: that is, that he is a good man, a believer,
and that he embraces Christians in the arms of love. And the Lord's
priests and multitudes of other believers from foreign countries began
all the more to assemble around him. And he received them kindly
and supported them as best he could. Then his name became famous
along with the names of the great ones who are on earth. For truly he
was a great man in his own right and the greatest among those chosen
for salvation, who fought against the rebelling enemies of the faithful,
as was mentioned above.

7

And his way of life was such that he either prayed, or taught the
ignorant faith and piety, or had himself instructed, or sat in the assembly and company of the righteous, or attended to the poor, or lent an
ear to the concerns of petitioners. But he also secretly carried a small
book on his person, and from it he would recite various prayers fitting
for this or that time, like a ruminant masticating its pure cud. And
when he was not occupied in this way, he had texts read to him, now
from the New Testament, now from the Old; for his delight was in the
law of the Lord day and night.[19] Thus, he trained himself in divine
decrees, always cognizant that in the hour of death there would be a
careful examination of how all of man's time provided for penance
was exerted. Thus, he provided estates for his soul, not of the earthly
life but of the coming one, according to the saying of the Apostle, "Set
your affection on things above, not on things on earth!" [Colossians
3:2]. He never delighted in the fleeting favor of men when it smiled
upon him, nor did he elevate himself for the flattery and applause of

actors. He wholly shunned contact with slanderers, calumniators, and with people whose God is their belly. And he was so constituted that from the character of the external, visible man it was possible to recognize the honorable and holy composition of the invisible spirit in him. For his mere appearance unquestionably showed his saintliness. Verily, he hastened to God with his entire being, and clinging to Him, he merged with Him as if into one spirit. Inasmuch as the hart thirsts after the water brooks,[20] so his soul thirsted after the Lord Jesus, and mostly to leave the tabernacle of his body by way of martyrdom. O, how many times, as I confidently believe, did he sigh and say with the Apostle: "Who shall deliver me from the body of death?[21] I have a desire to depart and to be with Christ."[22]

This saintly man was also not without a prophetic spirit. For, according to a revelation which God granted him, he foretold the death of his grandmother, the Blessed Ludmila, and said that she would be murdered under cruel bodily tortures by unbelievers for professing the name and faith of Christ. He also prophesied the expulsion of the priests from Bohemia; and later deeds confirmed them both. Verily, the Lord was with him, and none of his words were in vain. He even foresaw his own death, as will be shown below.

8

Now in those times, when that truly Christian prince, who, like the rising sun, drove away the darkness of unbelief with the rays of his virtue, was guiding them according to the will of God, everything was going well for the Christians. However, seeing that his intrigues were being undone, the enemy of mankind, who from the very beginning of the world has attacked throngs of the faithful, took up arms against the prince so as to scatter the sheep of the flock. And were the shepherd killed,[23] he could easily attain the end for which he was striving. Just as once he incited Cain against Abel, so he incited Boleslav to kill his brother, the Blessed Wenceslas. And adding to the sin, he took counsel with evil men, who bore with difficulty the fact that they had to abandon their customs and could no longer do forbidden things. For the Lord had aroused in them such a terrible dread before him, that they were afraid of him, although he did not utilize severe punishments. For in those times some refrained from evil out of good will, but others went contrary to their will, being devoted to pagan rituals, since at that time paganism had not yet been uprooted.

Thus his younger brother, named Boleslav, sat in counsel with the impious and schemed to murder the innocent one. And under the guise of peace he made ready for war, intending to kill him, unaware and unarmed, using a peaceful banquet as a pretext. And his mother, whom her kind-hearted son had summoned back from exile, though she was unworthy of this, was involved in this treacherous plot. Then his aforementioned brother, although he was of cruel heart, wild countenance, and inhuman manners—wherefore he was called The Cruel—nevertheless made of himself the angel of light from the angel of Satan, feigning love and mirth in his countenance.

9

On the occasion of a certain feast day he prepared a splendid banquet and sent messengers to the Lord's saint, requesting his participation in the banquet at Boleslav's castle, where he was staying at that time with his entire court. Knowing that death awaited him, he took leave of Christ's faithful, who were in Prague at that time. And he set off, after having kissed some of them as if he would never return and see them again with corporeal eyes.

And his brother, by his betrayal a Judas, came out to meet him. Offering him a kiss as if of peace, he seated him on a soft seat as in a house of peace. Then, like a host, he made the rounds, seeing to a table for his retinue, the food, and the others. The guests emptied many goblets and made merry, not knowing what the following day would bring—that on that day grief would be mixed with laughter and merriment would end in sorrow. For while they were feasting, Boleslav was scheming with villainous men as how to kill his brother without arousing the people. This villainy on the part of his advisers was rooted in their zeal for pagan error, which they were unwilling to give up, but on the part of the fratricide it was a longing to seize sovereign power.

In the meantime, having heard this conversation, one of the faithful quietly whispered about it to the prince, offered him a readied horse, and exhorted him to flee before the face of death. But he knew that this day was predestined for him, for on it he would reach the banquet of the heavenly court and attain his eternal reward. Thus, he was not anxious in the least about himself but said, "Let us also drink this cup in honor of Saint Michael, that he may lead our souls to paradise!" And, as I firmly believe, this man, filled with a divine spirit, said this about the cup of suffering, an account of which he already knew, and about which the Lord said to His disciples, "Are ye able to drink of the cup that I shall drink of?"[24] For after drinking of this cup, Michael leads souls to paradise, but not after drinking of the cup of material things, the drinking of which is often careless, rarely meritorious, and many times sinful, as it usually is with drunkards. For it is written, "Woe to those who tarry long at the wine and empty full cups."[25] Thus, since Christ's servant, Wenceslas, who was filled with a divine spirit, was of a moderate and temperate disposition, he was not in the habit of inviting others to drinking sprees, which he himself shunned. It is certainly not true what some others assert about him in this regard, to the detriment of the hearers, and as an excuse for sinners, excusing their sins.[26]

10

What need is there for more words! And when nighttime finally came, when everything was wrapped in silence and tranquillity, and when the night had covered half its course, those who would shed innocent blood ran ahead swiftly to the church so as to set the snares of treachery at the place, as they undoubtedly knew, where Christ's poor man had to pass. And they lay in ambush to murder the innocent.[27] And lo, the man of innocent hands and of pure heart, who was in the habit of rising in the middle of the night so as to praise the name of the Lord, and to whom to live was Christ and to die was gain,[28] walked alone, unarmed, self-confident like a lion that is unafraid of anyone's attack. But the first among them to stand in his way was his brother, whom Christ's servant greeted in peace, as was his wont. But since the latter had nothing in common with peace, he said: "Yesterday I served you as was appropriate for that occasion, brother, but now this is how I will serve you." And drawing his sword, he struck him in the head. And when the sword glanced off and left only a trace of a wound, he struck another blow. And when even this did not do him more harm, he tried to wound him a third time. And when he raised his hand against the holy head, the sword fell from it; and as his weapon fell, this greatly enraged tyrant himself also collapsed, for he was petrified with intense fright. And Saint Wenceslas seized his sword and said: "Look, O most cruel foe and erstwhile brother, your sword could well pierce your heart, although you have sharpened it against me. But far be it from me to become guilty of my brother's blood. I would, if you like, sooner have you finish what you began." And he gave him his sword. Though still trembling, he began to call his people with a cry to battle as if he had been wronged. In the meantime the saintly man ran to the doorstep of the church, knelt, commended his spirit into the hands of the Lord, and prayed for his persecutors. Then the villains burst from ambush with swords drawn, bows taut, and brandishing lances. And they came running as if in a race, hurrying to strike the Lord's saint. Inflicting a variety of wounds on him, they destroyed him cruelly.

And thus the prince became a king, for he took his place on the heavenly throne, crowned by the glory of martyrdom. Thus his cruel brother made him a martyr, as once Cain did Abel. Thus, after he had drunk of the cup of suffering, as he foretold, the soul of the righteous one hastened to the banquet of the eternal land. Thus the Lord's beloved, though being made perfect in a short time, fulfilled a long time [Wisdom of Solomon 4:13]. For his soul pleased God; therefore He hastened to take him away from the midst of an ignoble and foolish nation.[29]

Therefore hearken now, all you countries of the earth, poor and rich together: on this day a great prince fell mournfully. Did I say, fell? Rather than fell, he was raised higher; for He who elevated him surely had him, as it is written: "Though the righteous man fall, he shall not be cast down, for the Lord upholdeth him with his hand. I have been young and now am old; yet have I not seen the righteous forsaken."[30] And thus he could say to the Lord: "Thou hast holden me by my right hand and Thou shalt guide me with Thy counsel and receive me to glory,"[31] or also, "Thou hast put off my sackcloth, and girded me with gladness" [Psalms 30:11].

11

And then, after his holy body was buried by the hands of some of the faithful, his blood that was spilled could neither be washed away nor wiped off for many years—as if through this deed it cried out from the earth to the Lord against so terrible a crime. And when the most cruel Prince Boleslav ascended the throne not long after the death of the blessed man and in his fury raged against throngs of the faithful, he condemned to death the clergy and his relatives, and those courtiers who were devoted to him, having put some to the sword and having others thrown into the river. And thus his retinue, which journeyed with him over the road of earthly misery, followed their prince to the heavenly land. Verily, having beheld the sword of persecution, some of them, whom he chose as companions, fled beyond the reach of his truculence, as it is written: "I will smite the shepherd, and the sheep of the flock shall be scattered" [Matthew 26:31].

But since the grace of God and His mercy are with His saints and He respects His chosen, and since the righteous one who is dead condemns the ungodly who are living, and youth that is soon perfected condemns the long life of the unrighteous,[32] many of those who rose up against the Lord's saint with cruel intentions or who became participants in such a crime by their consent fled to desolate places, pursued by evil spirits. And they never appeared again, having perished a wretched and well-deserved death. And others among them died, barking with their mouths like dogs and gnashing their teeth; and their entire clan was, so to speak, torn out by the root. And thus in a short time was fulfilled that which was said about similar people: "But the Lord shall laugh them to scorn and they shall hereafter fall without honor and be a reproach among the dead for evermore; for He shall rend them that they shall be speechless, and He shall shake them from the foundation, and they shall be utterly laid waste."[33]

On His Translation

12

Three years after his martyrdom it was repeatedly made known to some of the faithful by divine revelation that the body of Christ's warrior Wenceslas should be translated to the Church of Saint Vitus, which he himself had built while still alive and about which he said with prophetic words: "This is my rest for ever: here will I dwell; for I have desired it" [Psalms 132:14].

Hearing about this, his brother realized that no one can resist divine Providence. And he thought that if his brother's body were translated to the Church of Blessed Vitus, then the miracles that would probably take place there would not be attributed to his brother but to Saint Vitus. Thus he ordered several of his people, under threat of capital punishment, to translate the holy body before daybreak on the stipulated night, that is, the fourth of March, so that, in my opinion, the people, were a great number to observe this, would not be reminded of his crime, and it would not come to light that he was a criminal were some miracle to take place.

Therefore the ones charged with this task came, took the holy body and carried it away. And when they came to a small river which was called the Rokytnica,[34] lo, its waters had risen so that it overflowed its banks and flooded all the meadows. Thus, finding themselves in this difficulty, the bearers did not know what to do. Finally they began to offer prayers to the one whose body they were carrying so that he, who in many revelations made known that his body should be translated, would not delay in giving them aid, especially in view of the prince's cruel threats, which were hanging over their heads. Thus they prayed but nevertheless labored to make some kind of bridge. In the midst of this work they suddenly looked around and saw that they, as well as the carriage which contained the body of the extraordinary martyr, were standing on the side of the river to which they had wanted to cross. Even if the tongue were silent, reason would tell us what joy the bearers of the body felt over this. Not only were they delivered from a difficulty, but a miracle of honored bodies was manifested through them and their horses for the sake of the merits of this great martyr. Therefore the church built in Prosec[35] in memory of this miracle celebrates the commemoration of the day of his translation. Joyfully they took the holy burden and proceeded as far as the river called the Moldau. Seeing that the bridge was damaged, they started to complain. Moreover, they began to feel fatigue and were unable even to lift the saint's body. Again they began to pray to him that he should help them according to his customary mercy so that they would not lose their earthly lives according to the prince's stipulation, for cockcrow had already passed. Having completed their prayers, they easily lifted the litter with the precious treasure and advanced with confidence. Upon crossing the bridge without harm, they praised God's mercy, which He manifested through His saint.

While they proceeded joyfully along the road near a gloomy prison in which many prisoners were held in fetters, a great earthquake took place and the prison was lit by a strange light. And immediately the hands and feet of all those who were being held were freed from the chains holding them. And after this sign, He who through His power leads the chained out of prison said to them in a clear voice from heaven, "Rise quickly and hurry out of the darkness and shadow of death to meet your renowned liberator, the blessed martyr Wenceslas!" Thus they left the prison without hindrance and with great joy proclaimed in the presence of all the people how and when, for the sake of the merits of the most gracious martyr Wenceslas, God delivered them from the terrible prison and from their chains and fetters as his glorious body was being carried past the prison. In memory of this miracle a church was built on the site of the prison in honor of the blessed martyr, and it stands there to this day.

13

Then the bearers came to the place which the saint had once prepared for himself. When they lit a lamp here and looked at him, they saw that his body was incorrupt, and that all the wounds were healed save the one which his most cruel brother had inflicted on his head. In fact, though this one was also healed, nevertheless it differed from the others, as if there were some kind of dirty mark on the wound. This too they tried to wash away, but it became evident that it was the same as the others.

At that time, they say, there was among the people who took care of the funeral a certain clergyman of a venerable life, who was a very loyal friend of the saint while he lived in this world. And as this man was stroking each limb of the most holy body, he took the saint's hand into his own hand—his eyes flooded with a torrent of tears—and, as he gently touched his fingernails, he noticed that one of them was loose. And in a sorrowful voice he said to his companions: "Woe to us sinners, it seems the most holy body is very close to decomposing. For, behold, the fingernails are obviously loose." But the others rebuked him and said: "Why do you speak thus, brother? Does your mind not grasp that he wishes to present you with a piece of the relics from his body for your devotion to him?" And now he beat himself on the breast with his fist and said, "Certainly, certainly, I also think that is so." But upon taking hold of the most holy hand again, he touched the fingernail once more but noticed that it was so firmly fixed in the flesh as if there had been no sign of loosening before this.

Also his ear, which had been cut off completely by a blow from the sword and which his sister found when informed through a revelation, was now found completely healthy and grown back in its place. For the aforementioned venerable lady, that is, the sister of the blessed martyr named Přibyslava,[36] was instructed from the cradle to serve Christ the Lord without blame, according to the precept of the Gospel. Thus, after the Lord freed her from the yoke of matrimony, she devoted herself completely to the service of God, for with pious intention she clothed herself in a holy garment and spent day and night in prayers, in vigils and fasts. Blessed Wenceslas appeared to her in a vision and said: "My persecutors have cut off my ear which from the time it was cut off until now lies between the tree standing by the church and the walls of the church itself." When she awakened she found the ear at the place that was indicated to her, and with great reverence she brought it to her brother's grave in the sight of the faithful, and placed it next to the holy body. Then, after the translation of his venerable body, this ear was incorrupt and grown back to the body, as we already stated, as if it had never been cut off.

Now a great number of priests and people came, and while singing hymns and songs they buried the most holy body in the basilica of the Blessed Martyr Vitus, where the Lord deigned to work many miracles for the sake of the merits of this extraordinary saint, as it will be possible to learn more fully in the next part. Thus Blessed Wenceslas was martyred in the year of grace, 929,[37] and he was translated three years after his martyrdom.

On the Miracles of This Saint[38]

14

Although it is obvious from what we have written previously that the sanctity of this venerable man shines brighter than the sun and it is no longer necessary to look for anything else besides that as proof of his sanctity, nevertheless we shall not place the other rays of his glory under a bushel but on the candlestick[39] of a Christian audience so that all who enter will see the light and concur with the view of the Gospel. Therefore, let us now proceed to those miracles which the Lord Jesus deigned to work after the translation of the holy body for the sake of the merits of such an eminent saint. We shall not utilize an artificial style but an honest one, for we intend to speak not with pleasing words of human wisdom but in a way that simply shows his miraculous power.

Thus, in those days, after the account of the martyrdom, miracles, and merits of this gracious prince had spread far and wide, there lived in the land of Franconia a certain man who for a long time was afflicted with gout. And because of the extreme weakness of his legs, at times he could hardly walk any distance, and that only by leaning on crutches. A man dressed in white came to him in a nocturnal vision and said: "Rise quickly and do not delay in being taken to the grave of the blessed martyr Wenceslas, which is in the capital city of Bohemia called Prague. You will regain the health of your legs when you come there for the sake of the merits of this extraordinary martyr." But when he tarried in fulfilling what he was told to do, or did not give credence to the clear vision, the same man appeared to him in his dreams a second time, rebuked him for his procrastination and distrust, and said: "Why do you tarry in doing what I told you to do for the sake of your health? See to it that you are taken as quickly as possible to the grave of this gracious martyr." And he answered, "I am going, lord, I am going, and I go gratefully, giving thanks to God." And when he awakened, he gained confidence in the promise. Hiring a carriage from travelers who happened to be going there, he hastened with them to the above-mentioned city. Upon entering the city and the Church of Blessed Vitus, he fell facedown before the grave of the frequently mentioned martyr and in tears begged that he might obtain the favor for which he had come. After he had prayed tearfully for a long time, he sensed that he had gained the health for which he had hoped. And rising, he joyfully glorified God who is wondrous in His holiness, and who restored his ability to walk for the sake of the merits of this martyr. And thus he bore witness that this saint is indeed a friend of God.

15

At that time a great number of accused persons lay shackled in fetters in the stench of a certain prison without hope of any help, and with moans they constantly awaited the terror of death. One night through God's influence, as we believe, it occurred to those who had been put through these agonies to beseech Blessed Wenceslas to help them. And when they prayed, wailing and sighing, "O Lord God, for the sake of the merits and mediation of Thy saintly friend Wenceslas, deign to deliver us from this torment," lo, divine grace did not tarry, and assistance came to them from the martyr whom they invoked. For the following night, while everyone in this world reposed in peaceful slumber—and only these poor wretches did not know what repose was—there was at first a ringing in their ears like the sound of a bell, and then a strange light began to shine for all of them in the prison. And suddenly the wood with which all their feet were enclosed bent like a bow, and soon all of them drew their feet out of the stocks. Witnessing the Lord's miraculous power helping them for the sake of Saint Wenceslas's merits, they now gained hope of salvation. And they were strengthened by this and cried out incessantly, "O God, Father of Our Lord Jesus Christ, help us, Thy servants who trust in Thee, for the sake of the merits and prayers of Saint Wenceslas, who for the honor of Thy name was destroyed by the hands of impious men." Immediately, Christ's miraculous power manifested itself, and the collar broke asunder and fell to the ground from each of their necks. And after they left the prison without hindrance, they went around the country and told about God's great wonder which they had seen before their own eyes.

After the account of this miracle had spread everywhere because of his greatness and glory, it came to pass that a certain imprisoned pagan heard that Saint Wenceslas is most concerned that people detained in prison be set free. Since he was oppressed by untold hardship, he made a promise, saying, "If through His goodness the God of Saint Wenceslas and the God of the Christians will extricate me from this misfortune and return me to my former dignity, I will believe in Christ the Son of God, I will receive the baptism of salvation, and with all my mind I will devote myself to religion and Christian charity, and consign my son to the everlasting service of this martyr." Scarcely had he finished speaking, and lo, all the fetters fell from him. And although he was freed from the shackles several times for the sake of the martyr's merits, the guards continually seized him anew and shackled him. But when the miracle was repeated again and again, his jailers, feeling pangs of remorse and fright, praised the saint whom the prisoners always invoked for help. And they released that man without ransom for his freedom. Thus, upon being released, he immediately had himself instructed in the holy faith and baptized. And when he had consigned to the martyr the son whom he promised to him, he lived for many years after.

Another accused man was also thrown into prison in the same way on orders. And when he invoked Saint Wenceslas aloud and with many sighs to take pity on him as he had on the preceding ones, all the shackles also fell from his hands and feet. But since they did not believe him, they seized him and sold him for foreign money to a distant land, not knowing that God is the Ruler of the whole world, and the earth is the Lord's and the fulness thereof [Psalms 24:1]. They also supposed that the blessed martyr cannot hear the prayers of people who are far away. But when they were leading him away, suddenly, for the sake of Blessed Wenceslas's merits, the shackles fell from his hands, as did the iron collar from his neck. And although those who bought him were pagans, they let him depart freely, having beheld such a divine wonder.

After a short time the prince ordered another man cast into prison. And after this man prayed to the Lord with many sighs and said, "O Lord God, for the sake of Blessed Wenceslas's merits, help me," it came to pass one night that he fell asleep with his agonies. And when he awoke suddenly, as happens to tormented people, he saw that he was standing outside of the castle in an open place, and there were no shackles on his feet, nor a collar around his neck, nor any fetters on his hands. Returning to the jailer, he told him how he was miraculously freed by the power of God. Then the jailer, discerning God's influence and the power of the blessed martyr in this wonder, gave the accused man his freedom.

16

It is fitting to relate yet another miracle concerning such an eminent martyr, which most certainly took place as well. There was a certain woman in the city of Prague who was blind and crippled over her entire body. She came to the Church of Saint Vitus and fell to the ground before the tomb of the wondrous martyr Wenceslas. Humbly turning her mind to God, she prayed until she regained her lost eyesight and became completely healthy again over her entire body through the intercession of the aforementioned martyr. And having obtained this favor, she praised God, bearing witness in the presence of all to His Saint Wenceslas, that he is a saint of wondrous goodness.

It came to pass at that time that a certain man was taken by his creditors and shackled in iron fetters because he could not pay the moneylenders. And by chance those who seized him put him next to the church where the body of Blessed Wenceslas is buried. Being in such agony here, he extended his hands laden with fetters toward heaven, and turning his eyes toward the church, he prayed that through the intercession of the holy martyr he might merit to be delivered from the heavy burden with which he was pressed. And as he prayed thus, immediately his hands were unshackled. Seeing this, they released him.

It is also wrong to pass over in silence a miracle that occurred as proof of the goodness of this renowned martyr, for all who are in anguish should seek to invoke him with fervent devotion. Therefore, hearken you who are in anguish. Once numerous prisoners were being held under guard in a fortified prison, some because of their guilt, but others because of the slander of accusers. Thus, they prayed tearfully to the Lord that He might deign to deliver them from their anguish of long duration, according to His usual mercy for the sake of the merits of His gracious martyr. Granting their prayers swiftly, He made it possible for them to leave freely for the sake of the merits of His saint whom they had invoked most piously. And lo, some accused the guard of accepting money from the prisoners, and that they had escaped for that reason. The guard, however, did not know how this happened but declared on oath that he had not released them, and that they were freed by a divine miracle and for the sake of the merits of Blessed Wenceslas, whom they invoked frequently. But when the judges of the land did not believe this and the accusers rejected it, he had to undergo trial by a fiery iron, according to the custom of the land. And in the presence of many people a white-hot iron was placed in the guard's hand. And he took it without fear, having commended himself to the goodness of the martyr, and walked beyond the point stipulated without feeling any burning. When they beheld this miracle, everyone believed him. And he was cleared of the charge and returned home. And God was glorified in His saint by those whose innocence was revealed, as well as by those who witnessed this, and those who heard about what happened.

17

When the glorious report about these and similar miracles of the blessed martyr had spread, some people, through the influence of the evil spirit, were tempted to possess the relics of the blessed body and keep them for themselves or distribute them to their relatives. Verily, some of them attempted this out of devotion and in good faith and with good intentions so that the martyr's name would spread everywhere. However, as a consequence vengeance overtook those who ventured this with bad intentions or out of greed for profit. Nevertheless, we do not excuse even those who dare to steal holy relics with pious intentions. For whenever sacrilege takes place it is a sin, though perhaps less so than the sin of those who commit such things out of greed for profit. Therefore, it is wrong to pass over in silence the fact that his sister, Přibyslava, who, as far as the human eye can judge, led a most saintly life in the sacred garb of a nun, took part in such a venture, having the priest of that very church, Stephen, as a helper in her plan. But a certain recluse, one who had a reputation for sanctity but contradicted it by his deed, took up residence near the church. And following his advice, they attempted this deed. In a word, they came on a predetermined night and made her an accomplice in their deed by forcing her to come with them. Upon exhuming the holy body, they took as much of him as they pleased, and placed the rest of the body into the grave. And among them there was also the son of the above-mentioned priest, who very disrespectfully pulled out the jaw from the holy body and wrapped it in his cloak. But divine vengeance soon overtook them all for the sin they committed.

In the land of Bohemia there was also a certain woman who descended from a noble family and who was united with Christ Jesus by faith and holy deeds. For a long time she was bereft of her hearing but bore her deafness in the fear of God. Once, when the feast of Saint Wenceslas was approaching, she came to the city of Prague so as to visit and pray before the holy relics and thus venerate them. Therefore, upon arriving there, she remained in the city for some time, resting from fatigue. And when the feast day came and the bells were ringing for vespers and a large crowd was entering the church where the sacrosanct body reposed, she had a carriage made ready for herself. After entering it, she began to drive out of the city, for she was afraid to enter the castle, ashamed of her deafness and that she would not know how to give a suitable answer were one of the gentlemen or ladies of rank to address her. Thus, when she was halfway across the bridge, she turned her eyes toward the Church of the Blessed Martyr and sent a silent prayer to the Lord, crying aloud tearfully with sighs. Distressed with great sorrow, she began to sense an itching in her ears when she was already near the city's gates. She now wanted to get rid of it and inserted her finger into her ear; but when she took it out again, she immediately regained her former clear hearing.

For the consolation of the faithful it is fitting to relate this miracle, which took place in the village of Bykoš. That is, one night thieves came and stole a heifer from the yard which belonged to the Church of the Holy Martyr. Immediately they were struck by total blindness, so that they wandered all night in the vicinity of the aforesaid village and were not at all able to find the road by which they could get away. When morning light put an end to night, the above-mentioned thieves recognized their sin and brought the beast back to the yard. And immediately they recognized the road and returned home without their plunder.

18

And we dare not let fall into oblivion the fact that even among foreign and distant nations the Lord Jesus deigned to manifest the glory and respect this blessed warrior enjoys in a wondrous and awe-inspiring way. Thus not only neighboring but also distant nations would know that it is pleasing to Christ when solemn respect is paid to such an eminent martyr. Hence, when the king of Denmark, named Erich, who was entangled in the snares of many sins, was residing in the forests for his relaxation and amusement and hunting game, lo, one night a crucified man appeared to him in a dream, with head bowed, eyes downcast and a pale face, sad and grieved, as though overwhelmed by anguish. When the king saw him, he became very frightened, for never before had he seen a man crucified. And although he was very afraid, nevertheless, upon summoning a little courage, he asked him who he was and why he was crucified. And the latter said in a quiet voice full of reproach, "I am Jesus Christ and you have crucified me." Trembling, the king now considered for awhile why Christ was blaming him for His crucifixion when, after all, he was in no way cognizant of such a deed. And he realized that he was being rebuked for the multitude of sins of which he was guilty and for which Christ is, so to say, crucified, according to the Apostle's words to the Hebrews: "They crucify to themselves the Son of God afresh and put Him to an open shame" [Hebrews 6:6]. That is, verily those who fall into and remain in sin crucify Christ afresh, so to say, for they spurn His grace through which they were delivered from sin. And that means, with regard to themselves, that is, by their behavior, they crucify to themselves the Son of God and disgrace Him, for they do not appreciate His grace and remain in sin. And that is the reason why people who have abandoned their original faith should not fall into sin, for they can no longer be baptized for the remission of their sins and, moreover, they spurn the Son of God and put Him to an open shame. However, this commentary does not come from us but was handed down by the saints of old. Thus, having digressed a little in commenting on the words of the Apostle, let us return to the continuing narrative. Therefore, the king did not dare oppose the words of Truth. Clasping his hands and kneeling, he replied in a penitent voice: "O God, mighty, just, and forbearing Judge, wilt Thou be angry for all days if they have penance and mercy in Thy sight? Forgive an atoner, I beseech Thee earnestly!" And the Lord said, "So as to obtain forgiveness for your sins, build a church in honor of my holy warrior Wenceslas." And to this he answered: " I am Thy servant and son of Thy handmaid, turn me not away from Thy face, I pray, and I will gladly fulfill what Thou hast commanded." When he said this he awakened and the vision vanished.

Having awakened from sleep trembling all over, the king began in his mind to consider the honor of such a remarkable vision. He reflected on Christ's anger and His accusation, and was seized by incredible fear. He also kept recalling what Christ commanded for making amends for sins; that is, that he should not tarry in building a church in honor of Saint Wenceslas. Although he did not know the saint about whom the Lord was so inordinately concerned, nonetheless he was uneasy on that account. And since the king was uneasy, all his knights were also uneasy. He would inquire of individual strangers whether by chance any of them knew who or from which nation Saint

Wenceslas was. Since no one knew this and all had become uneasy, lo, a certain bishop from the diocese of Ribe arrived so as to discuss official matters. But for those things there was neither place nor time, for a grave and difficult matter weighed on the king's heart. Yet he would always eagerly inquire of strangers about this. However, when the bishop did not know about this saint or who he was—for the name of Saint Wenceslas had never been heard in Denmark—an even greater sorrow flared up in the king's heart: for an urgency weighed on the king to carry out as soon as possible the penance which Christ had assigned to him.

Finally, after several days had passed and the king continued to be uneasy and sad, some knights arrived from the vicinity of Bohemia. And when the king inquired of them about the name and merits of Saint Wenceslas, they indeed set him right so that the king considered it sufficient. That is, they told him that he was the prince of Bohemia, who was obedient to Christian law, zealous in carrying out the truth of the Gospel, and a great propagator of the holy faith. And those who were still living in pagan delusion hated him for his good deeds, and incited his brother to kill him and seize his princedom. And when that took place, he entered the kingdom of heaven by way of martyrdom. Upon hearing this, the king rejoiced greatly and without delay began to build a cloister, as he was commanded. And when with the help of God he completed it, he installed monks of Saint Benedict and provided it sufficiently with implements, books, and the requisite properties.

Ultimately, the death of this king was nearly the same as the death of Saint Wenceslas: for he was seized and killed by his own brother when he showed regret for his sins and did penance. And this final grace, that is, the regret and penance by which the kingdom of heaven is gained for certain, the Lord granted him, as is believed, for the service which he rendered to the holy martyr Wenceslas, according to His command.

19

In the parish of Usti in the diocese of Prague it happened that a little girl died. She had not yet been regenerated in the fountain of holy baptism but had become a catechumen. As one awaiting baptism, she was named Wenceslasa. And when her parents—their hearts laden with sorrow and eyes flooded with tears—brought her to the church expecting that the priest of the aforesaid place would deign to bury the little body in the cemetery of the faithful, the latter hesitated for a long time. And lo, while several people stood around the dead girl, a certain woman appeared at that moment. She had consecrated her virginity to God, and had her hair shorn and herself covered with a sacred veil as a sign of her pious chastity. And when she learned the reason for the great sorrow of the parents in particular, that is, that their daughter whom they had brought dead had died without the regenerating bath, and when she also heard her name, with a sigh she said before those who stood there, "O Saint Wenceslas, you who kindly listen to prayers and who have always been merciful, do not allow the soul named after you to remain in hell, but let it return to the body and become worthy of being regenerated to life eternal by the water of baptism." O miraculous power of Christ, O charity of the martyr invoked! Hardly had the woman finished her prayer and, lo, the little girl yawned, opened her eyes, and began to cry. And to all who were standing around she showed signs of her return to life. What need is there of more words! While all were astonished and praised God in His holiness, she was baptized without delay. And having received baptism, she lived for fourteen more days. And thus, for the sake of the merits of this most gracious martyr, the little girl was returned to life temporal and eternal.

Verily, the Lord Jesus, whose deeds were not written down because of the negligence of those whom they concern, also worked many other miracles for the sake of His martyr Wenceslas: he freed some from prison, he delivered them from fetters and plucked them from misfortune; he cured many of various maladies; he helped them in war and protected them from enemies. However, this, which we found in various books, we have transcribed briefly in this work so that all those who read it without doubting might be moved to pious veneration of such an eminent saint; and so that those who heard about these miracles would in their need seek to invoke him without any uncertainty. And as concerns some of these miracles, that is, as concerns Christ's appearance to the king of Denmark and the resurrection of the dead little girl, we learned of them from the reliable narratives of the brothers of the Order of Preachers,[40] and we have included them in this work in abridged form.

On the Companion of Saint Wenceslas[41]

20

Since on the preceding pages we promised to elaborate on the faithful servant of this saintly prince and confidant of all the deeds that pertain to his sanctity, and having completed the exposition about the miracles concerning this same saint, we shall now relate how that man ended his life. Thus, after the martyrdom and victory of Christ's glorious warrior, and after the star which irradiated the entire land fell, and after those who had been devotedly attached to him, as I have said, and whom he had gathered around him to serve Christ were either put to the sword by the impious one, or buried in the river, and others fled from the land, one of the knights, Podiven by name—about whom we said he was acquainted with all the actions and deeds which the martyr performed without other people knowing—escaped to the Germans after his Lord departed from this world to Christ and found protection in exile. But after a long period of time, when he thought that peace had been restored in the country, he returned to his home and stayed there for awhile. With what fervent love and inviolable loyalty he was united with his lord while he was still alive is evident from how he always helped him, and how he would secretly go out with him at night and walk with him from church to church so as to pray.

One day, feeling excessively great sorrow over the loss of his gracious lord, he seized a sword and hurried to the home of a certain knight whom he knew to have been the head of the conspiracy that strove to murder Saint Wenceslas and, above all, the one at whose hands the blessed one was put to death. And upon finding him lying in a bath, he killed him with the sword. Then, hoping he could save himself through flight, he hastily went into a thick forest. But the death of the latter and the hiding-place of this knight were reported to the above-mentioned fratricide, and he had the forest quickly surrounded by his knights. And when the servant of his brother was found, he ordered him hanged in that very forest. And that man remained hanging from a tree for three years, but neither a bird nor a beast of prey dared to mangle him. Nor did the body succumb to decomposition and putrefaction; rather, his fingernails and whiskers grew as if he were alive, and the hair on his head turned gray and even became completely white.[42]

When this was brought to the attention of the fratricide, he ordered him buried, for talk of these wonders had spread among almost all the inhabitants of the land. But neither in this way could the acts of God remain concealed; for those that passed this way would very frequently see a heavenly light over his grave so that the merits of His servant would be revealed to the people. This continued for a long time until great numbers of the faithful came from many places and began to bring sacrificial gifts. And in the anxieties of their lives they appealed to God and this murdered man for help. After a long time the body was raised from this place and translated in a pious procession of priests and devout men and women who thronged there joyfully. And it was taken to the graveyard of the Church of Saint Vitus, where it was buried. Thus, Saint Wenceslas, who is buried inside the church, and that courtier, who is buried outside of it, are separated from each other only by a wall. However, the body was translated from there; now it reposes under the great tower in the chapel of Saint Nicholas the Confessor.[43]

While this man was alive he was steward over all at the court of Saint Wenceslas. And he educated all the domestics, down to the last cook, in such a way that among the court servants there were hardly any that did not know how to sing almost all the Psalms[44] or who did not learn something useful about church ceremonies. He loved them all like his own sons and was respected by them all like a father. If at times his lord ordered him to disburse ten coins to the poor, he added five more; if thirty, he added fifteen more. We are relating this so that stewards should not think that they sin against their lord if at times it happens that they disburse more to the poor than the amount commissioned by him. For this is not a sign of unfaithfulness but a confirmation of faithfulness. For as it is a crime to take from what belongs to the poor, so is it a virtuous act to add to them, provided, of course, that he who adds to them knows that he is causing his lord little or no harm by this, and that he also knows that it conforms to his piety. Thus, since the gracious lord had a gracious steward who was aware of his generosity, piety, and mercy, what he did was right, and both of them gained merit, the one who gave as well as the one who added. Thus, that faithful servant deserved to hear the words of the Gospel:

"Well done, good and faithful servant: because thou hast been faithful over a few things, I will make thee ruler over many things; enter thou into the joy of thy lord" [Matthew 25:21]. And signs of this joy appeared in the church where the venerable bodies of the servant and lord repose: for many have frequently heard the voices of angels singing psalms there.

For the sake of the merits and intercession of both, O Christ, deign to succor us in our troubles and needs, Thou who art blessed forever and ever, amen.

✝ A Brief Account of Saints Cyril and Methodius and the Baptism of the Moravian and Bohemian Lands (*Diffundente sole*)

Cyril and Methodius creating the Slavic alphabet and translating the Gospel into the Slavic language, thirteenth-century. Radziwill Chronicle.

✝

1

DURING THE TIME of the renowned teacher, Blessed Augustine, after the sun of justice had diffused the holy Christian faith throughout the earth with rays, Saint Cyril came to Moravia,[1] where he won a number of people for Almighty God with His help. Being a highly educated man in Greek and Latin letters, he previously converted Bulgaria[2] to the faith of Jesus Christ in the name of the Holy Trinity and Indivisible Unity. And having invented new signs or letters, he translated the Old and New Testaments from Greek and Latin into Slavic speech, determining that the mass and the other canonical hours be celebrated in church in the Slavic language, which to this day is observed in Bulgaria and in many Slavic regions.[3] And in this way many souls were won for Christ the Lord.

2

Then, after this Cyril had gathered many sheaves into the Lord's barn, he left his brother, named Methodius—a zealous man, adorned with all manner of sanctity—in Moravia, and went to Rome for devotional purposes.[4] There he was accused of introducing the custom of singing divine services in the Slavic language by the pope and other authorities.[5]

Taking hold of the Psalter and finding the verse which says, "Let every thing that hath breath praise the Lord" [Psalms 150:6], he vindicated himself humbly. Now he said: "If every thing that breathes is to praise the Lord, why, o chosen fathers, do you forbid me to celebrate divine services in Slavic when God created this speech as well as the others? And when I was unable to help those people with the salvation of their souls in another way, God inspired me through this means, by which I have won a great many of them for Him. Therefore, pardon me, O holy fathers and lords. For the Blessed Apostle Paul, the best teacher of the pagans, also says in his epistle to the Corinthians, "Forbid not to speak with tongues" [1 Corinthians 14:39]. Hearing this and marveling at the faith of this great man, they now decreed in an apostolic decision and confirmed in writing that the mass and other canonical hours be sung in those regions in the language mentioned above.

3

Remaining in Rome, Blessed Cyril made known to that nation the favor of the Apostolic See, and having clothed himself in monastic habit, he completed the last day of his life there.

His aforementioned brother, Methodius, was then appointed archbishop by the Moravian king named Svatopluk, a pious and God-fearing man who at that time had a very extensive realm which later collapsed[6] through the imprudence of Svatopluk the Second, a nephew of Svatopluk the First. And there were seven other suffragan bishops subordinate to him.[7]

4

But the Bohemian Slavs,[8] who were settled under Arcturus in the climes of the Rhipaen Mountains[9] and given to idol worship, long remained without law or a prince. Finally, at the prompting of a prophetess, they founded the city of Prague.[10] Finding a very shrewd and prudent man named Přemysl, they elected him as their prince, having married him to the aforementioned prophetess, who was named Libuše.[11]

And in the course of time a most gracious prince, Bořivoj,[12] was born of this famous family. Shining with the bloom of outstanding beauty and youthful strength, he took a wife by the name of Ludmila[13]—the daughter of a prince named Slavibor from the land of the Milčane[14]—who as a young girl made offerings to the idols.

5

Thus, this Bořivoj once visited the Moravian king, Svatopluk the First, and was kindly invited by him and his magnates to a banquet. However, he was not allowed to sit among the Christians, but was seated before the table on the floor in the pagan manner. And here, they say, Bishop Methodius regretted his humiliation and said to him:

"What a pity, you are such an outstanding man but not ashamed to be excluded from sitting with princes although yourself of princely rank! You would rather sit on the ground for the sake of shameful idol worship!"

Then he said: "To what danger would I expose myself for this matter? What good will the Christian religion bring me?" Bishop Methodius said, "If you renounce idols and the evil spirits residing in them, you will be the lord of your lords, and all your enemies will be subordinate to your power, and your progeny will increase like a great river into which pours the flow of various streams."

And, verily, this prophecy was fulfilled in the Bohemian princes.

And Bořivoj said, "If that is so, what prevents me from being baptized?" Bishop Methodius said, "Nothing, but be prepared to believe with all your heart in God the Father Almighty and in His only begotten Son, Our Lord Jesus Christ, and in the Consoler, the Spirit, the Enlightener of all faithful souls, not only for the sake of worldly bliss, but also to attain salvation of body and soul, and to win the glorious palm of eternity and become a partaker of ineffable joy in the community of saints."

The youth's mind was roused by means of this and similar encouragement which flowed like honey, and he longed to receive the grace of baptism. Casting himself, together with all those accompanying him, to the ground at the bishop's feet, he besought him most earnestly that this take place without delay.

6

What need was there for more words! On the following day he instructed the prince and the thirty men accompanying him in the fundamentals of the faith and regenerated them in the sacred fountain of baptism after they had observed the customary ritual of the fast. And when he had educated him thoroughly in Christ's faith, he allowed him to return home, having enriched him with many gifts. And he gave him a priest of the venerable life named Kaich. Then, after returning home to the town called Hradec,[15] they appointed the aforementioned priest. And they founded a church there in honor of Blessed Clement, and caused Satan much harm by winning people for Christ the Lord.

After a short time Methodius, mentioned above, came to Bohemia and baptized Saint Ludmila,[16] along with many others. And thus did the Christian faith spread in a land of roughness and uncultivated wilderness.

7

But seeing that Christ's gains were multiplying daily and that he was suffering a great loss, the Devil provoked his members against the members of Christ, causing the prince to be banished from Bohemia on account of Christ's faith.[17] Having been banished, he again turned to King Svatopluk and Bishop Methodius. And they received him with great honor, as was fitting, and he stayed with them for awhile, enduring exile for the sake of propagating the true faith and becoming more thoroughly acquainted with Christ's science.

Now the Devil's members, mentioned above, elected another prince for themselves. But injustice cannot last, even if it prevails for a time, and the aforementioned gracious prince was called back from Moravia with honor. And he built a church in Prague in honor of Mary, the Mother of God, as he had promised while living in exile.

8

This first founder of holy places, assembler of priests, and supporter of the Christian religion had three sons and as many daughters with his wife, the aforementioned Ludmila. And as Blessed Methodius had predicted to him, not only did he gain worldly power day by day, but he also flourished in all virtues, blossoming like a lily.

And Blessed Ludmila became a true handmaid of Christ, emulating him not only in the religion of Jesus Christ, but even rising above him. Completing the course of his life and filling his days with good deeds, the aforementioned Bořivoj paid the debt of humankind and received a heavenly share in place of an earthly.

9

And after him his firstborn son, Spytihněv,[18] who shone in all virtues, began to reign. Emulating his father, he founded churches of God, assembled priests and clerics around him, and was perfect in Christ's faith. And upon completing the years of his life, he ended his last day and departed for the stars.

After him Vratislav,[19] the father of Saint Wenceslas,[20] ascended the princely throne. Having strengthened his realm, he built the basilica of Saint George the Martyr. Radiant with all manner of sanctity and with his noble way of life, he exchanged this fleeting world for life eternal.

✝

Notes

Introduction

1. Though the occupation of Bohemia by the Slavs almost escaped the notice of the early historians of Europe, it did not fail to capture the popular imagination, which created the legend about Čech, the mythical forefather of the Czech nation. After crossing three great rivers with his Slavic followers, Čech surveyed the land from the heights of Mount Říp in Northern Bohemia and decided to make this territory his new home.

2. Francis Dvornik, *The Slavs: Their Early History and Civilization* (Boston, 1959), pp. 60–61. The view that Samo's state disintegrated is not shared by Dittrich. He believes that it remained strong and that Mojmir's Moravian empire was its political and dynastic continuation. See Z. R. Dittrich, *Christianity in Great Moravia* (Groningen, 1967), pp. 9–12.

3. There is indirect evidence of Mojmir's baptism, which has been dated variously but may have taken place sometime between 818 and 838. If acceptance of his baptism is strained because of lack of evidence, then his successor, Rostislav, must be considered the first Christian ruler of Moravia. Rostislav's baptism in 846 is a generally accepted fact. See A. P. Vlasto, *The Entry of the Slavs into Christendom* (Cambridge, 1970), pp. 23–24.

4. An English translation of the *Lives* of Constantine and Methodius can be found in M. Kantor, *Medieval Slavic Lives of Saints and Princes* (Ann Arbor, Mich., 1983). For details in English about the Moravian Mission, see F. Dvornik, *Byzantine Missions among the Slavs: SS. Constantine-Cyril and Methodius* (New Brunswick, N.J., 1970).

5. This was probably the main reason for the failure of the Germanic missions among the Slavs of central Europe—namely, that their missionary activities were commonly accompanied by rampant colonization. The argument that their missions failed because they were poorly understood by the local populace is perhaps an oversimplification. However, the extent to which the German missionaries mastered Slavic and were able to provide their neophytes with translations in the vernacular of the basic sacred texts of Christianity is a matter of conjecture. Dittrich's argument (*Christianity in Great Moravia*, p. 5) that they had a proper command of the Slavic language and produced standard translations in that idiom, which "surpasses in

purity of language the meticulously graecing (sic) vocabulary of the Byzantine missionaries," is his opinion and is totally unsupported by the weight of textual evidence. Indeed, one of the criticisms of his book by Graus is that in places it has an abundance of unproven hypotheses. See F. Graus, "Říše velkomoravská, její postavení v současné Evropě a vnitřní struktura," *Konferencia o vel'kej Morave a Byzantskej Misii* (Nitra, 1963), p. 63.

The question of translations made by German missionaries among the Slavs is dealt with in detail in an article by B. Floria, which discusses the views that F. Zagiba advanced in his book, *Das Geistesleben der Slaven im frühen Mittelalter* (Vienna and Graz, 1971). See B. N. Floria, "K ocenke istoričeskogo značenija slavjanskoj pis'mennosti v Velikoj Moravii," *Velikaja Moravija ee istoričeskoe i kyl'turnoe značenie* (Moscow, 1985), pp. 195–217.

6. At its height, Great Moravia encompassed the territories of Bohemia, Moravia, Slovakia, Southern Poland, and Western Pannonia.

7. Horace G. Lunt, *Old Church Slavonic Grammar* (The Hague, 1955), pp. 1–3.

8. However, some scholars have unjustifiably challenged the notion of the comprehensibility of Old Church Slavonic. The question of how well it was understood by the Slavs in central and eastern Europe, or elsewhere, has been a subject of dispute among Slavic cultural historians and linguists, as has the question of whether these Slavs viewed this language as their own and not a foreign one. Such scholars as Roman Jakobson, Horace Lunt et al. concluded that the language of Constantine and Methodius was indeed close to the regional Slavic dialects, because in the ninth century the differences among these dialects were negligble over the vast territorial expanse of Europe that the Slavs occupied. Hence, Old Church Slavonic was entirely intelligible in the Slavic west among the Moravians, and also in the Slavic east among the Russians. This view was rejected as a myth by George Shevelov and Alexander Issatschenko. They maintained that Old Church Slavonic was an artificial and incomprehensible sacred language, and that it should not be identified with Common Slavic (Shevelov) or with the regional Slavic colloquial languages (Issatschenko). A similar view was also espoused by F. Zagiba.

Since a detailed discussion of this question is inappropriate in the present work, I shall confine my remarks to the following observation. In my opinion, linguistic and textual evidence raises serious doubts about the position espoused by Shevelov, Issatschenko, and Zagiba. For example, a glottochronological analysis of the Slavic languages by M. Čejka and A. Lamprecht has proved that the differences within the regional Slavic dialects of the ninth century were minimal phonologically, morphologically, and lexically. Also, L. Matějka has pointed out that the texts of the "Novgorod Pilot Book of 1282" (*Novgorodskaja kormčaja kniga*) was compiled for domestic needs, that is, for the clergy and the enlightenment of Novgorod Christians, whether literate or illiterate. And the texts of this codex—which included the "Russian Law Code" (*Rusьkaja pravda*) and

"Court Law for the People" (*Zakonъ soudnyi ljudemъ*)—were read aloud in the Church of Saint Sophia in Novgorod for the benefit of illiterate Christians. Indeed, this is stated explicitly in the preface to the "Novgorod Pilot Book."

The works in question are: R. Jakobson, "The Czech Part in Church Slavonic Culture," *Selected Writings* (Berlin-New York-Amsterdam, 1985), 6:130; Lunt, p. 3; G. Y. Shevelov, review of H. G. Lunt, *Old Church Slavonic Grammar*, in *Word* 12 (1956): 337; A. Issatschenko, *Mythen und Tatsachen über die Entstehung der russischen Literatursprache* (Vienna, 1975), p. 23; Zagiba, pp. 165–71; 219–22; M. Čejka and A. Lamprecht, "K voprosu o slavjanskom jazykovom edinstve v period prixoda v Moraviju Konstantina i Mefodija," *Magna Moravia* (Prague, 1965), p. 461–67, and "K otázce vznika a diferenciace slovanských jazyků," *Sborník praci filosofické fakulty Brněnske university*, A II (1963), pp. 5–20; L. Matějka, "Church Slavonic as a National Language," *Semiosis* (Ann Arbor, Mich., 1984), pp. 333–34.

9. The historian R. W. Seton-Watson claims that this dynasty arose late in the eighth century. He does not, however, indicate the source of his information. See his *History of the Czechs and Slovaks* (London, 1943), p.12. The last of the Přemyslide rulers was Wenceslas III (d. 1306).

10. See René Wellek, "Bohemia in English Literature," *Essays on Czech Literature* (The Hague, 1963), pp. 81–147.

11. Czechs made up one of the legions in the army of Otto I, which finally put an end to Magyar militancy and forced them to pursue a more peaceful existence.

12. A. P. Vlasto (n. 3 above), p. 106.

13. Only parts of Croatia (e.g., Krk) remained recalcitrant, and the Slavic liturgical language survived there into modern times.

14. As quoted by A. I. Rogov in *Skazanija o načale češskogo gosudarstva* (Moscow, 1970), p. 12.

15. According to this principle, the eldest son of the reigning prince would be sovereign of the undivided State of Bohemia, while the younger princes would receive lands in Moravia.

16. The present work is translated from the critical edition of J. Vajs, *Sborník staroslovanských literárnich památek o sv. Václavu a sv. Lidmile* (Prague, 1929), pp. 36–43.

17. O. Králík, *K počatkum literatury přemyslovských Čechách, Rospravy československe akademie věd* (Prague, 1961), p. 89; R. Urbánek, *Legenda tak zvaného Kristiána ve vývoji předhusitských legend ludmilských a václavských a její autor* (Prague, 1947), 1: 285; Z. Fiala, "Dva kritické přispevky ke starým dějinám českym," *Sborník historický* 9 (1962): 5–65 (see esp. p. 38); V. Novotný, *Český kniže Václav svatý* (Prague, 1929), p. 34; F. Vacek, "Úvahy a posudky o literatuře svatováclavské," *Sborník historického kroužku*, 27–30 (1926–29): 33–57 (1926): 1–10; 89–96 (1927): 44–48; 81–112 (1928): 6–30; 82–113 (1929); F. M. Bartoš, "O Dobrovského pojetí osudů slovanské bohoslužby v Čechách," *Historický sborník* 1 (1953): 7–26;

Z. Kalandra, *Česká pohanství* (Prague, 1946); Vajs, *Sborník*, pp. 36–43. R. Jakobson, "Some Russian Echoes of the Czech Hagiography," *Annuaire d'Institut de Philologie et d'Histoire Orientale et Slaves* 8 (New York, 1944): 155–168; M. Weingart, "První česko-cirkvenéslovanská legenda o svatém Václavu," *Svatováclavský sborník* (Prague, 1934), 1: 863–1088.

18. J. Slavík, "Mladši slovanská legenda o sv. Václavu a její význam pro kritiku legend latinských," *Svatováclavský sborník* (Prague, 1934), 1: 842–62; F. Vacek, "Poměr Gumpoldový legendy o sv. Václavu k legendě Crescente fide," *Sborník k 60. narozeninám J. Pekaře* (Prague, 1930), pp. 47–64.

19. The present translation is based on the text edited by V. Chaloupecký. Believing that originally the concluding section in both recensions was the same, he added to the "Bohemian Recension" the account of the *translatio* and first miracles according to the "Bavarian Recension." These texts can be found in Chaloupecký's "Prameny X Století," *Svatováclavský sborník*, 2: 495–50, and in *Fontes rerum boemicarum* I, *Vitae sanctorium*, fasc. 1 (*Prameny dějin českých*, I Ž ivoty svatých, fasc. 1, ed. Palecký; Prague, 1871), pp. 183–90. A Czech translation of this work was made by J. Ludvíkovský and can be found in V. Chaloupecký, *Na úsvitu křesťanství* (Prague, 1942), pp. 79–86. It should be noted that because my knowledge of Latin was at times insufficient to translate reliably the complexities and subtleties of the Latin texts, modern Czech translations served as ancillae.

20. In a recent article, Ingham also claims that *Fuit* is "a Latin translation or paraphrase," of the *Life of Ludmila*. However, no convincing proof of this is offered. See N. W. Ingham, "The Lost Church Slavonic Life of Saint Ludmila," *Studia Slavica Mediaevalia et Humanistica* (1986), 1:350. For an additional discussion of the relationship among the preserved manuscripts dealing with Saint Ludmila and her lost *Life*, see his earlier article, "Sources on Saint Ludmila, II: The Translation of Her Relics," *International Journal of Slavic Linguistics and Poetics* 31–32 (1985):197–206.

21. The Latin critical edition of this text is found in V. Chaloupecký, "Prameny X století," *Svatováclavský sborník*, 2:467–81. A Czech translation of this work was made by B. Ryba and can be found in V. Chaloupecký, *Na úsvitu*, pp. 60–66.

22. A. I. Rogov, "Legenda Nikol'skogo," *Skazanija o načale češskogo gosudarstva v drevnerusskoj pis'mennosti* (Moscow, 1970), p. 70; J. Vašica, "Druhá staroslověnská legenda o sv. Václavu," in Vajs, *Sborník*, pp. 78–79.

23. Gumpold's Latin work can be found in Vajs, *Sborník*, pp. 124–35, and in *Fontes rerum boemicarum*, 1:146–66, where it is accompanied by F. Zoubek's Czech translation.

24. The present translation of *CL* is based on the critical edition of the Latin text prepared by J. Ludvíkovský in his book, *Kristiánova legenda*, pp. 8–102. This text is accompanied by his modern Czech translation. *Fontes rerum boemicarum*, 1:199–227, also contains the text of *CL* with a Czech

translation by J. Truhlař. The text of the prologue and the ten chapters of this work can also be found in J. Pekař, *Die Wenzels- und Ludmilalegenden und die Echtheit Christians* (Prague, 1906), pp. 88–125.

25. The great majority of scholars believe that this legend originated in Bohemia. Notable exceptions to this view are V. Novotný and J. Slavík, who consider it to be Russian; see Novotný, *Český Kníže Václav svatý*, p. 37, and J. Slavík, "Svatý Václav a slovanské legendy," *Sborník statej posvjaščennyx P. N. Miljukovu* (Prague, 1929), pp. 137–54 (esp. p. 150).

26. N. K. Nikol'skij, *Legenda mantuanskogo episkopa Gumpol'da o sv. Vjačeslave Češskom v slavjano-russkom perevode, Pamjatniki drevnej pis'mennosti i iskusstva* 174 (St. Petersburg, 1904), pp. xii-xxxi; R. Urbánek, *Legenda tak zvaného Kristiána*, p. 325; J. Vašica, "Druhá staroslověnská legenda," in Vajs, *Sborník*, pp. 76–79.

27. A. I. Sobolevskij, *K xronologii drevnejšix cerkovnoslavjanskix pamjatnikov* (St. Petersburg, 1860), p. 4; V. Chaloupecký, "Kníže svatý Václav," *Český časopis historický* 47 (1946): 4–54 (see esp. pp. 4–5); J. Vašica, "Druhá staroslověnská legenda," in Vajs, *Sborník*, p. 79; J. Pekař, "Svatý Václav," *Svatováclavsky sborník*, 1:87 (previously he had dated this legend to the eleventh century—cf. *Die Wenzels- und Ludmilalegenden*, p. 51); Urbánek, *Legenda tak zvaného Kristiána*, p. 313; Bartoš, "O Dobrovského pojetí," p. 19; F. Graus, "Slovanská liturgie a pisemnictví v přemyslovských Čechách 10 století," *Československý časopis historický* 14 (1966): 491; O. Králík, "Prameny II staroslověnské legendy václavské," *Slavia* 31 (1962): 578–98. The present translation is based on the critical edition prepared by J. Vašica for Vajs, *Sborník*, pp. 84–124.

28. Novotný, *Český kníže Václav svatý*; W. Vondrák, *Kirchenslavische Chrestomathie* (Göttingen, 1910,) p. 169; J. Vašica, "Kanon ke cti sv. Václava," in Vajs, *Sborník*, p. 137, in *Slovanská bohaslužba*, p. 17, and again in Chaloupecký, *Na úsvitu*, p. 73; K. Krofta, *Naše stare legendy a začátky naseho duchovního života* (Prague, 1947), p. 46–48; M. Weingart, "La Première Legende de St. Venceslas, écrite en vieux slave est d'origine tchèque. Analyse philologique," *Byzantinoslavica* 6 (1935–36): 1–37. See also L. Matějka, "The Bohemian School of Church Slavonic," *Czechoslovakia, Past and Present* (The Hague, 1967), pp. 1035–43.

29. R. Jakobson, "Přehlédnutá památka velkomoravská," *Lidové noviny*, 23 December 1937, p. 7; J. Vašica, "Původní staroslověnský liturgický kanon o sv. Dimitrijovi Soluňském," *Slavia* 35 (1966): 513–24. The present translation is based on the manuscript prepared by J. Vašica for Vajs, *Sborník*, p. 139–45.

30. N. J. Serebrjanskij, "Prolozní legendy o sv. Lidmile a o sv. Vaclávu," in Vajs, *Sborník*, pp. 47–63; A. I. Rogov, "Slovanské legendy z doby vzniku českého státu," in *Staroslovenske legendy*, pp. 24–26; M. Weingart, "První česko-cirkevněslovanská legenda o svatém Václavu," *Svatováclavský sborník* 1:947–48. With regard to the connection between this work and the *Office of SS. Constantine and Methodius*, see R. Večerka, "Velkomoravská

literatura v přemyslovských Čechách," *Slavia* 32 (1963): 416. The present translations are based on the manuscripts prepared by N. J. Serebrjanskij for Vajs, *Sborník*, pp. 64–68.

31. The critical edition of this work is in V. Chaloupecký, "Prameny X století," *Svatováclavský sborník*, 2:542–56. A Czech translation of it was prepared by J. Ludvíkovský for Chaloupecký, *Na úsvitu*, pp. 162–67. This text is also found in *Fontes rerum bohemicarum*, 1:193–98, accompanied by a Czech translation by J. Truhlař.

32. The present translation is based on the manuscript prepared by J. Pekař in *Die Wenzels- und Ludmilalegenden*, pp. 409–30. A Czech translation of this work was made by J. Ludvíkovský for Chaloupecký, *Na úsvitu*, pp. 220–42.

33. A critical edition of this work was prepared by V. Chaloupecký, "Prameny X století," *Svatováclavský sborník*, pp. 486–93. J. Ludvíkovský made a modern Czech translation of it for Chaloupecký, *Na úsvitu*, pp. 98–101. This text is also found in *Fontes rerum bohemicarum*, 1:191–93, and is accompanied by J. Truhlař's translation into Czech.

34. A. I. Sobolevskij, "Mučenie sv. Vita v drevnem cerkovnoslavjanskom periode," *Izvestija otdelenija russkogo jazyka i slovesnosti* 8, no. 1 (1903): 278–96; J. Vajs, "Hlaholský zlomek nalezeny v Augustinianském klášteře v Praze," *Časopis českého muzea* 75 (1901): 21–35; J. Vašica, "Staroslovanské legendy o sv. Vítu," *Slovanske studie* (Prague, 1948), pp. 159–63; L. Matějka, "Dvije crkvenoslavenske legende o svetom Vidu," *Slovo* 23 (1973): 73–96; G. Kappel, "Die slavische Vituslegende und ihr lateinisches Original," *Wiener Slavistisches Jahrbuch* 20 (1974): 73–85; F. V. Mareš, *An Anthology of Church Slavonic Texts* (Munich, 1979), pp. 135–50; H. Birnbaum, "The Church Slavic Legends of St. Vitus: Some Unresolved Issues," *Language and Literary Theory* (Ann Arbor, Mich., 1984), pp. 1–7.

35. The present translation is based on the text found in the *Uspenskij sborník* (Moscow, 1971), pp. 220–29.

36. L. Matějka, "Tři církevněslovanské legendy svatovítske," *Litterae Slavicae Medii Aevi* (Munich, 1985), pp. 205–9; F. V. Mareš, "Prolozní legenda o svatém Vítu," *Slovo* 23 (1973): 97–113. It should be noted that Thomson maintains that the translation of the *Life of St. Vitus* was made in the South Slavic area; see F. J. Thomson, "A Survey of the Vitae Allegedly Translated from Latin into Slavonic in Bohemia in the Tenth and Eleventh Centuries," *Atti dell' 8 Congresso Internazionale di Studi Medioevo* (Spoleto, 1987), p. 344.

37. For a survey of the early literature on this issue, see N. K. Grunskij, *Pamjatnik i voprosy drevne-slavjanskoj pis'mennosti I, Pražskie glagoličeskie otryvki* 3 (Jur'ev, 1904), pp. 1–27. The other works in question are: M. Weingart, *Československý typ cirkevnej slovančiny* (Bratislava, 1949), pp. 68–76; F. V. Mareš, "Pražské zlomky a jejich předloha v světle hláskoslovného rozboru," *Slavia* 19 (1949): 54–61, and "Pražské zlomky a jejich původ v světle lexikalniho rozboru," *Slavia* 20 (1951): 219–31; B. Havránek,

"Počátky slovanského pisma a psané literatury v době velkomoravské,"
Velka Morava. Tisícileta tradice státu a kultury (Prague, 1963), pp. 77–96
(esp. p. 93); K. Horálek, "Rajhradské Martyrologium Adonis a otázka
cyrilice," *Listy filologické* 66 (1939): 23–43. The present translation is based
on the manuscript prepared by F. V. Mareš, *An Anthology of Church Slavonic Texts of Western (Czech) Origin*, pp. 41–45.

38. R. Jakobson, "An Old Church Slavonic Cantilena in the Czech Patrimony," in *Selected Writings*, 6:389–401; F. V. Mareš, "Stix češsko-
cerkovnoslavjanskoj pesni 'Gospodine pomiluj ny," in *To Honor Roman
Jakobson* (The Hague-Paris, 1967), 2:1261–63; J. Racek, "Sur la question de
la genèse de plus ancien chant liturgique tchèque 'Hospodine pomiluj ny,' "
Magna Moravia (Prague, 1965), pp. 435–60; Weingart, *Československý typ
cirkevnej slovančiny*, pp. 87–106; V. Flajšhans, *Nejstarši památky jazyka a
pisemnictví českého* (Prague, 1903), p. 86. The present translation is based
on the reconstructed text in R. Jakobson, *Nejstarší české písně duchovní*
(Prague, 1929), p. 23.

39. The works in question are: A. I. Sobolevskij, *Materialy i iz-
sledovanija v oblasti slavjanskoi filologii i arxeologii* (St. Petersburg, 1910),
p. 40; F. Dvornik, *The Slavs*, p. 172 (n. 2 above); N. W. Ingham, "The Litany
of Saints in 'Molitva Sv. Troicě,' " *Studies Presented to Professor Roman
Jakobson by His Students* (Cambridge, 1968), pp. 121–22. The present translations are based on the texts prepared by F. V. Mareš, *An Anthology of
Church Slavonic Texts of Western (Czech) Origin* (Munich, 1979), pp. 64–
70.

40. My review of this question is based largely on the works of J.
Ludvíkovský, *Kristiánova legenda* (Prague, 1978), and "Great Moravia Tradition in the Tenth Century: Bohemia and Legenda Christiani," in *Magna
Moravia* (Prague, 1965), pp. 525–66; *Magnae Moraviae Fontes Historici*, vol.
2 (Brno, 1967); A. I. Rogov, "Slovanské legendy z doby vzniku českého státu
a jejich osudy na Rusi," *Staroslovenske legendy českého původu* (Prague,
1976), pp. 11–53; and R. Večerka, "Velikomoravskie istoki cerkovnoslavjanskoj pis'mennosti v češskom knjažestve," *Magna Moravia*, pp. 493–524.
Ludvíkovský's work served as a general guide.

41. This came about through the mistaken identification by Balbín of
Bruno's Christian (from the *Legend of St. Vojtěch* by Bruno of Querfort) with
Cosmas Strachkvas (ostensibly the son of Boleslav I), whose monastic name
was Christian. Starting with Dobner, this would be used as an argument
against the veracity of *CL* . Ludvíkovský has shown that this identification
is clearly false. See his *Kristiánova legenda*, pp. 128–33.

42. Bohuslas Balbinus, *Epitome historica rerum Boemicarum*, vol. 1
(Prague 1677); J. F. (Gelasius) Dobner, *Examen Historica-Chronologico-
Criticum* (1755), and *Monumenta historica Boemiae nusquam antehac
edita* (Prague, 1768); J. Dobrovský, *Kritische Versuche die ältere bömische
von späteren Erdichtungen zu reinigen* (1803–26): 1, *Boriwojs Taufe* (1803);
2, *Ludmila und Drahomira* (1807); 3, *Wenzel und Boleslav* (1819); 4,

Mährische Legende von Cyrill und Method (1826); and his *Geschichte der böhmischen Sprache und Literatur* (Prague, 1818).
43. *Moskovskij Vestnik* 17 (1827); A. X. Vostokov, *Filologi českie nabljudenija* (St. Petersburg, 1865); R. Jakobson, "The Czech Part in Church Slavonic Culture," pp. 129–52 (n. 8 above), and "Some Russian Echoes of the Czech Hagiography" (n. 17); Weingart, "První česko-cirkvenéslovanská legenda o svatém Václavu" (n. 30); F. Palacký, *Dějiny národu českého*, vol. 1, (Prague, 1848); P. J. Šafařík, *Slovanské starožitnosti* (Prague, 1837), and *Rozbor staročeské literatury* (Prague, 1942); W. Wattenbach, *Die slavische Liturgie in Böhmen und die altrussische Legende vom heiligen Wenzel* (Breslau, 1857); J. Emler, *Fontes rerum Bohemicarum*, vol. 1 (Prague, 1873); I. V. Jagić, *Služebnye minei za sentjabr', oktjabr' i nojabr' v cerkovnoslavjanskom perevode po russkim rukopisjam 1095–1097* (St. Petersburg, 1886).
44. A. I. Sobolevskij, "Cerkovnoslavjanskie teksty moravskogo proisxoždenija," *Russkij filologičeskij vestnik* 43 (1900): 150–217, and *Materialy i issledovanija v oblasti slavjanskoj filologii i arxeologii* (St. Petersburg, 1910); Nikol'skij, *Legenda mantuanskogo* (n. 26 above); Pekař, *Die Wenzels- und Ludmilalegenden* (n. 24 above).
45. G. A. Il'inskij, "A. I. Sobolevskij, Cerkovno-slavjanskije teksty moravskogo proisxoždenija," *Izvestija otdelenija russkogo jazyka i slovesnosti* 5, no. 4 (St. Petersburg, 1900):1383–86; V. Jagić, *Entstehungsgeschichte der kirchenslavischen Sprache* (Berlin, 1913); F. Pastrnek, "Slovanská legenda o sv. Václavu," *Věstnik Kral. Česke Společnosti Nauk* 6 (Prague, 1903):1–88; V. Vondrak, *Spuren der altslavischen Evangelieubersetzung in der altbohmischen Literatur* (Vienna, 1893); B. Bretholz, *Geschichte Böhmens und Mährens bis zum Aussterben der Premysliden* (Munich and Leipzig, 1912), and *Die Chronik der Böhmen des Cosmas von Prag* (Berlin, 1923); V. Novotný, *České dějiny*, vol. 1 (Prague, 1912), and "Vratislav II a slovanská liturgie," *Časopis pro moderní filologii* 2 (1912): 289–93; 385–90; J. Pekař, "Svatý Václav," *Český časopis historický* (1929): 237–78; R. Jakobson, *Nejstarší české pisné duchovní* (Prague, 1929); N. I. Serebrjanskij, "Proložní legendy o sv. Lidmile a o sv. Václavu," in Vajs, *Sborník*, pp. 47–63; J. Vašica, "Druhá staroslověnská legenda o sv. Václavu," in Vajs, *Sborník*, pp. 70–83; Weingart, "První česko-cirkvenéslovanská legenda" (n. 30 above).
46. B. Ryba, "Kronika kristiánova s hlediska textové kritiky," *Listy filologicke* 59 (1932): 112–21, 237–45; J. Vilikovský, "V. Chaloupecký: Prameny X století. Legendy kristiánova o svatém Václavu a svate Lidmile," *Naše věda* 20 (1941): 81–94, and "O naše nejstarší legendy," *Řad* 7 (1941): 199–205; J. Ludvíkovský, "Great Moravia Tradition" and *Kristiánova legenda*; O. Jansen [R. Jakobson], "Český podil na církevneslovanské kultuře," in *Co daly naše země Evropě a lidstvu* (Prague, 1939), pp. 9–20; J. Vašica, *Slovanská bohoslužba v českých zemich* (Prague, 1940).
Chaloupecký had also proposed other solutions that were rejected—for example, his reconstruction of the unpreserved historical document

Privilegium Moraviensis ecclesie, which he drew from *Diffundente sole* and *Legenda Christiani* and from the Cyrillomethodian legends *Beatus Cyrillus* and *Tempore Michaelis imperatoris.* Also rejected were his opinion that *Diffundente sole* was identical with a document cited by Cosmas as *Epilogus eiusem tene (sc. Moravie) et Boemie* and his attempt to place all the possible models of *CL* before the years 992–94.

47. For a stimulating discussion of this theme, see Andrew Lass, "The Manuscript Debates," *Cross Currents* 6 (1987): 1–16.

48. Z. Kalandra, *Česke pohanství* (Prague, 1946); Urbánek, *Legenda tak zvaného* (n. 17 above); J. Ludvíkovský, "O Kristiána I," *Naše věda* 26 (1948–49): 209–39, and "O Kristiána II," *Naše věda* 27 (1950): 158–73; 197–216; J. Slavík, "Spor o podvrženou legendu," *Svobodny zitřék* 36 (1947); F. M. Bartoš, "O Dobrovského pojetí," pp. 7–26 (n. 17 above); J. Vajs, *Spisy a projevy Josefa Dobrovského,* vol. 12: *Cyrila a Method Apostolove slovanšti* (Prague, 1948), pp. 101–98.; R. Jakobson, "Minor Native Sources for the Early History of the Slavic Church," *Harvard Slavic Studies* 2 (1954): 39–73.

49. During excavations at Prague castle, graves were uncovered in which armaments and weapons were found that were identical with those found in Great Moravia.

50. O. Králík, "Josef Dobrovský a badání o počatcích českých dějin," *Pocta Zdeňku Nejedlému* (Olomouc, 1959), pp. 73–140; *K počatkum; Sázavské písemnictví XI století Rozpravy československe akademie věd* (Prague, 1960), and "Kreščenije Borživoja i vopros o nepreryvnosti staroslavjanskoj literatury v Čexii," *TODRL* 19 (1963): 148–68; Z. Fiala amd D. Třeštík, "K názorum O. Králíka o václavských a ludmilských legendách," *Československý časopis historický* 9 (1961): 515–31; R. Večerka, "Sázavské pisemnictví XI století," *Listy filologicke* 85 (1962): 190–93; J. Ludvíkovský, "Crescente fide, Gumpold a Kristián," *Sborník prací filosofské fakulty Brneňske university* 501 (1955): 48–66, and "Great Moravia Tradition, pp. 542–48.

51. F. Graus, "Velkomoravská říše v česke středověke tradici," *Československy časopis historický* 11, no. 3 (1963): 289–305, and "Slovanská liturgie a pismenictví," pp. 473–95; R. Večerka, "Cyrilometodějský kult v české středověké tradici," *Československý časopis historický* 12, no. 1 (1964): 40–43; O. Králík, "Nová fáze sporu o slovanskou kulturu v přemyslovských Čechách," *Slavia* (1968): 474–94; Z. Fiala, *Hlavní pramen legendy kristiánovy, Rozpravy československé akademie věd,* vol. 84 (Prague, 1974), and *Přemyslovské Čechy* (Prague, 1975).

52. J. Hamm, "Hrvatski tip crkvenoslavenskog jezika," *Slovo* 13 (1963): 43–67; F. V. Mareš, "Drevneslavjanskij literaturnyj jazyk v velikomoravskom gosudarstve," *Voprosy jazykoznanija* 2 (1961): 12–23; V. Tkadlčík, "Trojí hlalolské i v Kyjevských listech," *Slavia* 25 (1956): 200–16; R. Večerka, "Velikomoravskie istoki" (n. 40 above).

53. See V. Dokoupil, *List of Manuscripts from the Benedictine Library in Rajhrad (Soupis rukopisů knihovny benediktinské v Rajhradě).*

54. J. Ludvíkovský: "Rytmické klauzule kristiánovy legendy a otázka jejího datování," Listy filologické 75 (1951): 169–90; "Crescente fide, Gumpold a Kristián"; "Václavská legenda XIII století 'Ut annuncietur' její poměr k legendě 'Oriente' a otázka autorství," Listy filologické 78 (1955): 196–209; "Nově zjištěný rukopis legendy Crescente fide a jeho vyznam pro datování Kristiána," Listy filologické 81 (1958): 56–58; "Great Moravia Tradition"; "Latinské legendy českého středověku," Sborník prací filosofické fakulty Brneňske university E 18–19 (1973–74): 267–308; and, most recently, Kristiánova legenda.

55. D. Třeštík, "Deset tezí o kristiánově legendě," Folia historica Bohemia 2 (1980): 7–38, and "Kristián a václavské legendy 13 století," Acta Universitatas Carolinae, Philosophica et Historica 2 (1981), Studia Historica 21 (1983): 45–91.

Třeštík's ten theses can be summarized briefly thus: (1) CL is an integral literary work written by one author who is easily distinguished by his individual style; (2) the twelfth-century Ludmilian fragments cannot be the model for CL but only excerpts made for a prayer book; moreover, excerpts from some lost Ludmila legend that could serve as a model for CL are impossible, as they would be stylistically different; (3) CL served as the main source for the Wenceslas legends of the thirteenth and fourteenth centuries; thus it has to be older than the manuscripts dating therefrom; (4) CL could not have arisen during the time before the existence of the cult of Saint Vojtěch—i.e., before the translation of his relics in 1039—the work was commissioned by him; (5) hence, the legend arose either in 992–94, to which the original relates, or in the second half of the eleventh or first (perhaps even second) half of the twelfth century, and is a literary forgery; (6) to date, no one has proved that some author who was writing at the end of the twelfth century used Christian; (7) no one has as yet proved that Christian used any works written after 992–94; (8) to date, no one has found any anachronisms in Christian's work, which usually give the medieval forger away; (9) so far no one has found any motivation for compiling a falsification such as CL would be (why would a falsifier write a legend about four saints and the entire history of Bohemian Christianity instead of a simple legend of the Ludmilian type?); (10) until convincing evidence is found to prove that CL originated in the second half of the eleventh or first half of the twelfth century, we have to consider it genuine.

56. It need hardly be pointed out that, given the self-imposed limitations of this survey, some prominent names and important works have inevitably been omitted.

Prague Glagolitic Fragments

1. Exaposteilarion (Church Slavonic světilьna or světilьnь) is a verse read at matins after the Canon. Some of the exposteilaria in Fols. 1a and 1b are known from the Greek originals, while others are not known from the

Greek but from another Church Slavonic version from the *Sticherarion Chilandaricum*, and from early Russian and Bulgarian sources.

2. Mid-Pentecost (Church Slavonic *prĕpolovlenie*) is the feast halfway to Pentecost, on the twenty-fifth day after Easter, a Wednesday.

3. Cf. Psalms 10:16.

4. Antiphonon (Latin *antiphon*) refers to the verses from a psalm that are chanted or sung in reponse, alternating parts at the beginning of the Liturgy and matins and expressing the significance of the holiday.

5. Cf. Psalms 22:16.

6. *Service and Canon in Honor of Saint Wenceslas*, n. 3.

7. Cf. Psalms 35.

8. The Church Slavonic abbreviation *pĕl* stands for *otъpĕlo*, which is the refrain chanted after the antiphonon.

9. Cf. Psalms 41.

10. Since the vowel *i* (Church Slavonic и) has no "titlo" above it, it does not signify a numeral but the abbreviation of the Church Slavonic word *iskrъ* (Greek *plagios*), "plagal."

11. Kathisma (Church Slavonic *sĕdilьnъ*) is the part of the service when psalms are chanted and during which the congregration is allowed to remain seated. Indeed, the Greek Psalter is subdivided into numbered kathismata.

12. This designation seems to indicate that the Beatitudes (Greek *makarismoi*) are to be sung now.

13. If we can assume that this line follows the Greek original (*Triodion* [Rome, 1879], p. 674), it should read: "Let us imitate the righteous robber."

O Lord, Have Mercy on Us

1. This line in the original manuscript reads *Krleš*, which appears to be a Western Slavic adaptation of the Greek *Kyrie eleison* ("Lord, have mercy"). In the Miscellany (*Sborník*) of Milič from 1480, the hymn appears as follows:

Hospodine, pomiluj ny

Jezu Kriste, pomiluj ny
Ty Spase vseho mira
Spasiž ny i uslyšiž

Hospodine, hlasy nášě
Daj nam všěm, Hospodine
Žizn a mir v zemi
Krleš, krleš

For a detailed study of this work, see Jan Racek, "Sur la question de la genèse du plus ancien chant liturgique tchèque 'Hospodine, pomiluj ny,' " *Magna Moravia* (Prague, 1965), pp. 435–60.

2. I accept the reconstruction of this ancient hymn that was suggested by Roman Jakobson, which preserves the work's original octosyllabic meter

(see "An Old Church Slavonic *Cantilena* in the Czech Patrimony"). The reconstruction here differs slightly from the one he suggested in an earlier work, *Nejstarši česke pisne duchovní*, where lines 5 and 7 read, respectively: "Gospodi, glagoly naše," and "Žiznь i mir na zemli." As stated in the Introduction, F. Mareš's reconstruction of this hymn differs somewhat from Jakobson's but also preserves the octosyllabic meter:

Gospodine pomilui ny

Isu Kriste pomilui

Sъpase vьšego mira
Sъpasi ny i uslyši
Gospodine glasy naše
Dazь nam Gospodine
Žiznь a mirь vъ zemi

(Kъrьles, kъrьles)

The First Church Slavonic Life of Saint Wenceslas

1. The present translation is based on the manuscript that appears in Josef Vajs, ed., *Sborník Staroslovanských Literárních Památek O sv. Václavu a sv. Lidmile* (Prague, 1929), pp. 36–43. It should be noted that many of the following notes are identical with those that accompany my translation of another manuscript of the *First Church Slavonic Life of Saint Wenceslas* known as *The Slaying of Saint Wenceslas, Prince of the Czechs*, which was published in my book, *Medieval Slavic Lives of Saints and Princes* (Ann Arbor, Mich., 1983), pp. 141–61. However, the two works do differ, because the latter work (the so-called *Vostokov Variant*) was subjected to East Slavic redaction.

2. The first part of this passage appears to allude to the beginning of Acts 2:17: "And it shall come to pass in the last days, saith God. . . ." The second part of the passage paraphrases loosely the beginning of Mark 13:12: "Now the brother shall betray the brother to death, and the father the son. . . ." The allusion to the present in the opening lines has been interpreted as a definite indication that this work was written soon after the saint's death. See Václav Chaloupecký, *Na úsvitu kreštanství* (Prague, 1942), p. 257.

3. This passage is elliptic and reads, "i vrazi člvku domašti ego," which translated literally means "and man's foes of his household." I have embellished my translation by following Matthew 10:36 literally.

4. The first half of this passage paraphrases Matthew 10:35: "For I am come to set a man at variance against his father, and the daughter against her mother, and the daughter-in-law against her mother-in-law." The second part of the passage paraphrases Matthew 16:27: "For the son of man shall come in the glory of his father with his angels; and then he shall reward

every man according to his works." Cf. also Psalms 62:12, Jeremiah 25:14, Romans 2:6, and 2 Timothy 4:14. Indeed, the entire opening paragraph (see nn. 2 and 3 above) is made up of paraphrases of biblical texts, which attest to the author's familiarity with the Bible and indicate his mastery of the style of the ancient Cyrillomethodian usage.

5. Vratislav I was a prince of the Přemyslide dynasty and his brother Spytihněv's successor. He is believed to have been born around 883; however, the dates of his rule are uncertain, since Spytihněv's death is placed variously within the decade 905–15. He is a very vague figure in Czech tradition, which has him as a Christian prince and builder of the first Church of St. George in Prague. After the death of Louis III (899–911), taking advantage of the decline of the Eastern Frankish Empire, he extended his power over a considerable Moravian territory. It is generally assumed that he died while defending his country against a Magyar invasion in 920–21. He was succeeded by his son Wenceslas I (see n. 7 below).

6. Drahomira (Dragomira/Drahomir) was the daughter of a Veletian chieftain. The Veletians were a Baltic Slavic tribe who were known as *Ljutici* (Wild or Fierce Men) and for their long and vehement resistance to Christianity. Curiously, however, Drahomira was given in marriage to the Christian ruler of Prague. Upon the death of Vratislav, the government, as well as their children, were entrusted to Ludmila, the latter's grandmother; this gave rise to the ensuing conflict between daughter-in-law and mother-in-law. In the opinion of the Czech chronicler Cosmas of Prague, Drahomira remained a pagan even while living among the Czechs (see *Češskaja xronika* [Moscow, 1962], p. 58). She is also described as a hardened pagan by Gumpold. On the other hand, there are sources that attest to her being a Christian; see V. Novotný, *České dějiny* (Prague, 1912), p. 450. Attributed to her is the murder of her mother-in-law, Ludmila, and the building of St. Michael's church in Tetín.

7. According to tradition, Wenceslas I was born around 906–7 at Stochov near Libušin. Some sources give his date of birth as having been as early as 904. It is a generally accepted practice in translating from Slavic to use the Latin version of his name rather than the Czech, Václav, or the Russian, Vjačeslav.

8. There are two interpretations of the "tonsuring" of young Wenceslas. First, it has been understood to indicate that he was intended for service to the Church. Seven or eight was the usual age for dedicating a boy to a monastery, a practice that was known among the Slavs and other European peoples. Hence the ceremony of hair shearing was a form of commendation; see A. P. Vlasto, *The Entry of the Slavs into Christendom* (Cambridge, 1970), p. 93. This interpretation would be quite plausible were it not for the fact that Wenceslas was the eldest son and, by virtue of primogeniture, destined to succeed to his father's throne. If he had been the younger brother (as has been suggested by one source), how are we to explain why Boleslav was passed over in the succession? Second, this act has been viewed as a ritual

marking a boy's transition from boyhood to adolescence, a practice that was known among the Western and Eastern Slavs but not in the West; see *Skazanija o načale cešskogo gosudarstva* (Moscow, 1970), p. 56. It has also been pointed out that, as described in this work, the tonsure was administered according to the Eastern Rite; see Chaloupecký, p. 257.

9. No bishop of this name is known from any other source. It is possible that he was a bishop of the Slavic Rite in the Archdiocese of Moravia, although the name itself does not appear to be of Slavic origin. It is also possible that Notar is a misconstrued form of the noun for "notary" (*notarь*). The *Vostokov Variant* of this work omits the name of the bishop who performed the tonsuring, while the *Menology Variant* does mention Notar.

10. The present variant of the *Life* does not specify the church in which this ceremony took place. According to the *Vostokov Variant*, it was "in the Church of St. Mary," which was located in Prague. Many scholars have regarded this detail as proof that the *First Church Slavonic Life* was of Czech origin. Only someone intimately familiar with tenth-century conditions in Bohemia could have written about this church; see Chaloupecký, pp. 257–58.

11. The *Vostokov Variant* of the *First Church Slavonic Life* (and the *Second Church Slavonic Life*, chap. 7) notes that Wenceslas also knew Greek, an assertion which is suspect because of the origin of this variant.

12. Apparently, the principle of primogeniture, which was not universally observed at the time, was invoked here by the reigning prince on behalf of his eldest son.

13. Boleslav I of Bohemia (Boleslas I) was the younger brother of Wenceslas. (See also nn. 23 and 42 below.)

14. Cf. Matthew 25:35–36. The list of Wenceslas's good deeds is based on the six corporal works of mercy taken from Matthew 25:35–39 and is frequently included in medieval confessional formularies. Here it echoes the Western (Roman) prayer formularies, which once again indicates that the author of this work was a priest of the Slavic Rite but of Western (Roman) orientation.

15. This passage alludes either to Luke 22:3 ("Then entered Satan into Judas surnamed Iscariot, being of the number of the twelve . . .") or to John 13:2 ("And supper being ended, the devil having put into the heart of Judas Iscariot, Simon's son, to betray him").

16. I have not been able to trace the origin of this quotation. It is not from the Bible.

17. The precise cause of conflict between Wenceslas and Drahomira is a matter for speculation. Perhaps it was because Wenceslas, upon ascending the throne (924/925), had the property appropriated by Drahomira from Ludmila's priests (see *Prologue Life of Saint Wenceslas*, n. 4) returned to them (see Novotný, p. 463), or because Drahomira was fomenting trouble between the Christian and semipagan factions in the country—a charge that

was leveled against her by Wenceslas's friends. Whatever the reason, Wenceslas had his mother banished (see *Prologue Life of Saint Wenceslas*, n. 5).

18. In attributing this thought to his hero, the author uses a small relevant portion from Acts 7:60, changing only "their" to "my." The entire passage reads: "And he kneeled down and cried with a loud voice, 'Lord, lay not this sin to their charge.' And when he said this he fell asleep." Stephen, who spoke these words, was the first martyr of the primitive Christian Church.

19. The Slavic passage substitutes "ignorance" for "transgressions" in the passage from Psalms 25:7: "Remember not the sins of my youth, nor my transgressions: according to thy mercy, remember thou me for thy goodness' sake, O Lord."

20. The term "God's servants" is a metaphor for the clergy or clergymen used in the West. It seems that it became customary in Moravia from the time of Rostislav to assign priests from many nations to serve the newly founded churches. However, "many nations" can be reduced to three in particular, Germany, Italy, and Greece, as indicated in *The Life of Methodius* (see M. Kantor, *Medieval Slavic Lives*, p. 111).

21. The Church of St. Vitus (St. Guy), the patron saint of Saxony who became the national patron of Bohemia, was built in Prague during the years 926–29. Remnants of this ancient church were discovered during archeological excavations made in 1911 and 1928. The original church was built in the form of a rotunda, a shape that Cibulka claimed was inspired by Carolingian architecture and was rather widely imitated in Bohemia (see J. Cibulka, "Václova rotunda sv. Vita," *Svatováclavský sborník* [Prague, 1933], pp. 344–48). However, recent evidence has raised serious doubts about Cibulka's theory and speaks strongly in favor of this architectural style having come to Bohemia from Moravia (see V. Richter, "Die Anfange der Grossmährischen Architektur," *Magna Moravia* [Prague, 1965], pp. 121–360). Today at this location stands the magnificent Gothic Cathedral of Saint Vitus, which dates from the reign of Charles IV (1347–78).

22. St. Emmeram's Day was celebrated on 22 September. He was the patron saint of Bavaria and Regensburg, to which Bohemia was ecclesiastically subordinate. The pledge to Saint Emmeram is connected with events that followed the deaths of Vratislav and Ludmila. Uncertain about the direction Bohemia would take under Drahomira's regency, Arnulf, duke of Bavaria, made a trip to Bohemia, where he was assured by young Wenceslas that all would remain unchanged. As a gesture of good will, Wenceslas promised to dedicate the church he proposed to build to Saint Emmeram. As we know from the foregoing comment, Wenceslas, despite his promise, dedicated the church to Saint Vitus (see F. Dvornik, *The Slavs: Their Early History and Civilization* [Boston, 1959], pp. 106–7).

23. The conflict between Boleslav and his brother, it would seem from the legends, had its roots in their divergent personalities and commitments. Whereas Wenceslas is characterized in the legends as pious and inclined to

the ascetic life, Boleslav was worldly and eager to rule. Furthermore, Wenceslas, at least according to the sources, had identified himself with the Saxons and had personally supported Latin priests, while Boleslav favored the Slavic Church. All sources attest to Wenceslas's Christian virtues; none to the virtues of leadership. Since political realities had not changed after the acceptance of Christianity, Slavic rulers were forced to be military leaders, an ability which Wenceslas apparently lacked and Boleslav possessed. Thus, Boleslav was pushed into leadership of the anti-Saxon party and became an accomplice in his brother's assassination (see Vlasto, pp. 94–96).

24. The feast days of Saints Cosmas and Damian are celebrated on 30 June and 1 November in the Orthodox church but on 27 September in the Roman Catholic church. The church dedicated in their honor in Stará Boleslav no longer exists. In its place now stands St. Wenceslas Church, which some believe incorporated sections of the old church, an opinion not shared by all sources.

25. Boleslav's castle is in present-day Stará Boleslav, a town situated northeast of Prague.

26. A similar passage in the *Second Church Slavonic Life of Saint Wenceslas*, chap. 18, has this event taking place not at Boleslav's castle with friends but in Prague with his retinue. Furthermore, whereas here the expression *načetь igrati*, "began to sport," indicates engaging in sport, perhaps a knightly game, a similar expression in the *Second Church Slavonic Life* seems to refer to some military exhibition.

27. This is the third time counsel has been taken against Wenceslas by the conspirators. This number of occurrences can hardly be taken literally, given the mystical significance of the number three and the fact that "trebling" is a literary cliché in works of this type.

28. The mention of "bells" (*zvonь*) is significant on two counts. In the first place, this noun in Church Slavonic meant "sound," not "bell," which in its present use is an obvious Bohemianism. Second, it indicates that bells were used in Bohemia as early as the tenth century, a custom that probably came from Germany. In the *Menology Variant* of this *Life*, the abstract noun *zvonenie* ("ringing") is used.

29. The present account of the physical struggle between the brothers is similar to the one in the *Menology Variant*, but it differs from the *Vostokov Variant*, which does not mention Wenceslas knocking Boleslav to the ground (see Kantor, *Medieval Slavic Lives*, p. 149).

30. Apparently, Boleslav had ordered the priest to lock the doors to the church in order to prevent Wenceslas from seeking sanctuary. Indeed, an account of a traitorous priest, who on orders from the conspirators locked the church doors, is found in Christian's work.

31. The words of Jesus taken from Luke 23:46 serve as a formula in vitae, both East and West, for the dying words of a saint.

32. The present work refers to Mstina (Mastina) as "etera častna ma vešteslavla," literally, "an honorable man of Wenceslas." Perhaps he was a

nobleman who supported Wenceslas, or one of his retinue. Whichever the case, his is the only death that is mentioned specifically.

33. The persecution of the clergy after Wenceslas's death was limited to those clerics closest to the saint. It was not a resurgence of paganism among Boleslav and his followers.

34. Drahomira fled to the duchy of Croatia and apparently found refuge among the White Croatians, a tribe living north of Prague.

35. According to several legends dealing with Saint Wenceslas (e.g., Christian's), Paul was priest and confessor to Ludmila and Wenceslas. It is to him that Jakobson attributes the lost *Life of Ludmila*; see Roman Jakobson, "Minor Native Sources for the Early History of the Slavic Church," *Harvard Slavic Studies* 2 (1954): 57.

36. A verbatim translation of this line would read, "his blood did not deign to go into the ground" ("krьv že ego ne rači v zmju iti"). The exact meaning of this passage has been a point of controversy among scholars. For a discussion of this, see Chaloupecký, pp. 262–63.

37. Cf. John 2:19. It appears that this is an allusion to Christ's remark, "Destroy this temple, and in three days I will raise it up." There is also the legend of Saint Therapon and the great oak tree that sprang from the earth his blood had soaked; see Hippolyte Delehaye, *The Legends of the Saints* (New York, 1962), pp. 30–31.

38. There is some controversy concerning the significance of this passage. In the opinion of some researchers the expectation of more miracles attests to the great antiquity of this literary monument. On the other hand, O. Králík believed that the author of this work simply lacked sufficient information about the saint's miracles to enable him to enumerate them in a separate section. For further details, see *Skazanija o načale*, p. 58.

39. The year in which Wenceslas died was originally suggested by J. Pekař (*Die Wenzels- und Ludmilalegenden*), on the basis of *Legenda Christiani*, as 929. However, some evidence to shift this date to the year 935—a date claimed to agree more closely with current chronology—has been provided by Z. Fiala (see "Dva kritické přispěvky k starým dějinám českým," *Sborník historický* 9 [1962]). Indeed, the author of one of the most recent studies of medieval Czech culture, Pavel Spunar (see his *Kultura českého středověku* [Prague, 1987], p. 516), also dates the death of Wenceslas at 935. However, F. V. Mareš has argued persuasively for retaining the original dating (see "Das Todesjahr des hl. Wenzel in der I. kirchenslavischen Wenzelslegende," *Wiener Slavische Jahrbuch* 17 (1972): 192–208). The veneration of Wenceslas increased greatly after his death, which was soon accounted a martyrdom. He became a national hero, the national saint, and the celestial protector of the Czech nation.

40. The image of a stony heart is found in Ezekiel 11:19: "And I will give them an heart, and I will put a new spirit within you; and I will take the stony heart out of their flesh, and will give them an heart of flesh." This passage is repeated almost verbatim in Ezekiel 36:26.

41. This passage is a paraphrase of Psalms 51:3: "For I acknowledge my transgressions and my sin is ever before me."

42. In 932, Boleslav, who succeeded to power, had the relics of his brother brought to St. Vitus Church in Prague. It should be noted that Boleslav, like Wenceslas before him, had to accept the overlordship of the king of Saxony, Henry the Fowler (919–36). With the death of Henry in 936, Bohemia was again relatively free and continued to prosper throughout Boleslav's reign. Christianity spread from town to town under the hegemony of Prague, which was constituted a bishopric shortly before Boleslav's death in 967 (see Vlasto, pp. 96–99).

43. The conclusion of this supplication should read: "But Thou, O Lord, have mercy upon us [Ti že, gospodi, pomilui nasь]."

Second Church Slavonic Life of Saint Wenceslas

1. The entire prologue is written in a convoluted style, the result of the author's desire to adhere verbatim to the syntax of the original Latin text. Since he was more concerned with a lexical approximation on the word level than with the coordination of higher syntactic structures, the Slavic version often presents a rather scrambled conglomeration of words. This has caused problems for some of its modern translators. Apparently for this reason, the Czech translation by J. Vašica is based on the Latin text (see J. Vajs, *Sborník*, pp. 84–135), while the Russian translation by A. I. Rogov is very free and takes considerable license with the text (see *Skazanija o načale*, pp. 86–102). Unfortunately, both translations have basically ignored the Church Slavonic text. As opposed to Vašica's work, the most recent Czech translation does indeed offer solutions—with which I am not always in agreement—based on the Slavic text (see *Staroslověnské legendy českého původu*, pp. 154–222). The present translation is based exclusively on my reading of the Slavic text. I have translated everything in the prologue, no matter how obscure the passage.

2. This passage reads as follows: "sei poistině oumomь smyslenyi popravъ mirьskaę igrišta vyšnix želaet, onъže iskovanъ na vysotu čistii gorę duxomь uběgaę mirьskix, vyšnix želaet." I have translated it verbatim. Note, however, that the author seems to be contrasting the qualities of one with those of another; but whatever distinction he wished to make has been lost in the Slavic text. The Latin text does make the distinction: one desires the supernal; the other, the worldly, cf. "Hic namque mente moderatus, spreto caducorum ludicro, superna intendit, ille extructos in altum honores ardenti rerum fugacium siti exaestuans desiderat" ("For one with a well-ordered mind, having spurned the folly of fleeting things, seeks the supernal; another, with a raging thirst for fleeting things, desires high honors").

3. These words seem to indicate the use of an armillary sphere, an astronomical instrument utilized in ancient times to determine the position of heavenly bodies.

4. I have interpreted the noun *žatva* (reaping) in the sentence "kaa ili kakova měra zemskago veličestvia počatok, eterym aki tainym stroimь po obrazъcem geometrьskim na istinnouju žatvu obujati istegnęt" to mean "end of the world." The notion of the end of the world, expressed metaphorically by "reaping," is consistent with a biblical image (cf. Matthew 13:24; Revelations 14:14–16). It also appears in other saints' lives, cf. "žatva bo est člvčju rodu smrt" ("for reaping is death to the human race"); see *Žitie Nikolaja Mirlikijskogo i poxvala emu* as quoted in *Slovar' russkogo jazyka XI–XVII vv.* (Moscow, 1978), 5:77.

5. This statement reveals a familiarity with the monochord, an instrument used in ancient times to measure and demonstrate the mathematical relations of musical tones.

6. Otto II was emperor of the Holy Roman Empire during the years 973–83. The fact that he is mentioned by name helps in determining the approximate date the work was written. Since Gumpold's *Vita* was commissioned by him, we can date the manuscript around the year 980. This date is more likely when viewed in the context of the prologue (see following note).

7. On Christmas 980 or, at the latest, at the beginning of 981, there was a public disputation in Ravenna at the request of Emperor Otto II, who acted as arbiter. The dispute concerned the divisions of philosophy, and the principal opponents were Gerbert, an authority on astronomy, geometry, and mathematics, and Otric (Ohtrich), the learned rector of the episcopal school at Magdeburg (see Chaloupecký, p. 277). It would seem, therefore, that Gumpold's prologue is referring to these new pursuits, which, much to the chagrin of the hagiographer, were forcing the writing of saints' lives to take second place to the interest in and enthusiasm for philosophy and mathematics.

8. The reference here seems to be to the First Council of Nicaea, which was convened in 325 by Constantine the Great in an effort to put an end to the Arian doctrine that Christ was not divine because he was created by the Father and grew and changed as a man, hence was mutable and not coeternal with the Father. The Nicene Creed answered the charges of the Arians by stating that the Son was "of one substance with the Father."

9. Henry I, called Henry the Fowler (919–36), was the first of the Saxon line of German kings to rule Germany. He is generally recognized as one of the Holy Roman emperors, hence the reference to him as "King of the Franks and Romans"; cf. "prěsvtlym crmъ enr ěxom fratьskim i rimskimъ" (lit.: "serene Frankish and Roman majesty Henry").

10. Very little is known about Bořivoj, whose historicity is doubted by some researchers. According to Czech tradition, Bořivoj of Prague (his castle has been placed at Levý Hradec, just north of Prague) was the first of his line to be converted, having been baptized by Methodius himself in 894. The Czech chronicler Cosmas of Prague mentions this in two separate entries. One states that Bořivoj was baptized in 894, the other, that he was baptized by Methodius. However, both of these statements cannot be accurate, since

Methodius died in 885. Therefore, the date of Bořivoj's baptism, if it ever occurred, has to be placed before 885. In the opinion of A. P. Vlasto (*Entry of the Slavs into Christendom*, pp. 86–88), it should be placed in the mid-870s, during Methodius's second Moravian period. At this time Bohemia was falling under the domination of Moravia. Other Bohemian sources (cf. *Passion of Ludmila, Legenda Christiani, A Brief Account*) also speak of Bořivoj as the first prince of Bohemia to accept Christianity, as does the so-called Moravian Legend, in which, after being shamed by Svatopluk, he decides to be baptized together with thirty of his followers. Whatever the facts, it is not unreasonable to assume that Bořivoj did indeed exist, was Christianized, and died sometime around the year 891/892.

This is the approximate time that the reign of his son Spytihněv begins. A number of Latin sources (cf. *Crescente fide* and Gumpold's *Vita*) credit him with being the first to convert to Christianity. Bořivoj, however, is not even mentioned in Gumpold's Latin work, the reason being undoubtedly political. Since the German-Catholic hierarchy did not wish to recognize the activity of Saints Cyril and Methodius and their disciples among the Slavs in general and among the Bohemians in particular, they did not recognize the Bohemians as Christians until after 885, when Spytihněv seceded from Moravia and subjected his territory and church to German sovereignty. As a result, Bořivoj's Moravian connection was ignored, while Spytihněv's Roman orientation was emphasized.

Nowhere is there anything stated about Spytihněv's baptism. During his reign Bavaria became the dominant influence in Prague and the principal source of Latin-Christian culture in Bohemia. One result was that Bohemia became a bone of contention between Saxony and Bavaria, a rivalry that reached crucial proportions during the reign of Spytihněv's nephew, Wenceslas. Spytihněv's death, though generally believed to have been around the year 915, has also been given within the ten-year period 905–15. He was succeeded by his brother, Vratislav I.

11. According to Chaloupecký (p . 278), the first church was built in honor of the Blessed Mother the Virgin Mary by Bořivoj, and later rebuilt by Spytihněv. The second church, dedicated to Saint Peter the Apostle, was built at Budeč. Some, however, have claimed that it is not certain who built the first church in Prague.

12. See *First Church Slavonic Life*, n. 5.

13. The Church of St. George was founded by Vratislav I in Prague. It was rebuilt several times before approximately 1142. Since that time it has survived without any significant changes. At the end of the tenth century, a convent for Benedictine nuns was added to it. The daughter of Boleslav I, the blessed Mlada-Marie, was its first abbess.

14. See *First Church Slavonic Life*, n. 7.

15. See *Prologue Life*, n. 5. This work refers to the saint's tutor in Budeč as Učen, which could be an epithet meaning "learned." It is curious that this priest is not mentioned in Gumpold's Latin work. A priest by the name of

Uenno is mentioned in *Crescente fide*. If indeed Wenceslas knew Greek, it would confirm that this language was indispensable in Slavic ecclesiastical circles for as long as the Cyrillomethodian literary tradition was fostered in Bohemia.

16. The name Otto, an obvious error by Gumpold, is repeated in the Church Slavonic text in a confused form. The consonant *g* is added to the name, which then means "ready," rather than "Otto" (cf. *gotovoju* for *otovoju*). The emperor in question is Henry I (see n. 9 above).

17. It is curious that this work does not mention that Wenceslas also studied Slavic books, a fact confirmed by the *First Church Slavonic Life* (see n. 11 above).

18. The reference for this quotation is given by Chaloupecký (p. 140) as 2 Timothy 4:2. If this is indeed the source, the Slavic rendition of that passage is barely recognizable: cf. "Preach the work; *be instant in season, out of season;* rebuke, exhort with all long-suffering and doctrine" (italics mine). The Kazan' Manuscript inexplicably omits the verb "taught" (*uča*) which is found in the Petersburg Manuscript: cf. "dobrě i nedobrě obličaę" and "dobrě uča i nedobrě obličaę." My translation follows the latter source.

19. It has been suggested that the word for "host" in the Slavic text, *proskura*, rather than the Latin derivative for host, *oplat* (Latin: *oblatum*), was introduced into the text when it was being copied in Russia (see Chaloupecký, p. 278). This word is derived from the Greek *prosfora*, which indicates leavened bread; it is used in the Liturgy of the Eastern Rite to designate the bread for the Sacrifice of the Mass.

20. See *First Church Slavonic Life*, n. 35.

21. See *Prologue Life*, n. 4. The noun "vision" (*videnie*) is omitted from this passage in the Kazan' Manuscript but included in the Petersburg Manuscript: cf. "domu po istině razrěšenie moego" and "domu po istine razrěšenie viděnia moego." The translation is based on the latter source.

22. See *First Church Slavonic Life*, n. 6. There is a fundamental difference between the treatment of Drahomira in this work and in the *First Church Slavonic Life*. The latter work refers to her as a good Christian and fails to mention the part she played in the murder of Ludmila. This work refers to her as a vile pagan who had her mother-in-law strangled. The difference can be explained by the source of the present work. Gumpold's *Vita* was influenced by the Bavarian Recension of *Crescente fide*, which placed Drahomira in a dim light.

23. The name Drahomira (Dragomira/Dragomir') is constructed on the Slavic roots for "dear"/"precious" (*drah*) and "world"/"peace" (*mir*). Hence, the name would translate as something like "dear to"/"beloved of the world" or, perhaps, "precious peace." Either epithet, in the eyes of the author, could not be further from the truth—"an obvious mistake."

24. The word for Bohemia is corrupt in the text, reading *emъstě*. Apparently the beginning of the word was lost in transcription.

25. These are only the first and last parts of the quotation from 1 Corinthians 13:11. The entire passage reads: "When I was a child, I spake as a child, I understood as a child, I thought as a child; but when I became a man, I put away childish things."

26. In order to bring this passage closer to the scriptural passage to which it refers (cf. 1 Corinthians 13:11), I have added the words "the things of." The Slavic text simply reads "zavergox ounostь" (lit.: "I have done away with youth").

27. See *First Church Slavonic Life*, n. 17. Although both Slavic *Lives* mention Drahomira's banishment, the *First Church Slavonic Life* (as well as *Legenda Christiani*) speak of her being recalled to Prague. It is understandable that Gumpold would not have known about either event but surprising that a subsequent Slavic translator-author would include information about her banishment yet omit her recall.

28. That is, Boleslav I of Bohemia (Boleslas I).

29. See *First Church Slavonic Life*, n. 21.

30. Regensburg is corrupt in the Slavic text and reads *rezanьskomu* (? Rjazan'). This scribal error may reflect the similarity between this form and the Czech word for Regensburg, *Rezno*.

31. This work was written when Bohemia came under the jurisdiction of the bishop of Regensburg in Bavaria. His name was Tuto (893–930).

32. Opinions divide on the purpose of this trip. One view is that Wenceslas's strong ascetic leanings, coupled with his desire to be tonsured, prompted his wish to travel to Rome. But it has also been suggested that the object of this trip could have been to promote an independent bishopric for Prague.

33. That is, to the successor of the "Holy Apostle Peter," the pope.

34. The account of Wenceslas's "consorting with a woman," the birth of a son, Izbrjaslav (Czech: Zbraslav), and his vow of chastity are not included in any other source dealing with the saint's life. *Legenda Christiani* suggests that Wenceslas was married. It is possible that he was forced into marriage because his boyars wanted an heir to the throne. However, this seems to be contradicted by the account in this work (see also n. 36 below).

35. Cf. Peter's words to Ananias in Acts 5:4: "While it remained, was it not thine own? and after it was sold, was it not thine own power? why hast thou conceived this thing in thine heart? thou hast not lied unto men, but unto God."

36. These words are addressed to his wife as well as to his servant.

37. The meaning of this line can perhaps be best explained by remarking on the significance of a vow to God. Both Wenceslas and the woman vowed to observe chastity. Sinning against this vow did not in any way remove their basic obligation to remain chaste. Thus, the woman was obliged to live up to her vow to God even after sinning with the saint's servant. Although given in marriage to that servant to extricate her from an embarrassing situation at court, she nevertheless remained bound by her vow and, consequently, became a "sister" to her husband (see J. Pekař, *Die Wenzels- und*

Ludmilalegenden, p. 45). It should be recalled that the woman's sin is not called adultery but a breach of promise to God (thus Wenceslas's rebuke, "Why have you lied before God?"). This raises an interesting question. Did Wenceslas marry? The Slavic passage here is rather ambiguous. Literally, the phrase *priloži k sebě ženou* translates as "he joined to himself a woman," which would imply that he did not marry. Perhaps this is why the woman's sin was not called adultery and why no reference is made to any special ecclesiastical dispensation dissolving the "marriage." It also seems unlikely that Wenceslas's sense of morality would accommodate divorce.

38. See *First Church Slavonic Life,* n. 25.

39. See ibid., n. 24.

40 See ibid., n. 26. It would appear, on the basis of evidence from *Crescente fide* and Christian, that the *First Church Slavonic Life* recorded this incident in a confused form. This so-called game probably took place in Prague where Wenceslas, knowing that death awaited him at Boleslav's castle, bade his relatives and friends farewell after staging a military exhibition for the benefit of his brother's messengers. This was meant to suggest that, were he so disposed, he could command his retinue to do battle with his treacherous brother.

41. That is, Michael the Archangel, who escorts souls to heaven. In the Western Church the feast of Saint Michael is celebrated on the twenty-ninth of September. The day of the murder of Saint Wenceslas, Monday, 28 September, was the vigil of this feast. In the Eastern Church the feast of Saint Michael is celebrated on 8 November.

42. I have added the noun *men* to this elliptic sentence, which reads simply: "bratъ že ego ko svoim reče" (lit.: "Then his brother said to his").

43. According to the *First Church Slavonic Life,* Wenceslas was attacked and murdered on his way to matins, an account repeated in *Crescente fide* and *Legenda Christiani.* Only Gumpold's *Vita* states that Wenceslas was slain *after* matins.

44. At this point the Petersburg Manuscript adds: "takomu glu sladkomu" ("to this pleasant speech"). I note differences between the Kazan' and Petersburg Manuscripts only when they involve entire phrases; in other instances I simply made the change on the basis of the Petersburg Manuscript. The numerous differences in individual words have been noted by Vašica (see Vajs, pp. 84–124). Boleslav's reply to his brother is translated as it appears in both manuscripts, viz. "dnъ ti lěpěi pirъ ustroi." It has been suggested that the verb in this sentence should be read as a first-person singular rather than as an imperative (*ustroju* for *ustroi*), hence, "I'll arrange an even better feast for you today" (see Vajs, p. 111).

45. I have added the verb *shed* and the gerund *shedding* to Wenceslas's address to his brother. The Slavic construction in both cases is elliptic. Cf. "da by sę ot moeju rouku tvoe krovъ, brate, na poslědnem soudě ot mene vziskala" (lit. : "But I, brother, do not wish to be held accountable at the Last

Judgment for your blood from my hands"); and "a sam sę bratneju kroviju ne
ogrěši" (lit.: "but do not sin through a brother's blood yourself").

46. The first day of each month in the Roman calendar was called calends. From this day the days of the preceding month were counted backward
to the ides, which fell on the 15th of March, May, July, and October, and on
the thirteenth of every other month. In this system, both the calends itself
and the day in question were counted when calculating time. Hence, count-
ing October as the first day of calends, 28 September—the day of Wenceslas's
death—was the fourth day before the calends of October. Wenceslas died in
the year 929.

47. I have added the verb *began* to this elliptic sentence, which reads:
"priimšou že posemъ knęženie velikię nepravdy knęzju boleslavou" (lit.:
"Then, when Prince Boleslav took over, a reign of great injustice").

48. The "his" in the last two paragraphs refers to Wenceslas.

49. At this point the Petersburg Manuscript adds: "a druzii otlučeni
sluxa svoego i gla žitie svoe v nenavisti vsěm svoim bližnim zle okončasa"
("And some, after losing their hearing and speech, ended their life badly,
despised by all their neighbors").

50. The Rokytnice is one of the streams flowing into the Moldau, which
flows through Prague.

51. The reference to Peter walking on the sea is from Matthew 14:27–
29.

52. It has been pointed out by Chaloupecký (p. 281) that the passage
describing the incorrupt body of Wenceslas was taken from a Latin sermon
for the feast of the translation of the relics of Saint Wenceslas. This sermon
has been attributed to Saint Vojtěch (Adalbert of Prague), and was composed
between the years 992 and 994.

53. Cf. Jonah 1:17 and 2:10.

54. See *First Church Slavonic Life,* n. 42. The actual date of the translation was 4 March. The confusion of the numerals 3 and 4 resulted from the
differing numerical values of the letter *g,* in Glagolitic 4 but in Cyrillic 3. In
copying the text from the Glagolitic, the scribe apparently failed to change
the numeral to its proper Cyrillic equivalent.

55. Cf. Acts 5:18, 12:7–8, and 16:23–26. The theme of liberating prisoners expresses the new Christian morality, which criticizes the old moral
code. From a Christian viewpoint, the penalties formerly imposed upon
transgressors were unjust and cruel. It will be recalled that in chapter 7 the
saint destroyed every prison in every town (castle) and ordered that every
gibbet be struck down. This appears to be another aspect of this motif, a deed
for which Saint Wenceslas is exalted.

56. The prince referred to in this passage is Boleslav.

57. Chaloupecký (p. 281) mentions a legend concerning a certain King
Edmund (written around 980) which claims that his hair and nails kept
growing after his death and had to be trimmed each year. Only the present
work records the incident of an eagle guarding the body of the saint's ser-

vant. However, it is of interest to note that the bodies of Saints Bacchus, Vincent, Vitus, Florian, and Stanislaus of Cracow were protected from marauding dogs by birds of prey. Furthermore, Talmudic writings record that Solomon summoned an eagle to guard the body of David (see Delehaye, *Legends of the Saints*, p. 22).

58. The Kazan' Manuscript inadvertently omits the subject of this sentence (woman) which was added on the basis of the Petersburg Manuscript (cf. "Povědaetsę byvši v tomže gradě ideže stgo tělo počivaet viděnia očiju lišena" : "In the same town where the saint's body rests there lived who lost sight in her eyes").

59. The persons being referred to here are not specified. It seems, however, they they would be either the creditors or the jailors of the one who was seized.

Service and Canon in Honor of Saint Wenceslas

1. That is, the month of September.

2. See *Prague Glagolitic Fragments*, n. 11.

3. The Church Slavonic texts of the divine service in the Orthodox Church are sung in one of eight tones (*glas*), or modes, which are known as the Dorian, Phrygian, Lydian, Mixolydian (tones 1, 3, 5, 7, respectively) and Hypodorian, Hypophrygian, Hypolydian, and Hypomixolydian (tones 2, 4, 6, 8, respectively). This system is based on the eight Greek modes, a descending musical scale based on the tetrachord.

4. The books for the Divine Service indicate that a text is sung using the melody of another, better-known text, the first words of which are given.

5. The kontakion (Church Slavonic: *kondak*) is a hymn of praise. It is chanted to the glory of the Saviour, the Virgin Mary, or in praise of a saint.

6. According to Vašica, the word used to express "gift" (*rovanie*) in this passage is unknown in Eastern and Southern Church Slavonic. Thus, he considers its use as proof of the Western, specifically Czech, origin of this text (see *Na úsvitu*, p. 263).

7. The stichira (Church Slavonic: *stixira*) is a hymn the strophes of which follow the reading of certain verses of certain psalms. In the present context they belong to the standing evening psalm "I cried unto the Lord . . ." (cf. Psalms 3:4 and 142:1). This type of hymn is one of the most prevalent forms and is chanted in praise of a saint or a church feast. The stichira strophes are called "Apósticha" in modern liturgicological language.

8. These liturgical chants were intended to commemorate the anniversary of Saint Wenceslas's martyrdom, 28 September, as the words of this passage indicate. However, as Vašica pointed out, they were also used for the feast of the translation of his relics, 4 March.

9. Cf. Luke 23:46.

10. I have added the noun "hymn" (*stixira*) to the translation. The Church Slavonic text simply has the adjective "another" (*ino*). It is given in the neuter gender, since it would have modified the neuter noun *pěnije* ("ode").

11. The "highest calling" refers to martyrdom.

12. This appears to be a reference to Wenceslas's death at the doors of the church.

13. This passage has been interpreted as proof of the Czech origin of this text from a time before the Christianization of Rus'. However, the argument in favor of such an interpretation is weak and unconvincing (see *Staroslověnské legendy*, pp. 245–46).

14. That is, the Church.

15. See n. 10 above.

16. In the Eastern Church, the canon (not to be confused with the canon of the Roman Liturgy which is the eucharistic prayer used at mass) is a special group of hymns or odes that glorify a saint or a biblical event. Each canon is divided into odes, which consist of an introductory verse (*jermos*; Greek: *hiermos* or *hirmes*) and have a fixed rhythm and melody that set the rhythmic and melodic pattern for the following stanzas, and several strophes (*tropari*; Greek: *troparia*), which in part continue the theme of the *jermos*, following its rhythmic and melodic pattern and expressing the essence of the celebrated holy event, or delineating the principal features in the life and deeds of the glorified saint. The canon ended with a hymn to the Mother of God or "God-Bearer," called *Bogorodičen* in Church Slavonic (Greek: *Theotokion*). The canon itself is composed of nine (or eight) odes, the second being omitted if the Liturgy was celebrated at any other time than during Lent. Since the feast of Saint Wenceslas was never celebrated during Lent, the second ode was never composed. However, the Canon in honor of Saint Wenceslas has a "theotokion"-strophe at the end of each ode. This reveals an older liturgical tradition that is known from early Eastern Christian manuscripts.

17. The first verse contains only the initial words of the hymn in the Church Slavonic text. The entire first verse is given for the odes in the modern Czech translation of this work (see *Staroslověnské legendy*, pp. 229–35).

18. Cf. Exodus 15:19.

19. I have added the phrase "To the Mother of God." The Slavic text simply concludes each ode with the *Bogorodičen* (see n. 16 above).

20. A literal translation of this adjective (*dušegubьnyi*) would be "soul-destroying."

21. The reference here is obviously to the Church Slavonic *Lives* of Saint Wenceslas, where we read that the walls of the church were spattered with the saint's blood when he was martyred, and his blood could not be wiped clean.

22. This same motif is met in a hymn preceding the canon (see n. 13 above).

23. Every strophe of this ode ends with this phrase save the last one. Thus it is indicated in abbreviated form at the end of the second and third strophes.

24. The Latin designation for the land of the Czechs, Bohemia, has been viewed by some researchers (e.g., Novotný) as proof that the canon is a translation of a Latin original. However, Matějka has shown that this conjecture is most unlikely (see his "On Translating from Latin into Church Slavonic," *American Contributions to the Sixth International Congress of Slavists* [The Hague, 1968]).

25. Except for the last one, every strophe of this ode ends with this phrase. Thus it is indicated in abbreviated form at the end of the second and third strophes.

26. See *Prague Glagolitic Fragments*, n. 1. In Church Slavonic the name is derived from the root for "light" (*světъ*), since this morning prayer (or matin-song) was chanted after the matin's canon, as dawn was breaking.

Prologue Life of Saint Ludmila

1. The day referred to here is 16 September (920). This date has been observed in Bohemia from time immemorial as the feast-day of Saint Ludmila. It should be noted that, according to the Latin legends, *Fuit in provincia Boemorum* and *Legenda Christiani*, Ludmila died on the fifteenth of September. That date is unlikely, as Ludmila died on a Saturday, which in the year 920 fell on the sixteenth.

2. "Serbian" in this context undoubtedly refers to the Lusatian Serbs (or Sorbs) who were neighbors to the Czechs. This seems to be further reinforced by other sources, which report that Ludmila came from the land of the Milčane. Upper Lusatia was known as Milsko. Ludmila was the daughter of Slavibor who, according to the Czech chronicler Cosmas of Prague, was "a dignitary from the town of Pšov" (see *Staroslověnské legendy*, p. 276).

3. See *Second Church Slavonic Life*, n. 10.

4. Cf. Matthew 28:19.

5. See *Second Church Slavonic Life*, n. 11.

6. The Latin legend *Fuit in provincia Boemorum* states that Ludmila and Bořivoj had three sons and three daughters. Cosmas of Prague writes that "Bořivoj begot two sons." However, the majority of manuscripts agree with the number stated herein. Nevertheless, given the mystical significance and stereotyped usage of the number three, and the fact that only two sons are known by name (Spytihněv and Vratislav), the actual number of children remains uncertain.

7. Tombstone inscriptions in ancient Bohemia usually stated the year in which an individual died. However, no tangible evidence of the historical

existence of Bořivoj has ever been found. Nevertheless, he is treated historically, and it is generally assumed that he was born around the year 855,
married Ludmila around 873, was baptized around 874, and died around 891/
892. See *Second Church Slavonic Life*, n. 10.

8. Cf. Psalms 37:5.

9. See *First Church Slavonic Life*, n. 5.

10. See ibid., n. 7.

11. See ibid., n. 6.

12. The town of Tetín was located near the present-day city of Beroun
on the Mze River. It was given to Ludmila as her widow's grant.

13. *Legenda Christiani* records the names of Ludmila's murderers as
Tionam and Gommon (see *Legenda Christiani*, n. 32).

14. The translation of Ludmila's relics was part of the canonization
process (see *Prologue Life of Saint Wenceslas*, n. 4). It took place on 21
October 925. However, the feast of the translation of Ludmila's relics was
observed on 10 October, the day in the year 926 when her relics were depos-
ited in the Church of St. George.

15. See *Second Church Slavonic Life*, n. 13.

Prologue Life of Saint Wenceslas

1. That is, 28 September, the day of Saint Wenceslas's martyrdom. It
should be noted that the *Prologue Life* repeats in a highly condensed form
much of the information contained in the *First Church Slavonic Life*.

2. See *First Church Slavonic Life*, n. 5.

3. According to the Vostokov Variant of the *First Church Slavonic Life*,
Vratislav and Drahomira had four daughters in addition to their sons, Wenceslas and Boleslav. Of the former only the name of one, Přibyslava, who was
given in marriage to a Croatian prince, has come down to us. The present
work introduces a third brother, Spytihněv, into the family. Some scholars
have assumed that this is an error and that Wenceslas's Uncle Spytihněv was
mistakenly thought to be his brother. However, others maintain that there
were three brothers and that Spytihněv died. It is noteworthy that no other
manuscript, either Latin or Slavic, mentions three brothers, while Cosmas
of Prague speaks of only two sons. See also *First Church Slavonic Life*, nn.
13, 23, and 42, and *Second Church Slavonic Life*, n. 10.

4. Tradition holds that Ludmila (Ludmilla/Ljudmila) was an ardent
Christian. She was the unfortunate victim of Drahomira's abortive bid for
power. Encouraged, it seems, by a powerful party of semipagan nobles,
Drahomira had her mother-in-law strangled during a palace revolt immediately following Vratislav's death (16 September 920/921). Her death made a
deep impression on the people, and she was soon considered a martyr to the
faith. Her canonization has been dated variously as occurring between the
tenth and twelfth centuries.

5. The ancient site of the town of Budeč, located northwest of Prague, is remarkably well preserved to this day. Also preserved are the ruins of the Church of SS. Peter and Paul, to which was attached the school where Wenceslas was educated.

6. According to both the *First* and *Second Church Slavonic Lives*, Wenceslas came to Boleslav's castle to celebrate the Feast of Saints Cosmas and Damian, and not for the consecration of a church. See *First Church Slavonic Life*, n. 24.

7. There are two interpretations of how the sentence, "bě bo jazykomь lstisvymь pače života svoego ljubje . . .," should be understood. The question concerns the treatment of the aorist *bě*, whether it is an independent verb (as Vajs interprets it) or a passive participle that may translate a Greek passive, *bě ljubje*, "was loving" (as Mareš interprets it). My translation follows the former interpretation.

8. See *First Church Slavonic Life*, n. 30.

9. For some reason the present manuscript omits the name Tista, which is found in every manuscript that gives names, as one of the subjects of the dual form of the aorist *rassěkosta* ("cut down"). Some manuscripts simply mention "two boyars."

10. Cf. Luke 23:46. See also *First Church Slavonic Life*, n. 31.

11. See *Second Church Slavonic Life*, chap. 21.

12. Cf. Genesis 4:10.

13. See *First Church Slavonic Life*, n. 21.

Translation of Saint Wenceslas

1. That is, 4 March.

2. See *First Church Slavonic Life*, nn. 5, 6. The name of Wenceslas's mother is corrupt in this work and should read as Drahomira.

3. Boleslav was Wenceslas's younger brother, according to both the *First* and *Second Church Slavonic Lives*. See *First Church Slavonic Life*, n. 13. It has been suggested that this statement was motivated by a desire to compare Boleslav to Svatopluk, the elder brother and murderer of Saints Boris and Gleb.

4. See *First Church Slavonic Life*, n. 37.

5. Cf. Isaiah 48:4.

6. Cf. Psalms 51:3.

7. The last line in this sentence is elliptic, and I have added the words "he should be buried," cf. "iděže bě samь reklъ sъtvorь crkvь tou" (lit.: "where he himself had said, having built a church here"). "He," obviously, refers to Wenceslas.

8. There is a curious omission of the preposition "from" (otъ) in this passage, without which the sentence reads: "awaiting the resurrection of Our Lord Jesus Christ" ("čajušte vъskresenija ga našego isъ xa"). This same omission is found in the *Vostokov Variant* of the *First Church Slavonic Life*.

The *Croatian-Glagolitic Variant* of this *Life* reads: "awaiting the resurrection of their bodies in Christ Jesus Our Lord." Cf. also 1 Corinthians 1:7.

Life of Saint Vitus

1. Lucania, which derived its name from the Lucanians, its conquerors (fifth century B.C.), is the ancient designation of a territory in southern Italy that corresponded approximately to the modern-day region of Basilicata. It was there that the legend of Saint Vitus arose (ca. 600 A.D.) on the basis of the legend of Saint Potita. Later it was variously altered in France, northern Italy, and Germany. However, this legend relates that Vitus was martyred in Lucania rather than in Sicily (ca. 303–4 A.D.), as is the case in several Latin legends of Saint Vitus; see L. Matějka, "Dvije crkvenoslavenske legende o svetom Vidu," *Slovo* 23 (1973): 73–96, and G. Kappel, "Die slavische Vitus-legende und ihr lateinisches Original," *Wiener slavistisches Jahrbuch* 20 (1974): 71–85.

2. According to tradition, Vitus was martyred during the reign of the emperor Diocletian (284–303). Because of his Dalmatian origin (he was born in the town of Dioclea), Gaius Aurelius Valerius was named Diocletian (Diocletianus). He was the Roman emperor under whom the last extensive and bloody persecutions of Christians occurred. With regard to Antonius, no such ruler has been attested; but Diocletian did create a tetrarchy that shared rule of the empire in order to reduce the danger of usurpation. He appointed his friend Maximian as his equal (286), and in 293 he appointed two more emperors, Galerius and Constantius Chlorus—the former to serve under him, the latter, under Maximian. Hence, historically, the "other" emperor was Maximian.

3. Saint Vitus was a youthful martyr of the late third or early fourth century. The details of his life and martyrdom are legendary. He was reckoned among the Fourteen Holy Helpers and was invoked for protection against various diseases, including epilepsy and the nervous disorder called chorea (popularly known as St. Vitus's dance). Thus he became the patron saint of dancers and actors. Saint Vitus was first mentioned along with Modestus and Crescentia in the fifth-century Hieronymic *Martyrology*. Allegedly his relics were translated in 836 to the Abbey of Corvey in Westphalia, whence Saint Wenceslas is believed to have obtained part of them. He was venerated in Italy, Germany (particularly Saxony), and Bohemia, where he became the patron saint. The cathedral at Prague castle was dedicated to him (see *First Church Slavonic Life of Saint Wenceslas*, n. 21). Subsequently, more than thirteen hundred churches and altars were consecrated in his name.

The similarity between the names of this Christian saint and the West Slavic pagan god Sventevit is a rather curious phenomenon. According to Matějka, the monks of Corvey used the name of Saint Vitus as a substitute for the deity Sventevit in order to transform his pagan cult into a Christian one (see "The Creative Use of Church Slavonic," *To Honor Roman Jakobson*, p. 1308). The connection between the two names is also discussed in L. Niederle, *Slavjanskie drevnosti* (Moscow, 1956), p. 283. The practice of identifying pagan gods with Christian saints was commonly employed by the Church in its efforts to convert pagans. Of course, the political dominance of Saxony at the time provided an equally important reason for dedicating the church in Prague to its patron saint.

4. This type of activity is a hagiographical commonplace.

5. The wearing of a hair shirt to mortify the flesh was a common Christian ascetic practice; see *Second Church Slavonic Life of Saint Wenceslas*, chap. 8.

6. Cf. Psalms 111:1.

7. Cf. Matthew 3:17.

8. As Sicily was colonized by the Greeks, the Greek name of Vitus's father, Hylas, adds a touch of authenticity.

9. Cf. Genesis 1:2–5.

10. Cf. Exodus 20:11.

11. For the sake of clarity, I have substituted the word *father* for the ambiguous third-person pronoun *he* in this translation.

12. The names of these gods are corrupt in the Slavic text and read: "... ounobema erьkoulě i minьerьvamъ." The Latin breviary text has: "Nescis deos immortales esse Iovem, Martem, Vestam, Herculem et Minervam" (see Chaloupecký, *Na úsvitu*, p. 267). Diocletian and Maximian adopted the divine surnames Jovius and Herculus, respectively (i.e., Jupiter's representative on earth and the fulfiller of Jupiter's will—names symbolic of their relationship).

13. Cf. John 1:29.

14. Valerian was not the emperor but the administrator of Sicily.

15. It was specifically about the matter of sacrifice that the emperor felt most strongly, as he wished to revive the ancient pagan religion of Rome. At the close of the third century A.D., Diocletian is known to have ordered all Christians expelled from the civil and military service if they refused to make sacrifices. Indeed, refusal to do so was considered an affront to the gods, a view that led to an edict (ca. 304) commanding all subjects of the empire to make sacrifices. This period of intolerance lasted until the abdication of Diocletian and Maximian in 305. Diocletian died in 313 in Dalmatia, at Split.

16. The word *filled* is omitted from the Slavic text in the *Uspenskij sborník*; cf. "blaženyi že vitь čistъ sy dxa stgo" (lit.: "blessed Vitus, being pure of the Holy Ghost"). This addition was made on the basis of the Latin text.

17. Cf. Acts 7:55.

18. This entire phrase is omitted in the Slavic text. The addition was made on the basis of the Glagolitic fragment of the office in the honor of Saint Vitus.

19. Cf. Psalms 111:1.

20. Cf. 1 Kings 13:4.

21. For the sake of clarity I have substituted the words *the lad's* for the ambiguous pronoun *his*.

22. Cf. Matthew 14:26.

23. Cf. Matthew 8:26.

24. For the sake of clarity I have replaced the ambiguous pronoun *he* with *the youth*.

25. Cf. Psalms 51:17.

26. For the sake of clarity I have replaced the ambiguous pronoun *he* with *his father*.

27. Cf. Exodus 3:6.

28. Cf. Psalms 86:16.

29. Cf. Psalms 79:10 and 115:2.

30. This passage seems to allude to Revelations 8:2: "And I saw the seven angels which stood before God; and to them were given seven trumpets."

31. For the sake of clarity I have substituted *his father* for the ambiguous third-person pronoun *he*.

32. The Slavic expression in this instance is "děvy čisty" (lit.: "pure virgins"). Since the reference here is to the virgins consecrated to the goddess Vesta, the translation takes this into account.

33. Cf. Tobit 11:7–15.

34. Cf. Job 2:7 and 42:10.

35. These names are corrupt in the Slavic text and read: "otvьržeši li se dija i aroema i erkoulě ounouna i minegma." The translation follows in part the Latin text.

36. The Slavic text includes only Vitus's answer. Hence, I have added "Saint Vitus said."

37. Cf. Matthew 9:28–29.

38. Cf. Acts 9:18.

39. For the sake of clarity I have substituted *the boatman* for the ambiguous pronoun *He*.

40. This place name is corrupt in the Slavic text and reads *Alefarioum*. See n. 46 below.

41. The river Silar (Silarus) marked the northwest boundary of Lucania.

42. Cf. Matthew 8:29.

43. Cf. Psalms 116:10.

44. The subject of this verb is omitted and ambiguous. Because the reference is apparently to the "evil spirit," I have added the pronoun *it* to the translation.

45. Since this legend places Saint Vitus's martydom in Lucania, he is referred to as Vitus of Lucania.

46. As in the case of Alectorium (n. 40 above), this name is corrupt in the Slavic text (cf. "Fanьgritanьsta") and remains a mystery. It is not, as

pointed out in *Staroslověnské legendy českého původu*, p. 345, a reference to Tanagra, a town in the ancient republic of Boeotia in Greece.

47. It will be recalled that after Diocletian divided the empire among Maximian, Galerius, and Constantine Chlorus, he retained the eastern portion, the chief city of which was Nicomedia (modern-day Izmit in Turkey).

48. For the sake of clarity I have substituted *the youth* for the ambiguous pronoun *he*.

49. The Slavic passage reads: "čьto vъprašaješi stara ili ouna člvkъ." (lit.: "why do you question an old man or a young one?"). Obviously *ili* ("or") is incorrect and should read *aky* ("like"); cf. the Latin text: "senem uti invenem" ("an old man like a young one").

50. See n. 42 above.

51. For the sake of clarity I have substituted *Vitus* for the ambiguous pronoun *him*.

52. Cf. Mark 5:8.

53. See n. 15 above.

54. This passage in the Latin text reads: "Hoc et ego desidero ad illam palmam pervenire, quam Dominus repromisit electis suis" ("I wish to attain that palm, which God promised to His chosen ones"). "Palm" in this context refers to martyrdom. Apparently the Slavic translator either misunderstood or purposely changed the drift of this sentence, since it reads as translated, "azъ želaju kъ togo rouče iti jako že gь obešča izbьranyimъ ego."

55. Manuscripts differ on the amount of weight placed upon the saint. The *Vienna Manuscript* has 200 libras, while the *Acta Sanctorum* has 80 libras (an ancient Roman unit of weight equivalent to 327.45 grams). The Slavic translator changed "libra" into "measure" (one measure equaled the amount of metal it would take to fill nine liters). Moreover, the numerals *rm* translate differently in Glagolitic and Cyrillic—as 160 and 140, respectively. Thus, it is possible that the Slavic translator doubled 80 libras in order to make an equivalent amount in measures, but in the process of transcribing the manuscript from Glagolitic into Cyrillic a scribe failed to make the necessary change.

56. This sentence is elliptic and simply reads: "i svoimь pьrstenьmь zapečatьlě" (lit.: "and he sealed with his ring"). I have expanded my translation for the sake of clarity and added the phrase "upon the prison."

57. This passage seems to allude to Acts 12:7: "And behold, the angel of the Lord came upon him, and a light shone in the prison. . . ."

58. Cf. Psalms 40:13.

59. This phrase is elliptic and omits the verb, which I have added.

60. Cf. Daniel 3:23–28.

61. Cf. Susanna 20:60.

62. Cf. Matthew 28:20.

63. Cf. Daniel 3:15.

64. That is, the crown of martyrdom.

65. Cf. John 13:27.

66. It is quite unusual to encounter a martyr cursing and hurling reproaches at his antagonist(s). More commonly he rises above the base actions directed against him and ignores his worldly tormentor(s).

67. The Slavic word for "pitch" (pьkъlъ) is corrupt and reads bьkъlъ.

68. See n. 63 above.

69. Cf. Exodus 14.

70. This sarcastic humor in the face of death serves to underscore the courageous nature of the martyr.

71. I have added the words on them to my translation. The Church Slavonic text simply reads: i raspeša (lit.: "and they stretched").

72. I have corrected the text to read "servants of God" instead of the grammatically incorrect raba božija ("servant of God").

73. It seems that the number of people who perished in the earthquake was inspired by certain biblical accounts; cf. Ezekiel 5:12 and Revelations 9:18.

74. The Slavic text reads: "gore mně ot selika otročišča preselenou soušcou" (lit.: "Woe is me, I have been moved by such a child"). Obviously this is an error: preselenou ("moved") should read presilenou ("overpowered").

75. See n. 41 above.

76. This sentence reads as follows in the Church Slavonic text: "i molju te da na semь městě čeresъ četyri dni mouka se da ne javleet rodьstva mojego" (lit.: "and I beseech Thee that no torture [flour ???] appear on this spot for four days after my birth"). There are several problems in this sentence. In the first place, the word torture (or flour) clearly does not fit the general context of the sentence; and, second, the end of the sentence is rather elliptic. It is clear from the Latin text that mouka ("torture"/"flour") should read mouxa ("fly"); cf. "et per dies qutuor natalis mei, musca non appareat." It has been pointed out (see Chaloupecký, Na úsvitu, p. 268) that the fly motif was borrowed from pre-Christian legendary traditions which viewed as miraculous the fact that flies would not touch animals slaughtered for sacrifice during the summer, returning to feed only after the festive days were over. Although this type of "miracle" might make sense in certain contexts, it hardly does so in a saint's life, where it simply appears to be in bad taste and is given a forced explanation in the Latin text, viz., "quae imago est daemonum" ("which [the fly] is an image of a demon"). Hence, the sense of the passage is that for four days following the saint's death no symbol of a demon was allowed to appear at the place where he died. As regards the phrase "after my birth," it should be borne in mind that the death of a martyr is his feast-day or birthday (i.e., his birth into heaven).

77. See Second Church Slavonic Life of Saint Wenceslas, n. 57.

78. This name in the Church Slavonic text reads "Florьnovija." The name Florentia is found in the Latin text.

79. Cf. John 11:22.

80. Cf. John 19:40.

Glagolitic Fragment of the *Office in Honor of Saint Vitus*

1. See *Life of Saint Vitus* (*Passion of the Blessed Martyrs Vitus, Modestus and Crescentia*), n. 76.

2. The term for a high official is the Greek word *strategos*. He possessed supreme power in both civilian and military matters.

3. For the sake of clarity I have substituted *Vitus* for the ambiguous third-person pronoun *he*.

4. See n. 3 above.

5. The manuscript is unclear at this point and simply reads *i lьži* (lit.: "and false"). I have added the word *gods* to the translation.

6. The names of the gods are corrupt in the Church Slavonic text and read "arkoula i juvěě."

7. This sentence contains an anacoluthon and is translated according to the notion of what is expected in this context.

8. Cf. Colossians 1:14.

9. See *Life of Saint Vitus* (*Passion of the Blessed Martyrs Vitus, Modestus and Crescentia*), n. 14.

10. Cf. Psalms 111:1.

Prayer Against the Devil

1. The abbreviation is *imrь*, which stands for *imjarekъ* (lit.: "name spoken"), an expression indicating the place in the text for the person's name.

2. Cf. Hebrews 11:5.

3. Cf. 2 Peter 2:5.

4. Cf. 2 Chronicles 20:7, Isaiah 41:8, and James 2:23.

5. Isaac's name in Hebrew translates as "laughter."

6. One of the meanings of Jacob's name is "heel."

7. I am assuming that the omitted object of the verb is "it"—i.e., the evil serpent.

8. Cf. Job 42.

9. I am assuming that the finite verb which this sentence lacks is "save."

10. The word for sea is corrupt and reads *morьste*. Cf. Exodus 14:23.

11. The name Joshua means "Redeemer" or "Saviour."

12. This sentence lacks a finite verb, which I am assuming is "bring."

13. I am assuming that *izlьmь* is the abbreviation for *izrailь* ("Israel"). In Scripture, Israel frequently indicates the people of God (cf. Exodus 6:6–7). Hence I have translated this rather confusing sentence utilizing the aforementioned interpretation.

14. The name Samuel translates as "heard of God."

15. This name is an obvious mistake and should be changed to read Ezekiel.

16. Cf. 1 Kings 18:40.

17. Cf. 2 Kings 2:21–22.

18. It appears that the verb *světovavъše* is corrupt and should read *sъvestovavъše*.

19. Saint Thecla is referred to here as the first female martyr (*pervomčica*). Since Saint Stephen was the first martyr, I have added the words "among women" to the text. Saint Anastasia's agnomen is "the woman who delivers from poison."

20. I believe that Saints Marina and Margaret are one and the same person, since Saint Marina is known as Margaret of Antioch.

Prayer to the Holy Trinity

1. See *Prayer Against the Devil*, n. 1.

2. I am uncertain as to the correct English form for this name.

3. At this point some manuscripts of this prayer add the names of three additional saints: Magnus, Canute, and Alban.

4. Mareš conjectures that the reference here is to George the Hermit. See F. W. Mareš, *An Anthology of Church Slavonic Texts of Western (Czech) Origin* (Vienna, 1979), p. 70.

Life and Martyrdom of Saint Wenceslas

1. It should be noted that in the so-called Bavarian Recension of this work Christianity begins not with Bořivoj but with his son, Spytihněv. See *Second Church Slavonic Life*, n. 10.

2. See *Second Church Slavonic Life*, n. 11.

3. See *Prologue Life of Saint Wenceslas*, n. 5.

4. See *Second Church Slavonic Life*, n. 15. The *Vostokov Variant* of the *First Church Slavonic Life* (not the *Croatian Glagolitic Variant* included in this work) notes specifically that Wenceslas was sent to Budeč to study Latin. This has led to speculations that the church at Budeč, St. Peter's, was of the Latin Rite rather than the Church Slavonic. However, this need not necessarily be the case. The name of Wenceslas's priest-tutor, Učen—if this name is not an epithet—would indicate that he was a Slav. Especially interesting is the fact that all the works dealing with Wenceslas stress his literary training in Latin and/or Church Slavonic and/or Greek. This was indeed a remarkable achievement on the part of the young ruler—all the more so in view of the fact that illiteracy was not an uncommon phenomenon among rulers in the Middle Ages. Indeed, Wenceslas's contemporary, Otto I, taught himself to read and write at a relatively late age, approximately forty.

5. See *First Church Slavonic Life*, n. 5.

6. See ibid., n. 14.

7. See ibid., n. 35. The motif of the forsaken house may have been drawn from the words of Christ: "Behold, your house is left unto you desolate." Cf. Matthew 23:38 and Luke 13:35.

8. The name of Wenceslas's mother was Drahomira. See *First Church Slavonic Life*, n. 6, and *Second Church Slavonic Life*, n. 23.

9. See *Prologue Life of Saint Wenceslas*, n. 4.

10. Chapter 7 of the *Second Church Slavonic Life* refers to these same vestiges of paganism in Bohemia. It is clear from this work that pagan rites were practiced alongside Christian ones well into the tenth century and probably beyond.

11. According to chapter 14 of the *Second Church Slavonic Life*, the lands from which priests came with relics and so on were Bavaria, Franconia, and Saxony. Since Wenceslas had established close ties with Saxony in particular, it is surprising that it goes unmentioned in this work.

12. The metaphor of the pearl seems to be an allusion to Christ's parable in Matthew 13:45–46: "Again, the kingdom of heaven is like unto a merchant man, seeking goodly pearls: who, when he found one pearl of great price, went and sold all that he had, and bought it." Here the "pearl of great price" is, of course, the kingdom of heaven.

13. It is difficult to say which "victories" are being referred to in this passage. Wenceslas was not known for his military prowess. It is quite certain that he did not wage war upon any of the German lands. Hence, it is possible that he fought with the Magyars, as did both his father and brother.

14. Cf. 2 Timothy 4:2.

15. See *First Church Slavonic Life*, nn. 13, 23, and 42.

16. See *First Church Slavonic Life*, n. 21, and *Second Church Slavonic Life*, n. 31.

17. See *Second Church Slavonic Life*, n. 32.

18. The year of Wenceslas's death is 929. See *First Church Slavonic Life*, n. 39.

19. See *First Church Slavonic Life*, n. 33. The slaughter of Wenceslas's family reminds one of the slaughter perpetrated against the Slavníks by the Přemyslide Boleslav II. See *Homily for the Feast of Saint Ludmila*, n. 8.

20. This river is the Rokytnice, which is mentioned by name in the *Second Church Slavonic Life* (see chap. 23 and n. 50).

21. See *Second Church Slavonic Life*, n. 52.

22. The year of the translation is 932.

23. See *Second Church Slavonic Life*, n. 55.

24. The selling of prisoners into slavery was a rather common phenomenon. And though Christianity was attempting to ban trafficking in slaves in general, it was not very successful, as it was a regular part of life in tenth-century Bohemia. Indeed, according to Christian's account in the *Life and Martyrdom of Saint Wenceslas*, Wenceslas himself bought slaves and donated them to the church.

25. Cf. Matthew 25:33.

Passion of the Martyr Ludmila

1. The original *Fuit* probably consisted of chapters 1–7 only. Chapters 8–10 were tacked on later; the Translation (*"Recordatus"*) was a separate work. See N. W. Ingham, "Sources on Saint Ludmila, II: The Translation of Her Relics," *IJSLP* 31–32 (1985): 197–206. Chaloupecký believed that this work was the oldest preserved Latin legend dealing with ancient Bohemia. Although the question is controversial, the honor should probably go to *Crescente fide*. See *Second Church Slavonic Life*, n. 10.

2. See *Prologue Life of Saint Ludmila*, n. 4.

3. See ibid., n. 6.

4. It was thought that Bořivoj ruled only over the Prague territory or, at most, over the Czech tribe in central Bohemia, and that the political unification of Bohemia took place under his grandson and great grandson, Boleslav I and Boleslav II.

5. See *Second Church Slavonic Life*, n. 10.

6. See *First Church Slavonic Life*, n. 5.

7. Cf. Job 29:15.

8. See *First Church Slavonic Life*, n. 6.

9. See *Prologue Life of Saint Ludmila*, n. 12.

10. See *First Church Slavonic Life*, n. 35.

11. See *Prologue Life of Saint Ludmila*, n. 1.

12. See ibid., n. 13.

13. Apparently the basilica was only a small wooden structure.

14. See *Prologue Life of Saint Ludmila*, n. 14.

15. It is assumed that the church in question is that of the Blessed Virgin Mary, which was built by Bořivoj in Prague, at least according to tradition.

16. Only the second part of this citation is from the Scriptures, cf. Genesis 3:19.

17. See *Second Church Slavonic Life*, n. 31.

18. This date would be 21 October 926.

Life and Martyrdom of Saint Wenceslas and His Grandmother, Saint Ludmila

1. This is the most controversial work in early Bohemian literature and has been the subject of debate since the dawn of Slavic philology in the eighteenth century. Undoubtedly the last word about it is yet to be heard. For further details see the Introduction.

2. See *Homily for the Feast of Saint Ludmila*, n. 8.

3. It is here that we learn the name of the author of this work. Christian (Kristian or Krist'an) was a monk in the Břevnov Abbey, a monastery founded by his nephew (?), Saint Vojtěch (Adalbert of Prague). Whether these two men were actually related is unresolved (see Ludvíkovský, "Great Moravian

Tradition," p. 557). The name of a monk Christian is attested in historical sources of the ninth and tenth centuries.

4. See *First Church Slavonic Life*, n. 7, and *Prologue Life of Saint Wenceslas*, n. 4.

5. All Christian's sources of information are not known and are a matter of debate. Nevertheless, arguments have been made in favor of his knowledge, not only of the Latin works associated with Wenceslas (e.g., *Crescente fide*), but of the *First Church Slavonic Life* and the literature of the Cyrillomethodian tradition, that is, the *Life of Constantine*, the *Life of Methodius*, and the *Life of Naum*. For a detailed discussion of this problem, see O. Králík, "Kreščenije Boriživoja," *TODRL* 19 (1963): 148–68.

6. The expression "lands of the Lothairians or Carolingians" is an ancient designation for Germany and France, respectively. When Charlemagne's successor, Louis the Pious, died, his sons, Lothair, Louis the German, and Charles the Bald, partitioned the Frankish Empire. The eastern part was under the former two; the western, under the latter.

7. This passage, with its obvious anachronism, has been used as an argument for the late origin of *Legenda Christiani* by those who opposed the authenticity of it. Most troublesome has been the reference to Augustine. However, the historian F. Graus has pointed out that similar tendencies are found in the works of numerous other medieval authors who (for obvious reasons) moved back the date of Christianization of their country as far as possible (see F. Graus, "Velkomoravská říše v české středověké tradici," *Československý časopis historický* 11, no. 3 (1963): 289–305; see also *A Brief Account*, n. 1. It should be noted, however, that Jakobson rejected this notion many years earlier (see R. Jakobson, "Minor Native Sources," pp. 49–50).

8. Svatopluk was the nephew and successor of Rostislav (or Rastislav, 846–70) and ruled Moravia from 870 to 894. Hence, the "prince or king" is Rostislav.

9. Cf. 2 Corinthians 6:14–15.

10. This entire paragraph is clearly tendentious. Christian suggests that, just as Moravia declined under Svatopluk because he refused to heed Bishop Methodius, so did Bohemia fall to Boleslav for persecuting the Slavníks and Bishop Adalbert (Vojtěch). There is, nevertheless, some basis in fact for the statement "they were surrendered to plunder," for Moravia was indeed plundered by the Magyars in 895, the year following Svatopluk's death.

11. The expression "under Arcturus" simply means "in the north." Arcturus is the brightest star in the constellation of Boötes.

12. The account of the people being stricken by the plague and then saved by a prophetess and "wise man" by virtue of their marriage is strongly reminiscent of ancient magical traditions. Prague, the cultural and political center of medieval Bohemia, derived its name from the castle Praha (Prague), which was founded around the ninth century.

13. The name Přemysl can be translated literally as meaning "very wise."

14. See *Second Church Slavonic Life*, n. 10.

15. An account of Bořivoj sitting on the floor at the feet of the Christian ruler while he is eating is repeated in a later Latin work (*Tempore Michaelis Imperatoris*), which is also known as the *Moravian Legend*. This story is analogous to the one dealing with Ingo, the prince of Carinthia. Some historians find this incident anecdotal and fanciful. However, this practice is known to have been followed in Bavaria.

16. The description of Bořivoj's conversion as progressing in stages—basic instruction in the faith, baptism, further instruction—is reminiscent of the methods recommended by Alcuin, Charlemagne's ecclesiastic adviser (see Vlasto, *Entry of the Slavs into Christendom*, pp. 18–19). However, by this time Alcuin's recommendations were no longer followed. Christian's mention of them has been viewed as a survival from Great Moravia. It should be noted that most of the following paragraph was omitted from Chaloupecký's work because he considered it a later, twelfth-century interpolation (see *Prameny*, p. 232). The entire incident seems to be artificial. For a more detailed discussion of this passage, see F. Graus, "Říše velkomoravská, její postavení v současné Evropě a vnitřní struktura," *Konferencia o vel'ky Morave a Byzantskej missii*, Brno-Nitra 1–4 (Nitra, 1963), p. 70.

17. See *Prologue Life of Saint Wenceslas*, n. 4.

18. Other manuscripts report that Bořivoj died at age thirty-six.

19. See *Second Church Slavonic Life*, n. 10.

20. See *First Church Slavonic Life*, n. 5.

21. See ibid., n. 6.

22. It seems that Christian portrays Drahomira as an even more negative and evil person than does the majority of the authors of the other works (see *Second Church Slavonic Life*, n. 22). It is curious to note that, with the exception of the *First Church Slavonic Life*, all the other works emphasize that Drahomira was of pagan descent. However, so was Ludmila, which fact, of course, is not mentioned.

23. See *First Church Slavonic Life*, n. 13.

24. Cf. Romans 6:19–21.

25. Cf. Job 31:31, 29:15.

26. See *Prologue Life of Saint Wenceslas*, n. 5.

27. Christian is the first to state explicitly that Ludmila rather than the boys' mother, Drahomira, was put in charge of their training. The Vostokov Variant of the *First Church Slavonic Life* alludes to this fact by stating that Ludmila entrusted Wenceslas "to the guidance of a priest, to be taught Slavic letters." See M. Kantor, *Medieval Slavic Lives*, pp. 142–43.

28. See *Prologue Life of Saint Ludmila*, n. 12.

29. Cf. Romans 12:19.

30. Cf. Matthew 10:23.

31. See *First Church Slavonic Life*, n. 35. It had been pointed out that the description of the priest's home is probably an imaginative embellishment. Paul's residence was undoubtedly a simple wooden structure.

32. This is the first work that mentions the names of Ludmila's murderers. The names are unusual and have been shown to be of Scandinavian origin. However, whether they are connected with mythological or historical figures is still unknown. Earlier hypotheses assumed that these names derived from German (Pekař) or were connected with the Russian word *gomon*, meaning "uproar"/"din" (Jakobson).

33. Cf. Wisdom of Solomon 4:7.

34. That is, 16 September 920.

35. Cf. Ecclesiastes 12:11.

36. That is, 19 and 21 October 925. It is interesting to note that the *Passion of the Martyr Ludmila* (chap. 11) states that Ludmila's body was found during the "ninth hour."

37. See *Second Church Slavonic Life*, n. 31. At this time Tuto was too feeble to travel and sent his coadjutor bishop, Michael, in his place. He later became bishop of Regensburg.

38. Cf. Genesis 3:19.

39. See *Life and Martyrdom of Saint Wenceslas*, n. 12.

40. Cf. 2 Timothy 4:2.

41. Cf. Psalms 42:1.

42. The ascendency of Saxon influence in Bohemia was certainly due in part to the mutual cultural and political concerns and interests that Wenceslas and Henry I, the Fowler (919–36), shared. Henry had helped Wenceslas in the court revolt fomented by Drahomira, and they were allied in their struggle against the Magyars. Also, the Saxon patron saint, Vitus (Guy), eclipsed the popularity of the other (principally Bavarian) foreign saints venerated in Bohemia.

43. See *First Church Slavonic Life*, n. 24.

44. See *Life and Martydom of Saint Wenceslas*, n. 24.

45. Cf. John 18:28.

46. Although this is the generally accepted date of Wenceslas's martyrdom, arguments have been made to date this event 28 September 935 (see Chaloupecký, *Na úsvitu*, p. 275, and *First Church Slavonic Life*, n. 39). It should be borne in mind that all the manuscripts translated in this work are transcriptions of manuscripts of a much earlier date—at times as much as five hundred years earlier. Hence it is difficult to determine how faithful the extant manuscript is to the lost original. Generally speaking, however, numerals and dates are quite frequently far from certain.

47. Apparently, Christianity had not softened former pagan attitudes toward bloody revenge—nor those of the "humble" author himself. The major difference here is that it is transferred to the Christian God.

48. See *Second Church Slavonic Life*, n. 50.

49. See *Prologue Life of Saint Wenceslas*, n. 3.

50. Cf. Luke 1:6.

51. See *Second Church Slavonic Life*, n. 57.

52. If this statement can be accepted as historically true, it speaks well for the cultural level of Bohemia during the reign of Wenceslas. It would have indeed been quite remarkable for lay members of the prince's retinue to be literate, not to mention servants in his household.

53. Cf. Matthew 25:21 and Luke 19:17.

54 . The so-called old miracles are those which Christian found recorded in other literary sources, viz., *Crescente fide*.

55. A trial by "God's court" is a trial by fire.

56. As Chaloupecký, *Na úsvitu* (p. 276), pointed out, the setting of this miracle is clearly the tenth century, when tribal princes were subject to the rule of the Přemyslides. Kouřim (originally called Zlicko) was a separate principality that extended north to the Elbe River and south to the territory of Sázava. The prince who rebelled against Wenceslas has been identified as Radslav, the "prince of Zlicko (Kouřimsko)." This region became part of the Slavníks' territory by the end of the tenth century; its center was at Libice castle.

57. This miracle calls to mind the one described in the Legend of Saint Eustathius, who saw a cross and the figure of Christ between the antlers of a stag. See M. Kantor, *Medieval Slavic Lives*, p. 81.

Homily for the Feast of Saint Ludmila, Patroness of the Bohemians

1. This *Homily* is based on *Legenda Christiani* and simply reworks a portion of it. However, it is not entirely consistent with its source in the treatment of Drahomira. Cf. the latter work, as well as the *Passion of the Martyr Ludmila* and the *Second Church Slavonic Life*. See *A Brief Account*, n. 1.

2. In this context "both natures" refers to the spiritual and carnal aspects of life.

3. Cf. Judges 4:17–21.

4. Cf. Colossians 3:5.

5. The allusion in this passage is clearly to Psalms 119:83: "For I am become like a bottle in the smoke; yet do I not forget thy statutes." In order to sustain the metaphor, the noun *smoke* (which can connote "frozen mist"/ "hoarfrost") was changed to *frost*.

6. See n. 5 above.

7. Cf. Judith 8:8.

8. Cf. Genesis 40:9–10. The order in which these saints were canonized is questionable. It is certainly the order in which they died. Apparently this work was written after their cults had become established.

After the death of Bishop Thietmar (January 982), who was acceptable to both the Přemyslides and Slavníks, Adalbert (?956–997) became bishop at

Prague cathedral. The appointment of a Slavník was made by Otto II in order to assure the loyalty of the Bohemian Church and the Slavníks, since relations between the two leading houses of Bohemia were deteriorating. However, Adalbert did not turn out to be the politician that the situation required and he inadvertently became a factor in the political rivalry between the Přemyslides and the Slavníks, the latter being suspected by Boleslav II of separatist tendencies and intrigues with Poland. Thus, when Adalbert departed for Rome in 995, Boleslav massacred all the Slavníks he could lay his hands on. Fearing to return to Prague, Adalbert then devoted himself to missionary work and visited Hungary and Poland. And from Poland he set off on a mission to convert the Prussians, at whose hands he met a martyr's death (April 997). His relics were redeemed for their weight in gold by Bolesław III and laid to rest in Gniezno. Two years later he was canonized in Rome (29 June 999). It was not until 1038/39 that his relics were returned to Prague. See Vlasto, *Entry of the Slavs*, pp. 100–105.

It is interesting to note that there is evidence indicating that the Přemyslides and Slavníks were in fact relatives, perhaps even close relatives (see Ludvíkovský, "Great Moravian Tradition," pp. 553–57).

9. Cf. John 15:1.

10. That is, Drahomira. See *First Church Slavonic Life*, n. 6.

11. Cf. 1 Kings 18:4; 19:2.

12. See *Prologue Life of Saint Ludmila*, n. 13.

13. See ibid., n. 12.

14. Cf. John 10:23–40.

15. Cf. Psalms 60:5.

16 Cf. Philippians 1:23–24.

17. Cf. Wisdom of Solomon 4:14.

18. Cf. Psalms 58:4.

19. Cf. Esther 2:8.

20. Saint Ludmila's relics were enshrined in Prague at the Convent of Saint George.

21. Cf. Luke 19:15–29.

22. Cf. Esther 7:1–10.

23. That is, the archangel Michael. See *Passion of the Martyr Ludmila*, n. 13.

Legend of Saint Wenceslas

1. See *First Church Slavonic Life*, n. 7.

2. Cf. Psalms 107:10.

3. See *First Church Slavonic Life*, n. 6. This description of Drahomira seems to be based on the one given in the *Passion of the Martyr Ludmila*.

4. See *First Church Slavonic Life*, n. 5.

5. Cf. Psalms 119:99–100.

6. See *First Church Slavonic Life*, n. 13.

7. See *Prologue Life of Saint Wenceslas*, n. 4.

8. Cf. 1 Kings 16:31–34.

9. Cf. Genesis 9:25.

10. Cf. Psalms 145:3.

11. Cf. 2 Chronicles 15:8.

12. The author's opinion that Wenceslas, because of his goodness, "would have undoubtedly yielded to the rein of justice" differs markedly from the earlier view expressed in the *Second Church Slavonic Life*. This difference has been attributed to later concepts of the role of the legal system.

13. The reference here to man's love for liberty has led some scholars to suggest that perhaps Aristotle is the unnamed philosopher. Also cf. Proverbs 8:20.

14. Cf. Wisdom of Solomon 8:1.

15. See the final chapter of the *Life and Martyrdom of Saint Wenceslas and His Grandmother, Saint Ludmila*. Note that in Christian's work this incident is presented as an attempt by a local prince to usurp the power of Wenceslas, and hence as a political uprising and not an evangelizing mission, as we find it in this work.

16. Cf. Ecclesiasticus 31:9.

17. This appears to be the first account of the receipt of the relics of Saint Vitus by Saint Wenceslas. It is not found in any earlier works.

18. See *First Church Slavonic Life*, n. 21.

19. Cf. Psalms 1:2.

20. Cf. Psalms 42:1.

21. Cf. Romans 7:24.

22. Cf. Philippians 1:23.

23. Cf. Matthew 26:31.

24. Cf. Matthew 20:22.

25. Cf. Proverbs 23:30.

26. This passage attempts to counter the view expressed by Christian (chap. 6) that at times Wenceslas "drank more than usual." It was not the image of the nation's patron saint the author of this work wished to preserve.

27. Cf. Psalms 10:8–9.

28. Cf. Philippians 1:21.

29. Cf. Wisdom of Solomon 4:14.

30. Cf. Psalms 37:24–25.

31. Cf. Psalms 73:23–24.

32. Cf. Wisdom of Solomon 4:15–16.

33. Cf. Wisdom of Solomon 4:18–19.

34. See *Second Church Slavonic Life*, n. 50.

35. The church in Prosec was located near Prague and was dedicated in memory of the translation of the relics of Saint Wenceslas.

36. See *Prologue Life of Saint Wenceslas*, n. 3.

37. That is, 28 September. See *First Church Slavonic Life*, n. 39.

38. The majority of the miracles described in the following chapters follow those included in Christian's work.

39. Cf. Matthew 5:15.

40. This appears to be a reference to the Dominican friars, which is unlikely. The author was probably a priest at the Church of St. Vitus in Prague.

41. This account is borrowed from Christian's work (see chap. 9).

42. See *Second Church Slavonic Life*, n. 57.

43. The concluding sentence was added to the material which the author of this work borrowed from Christian.

44. See *Life and Martyrdom of Saint Wenceslas and His Grandmother, Saint Ludmila*, n. 53.

A Brief Account of Saints Cyril and Methodius and the Baptism of the Moravian and Bohemian Lands

1. Following Dobner and Dobrovský, Chaloupecký maintained that this work was a source for *Legenda Christiani*. Subsequent studies by B. Ryba and J. Vilikovský (see Introduction) have shown the contrary to be true. In actuality, *A Brief Account* is drawn from Christian's work. Originally it was combined with the *Homily for the Feast of Saint Ludmila*, and they together were known as *Diffundente sole*. It was subsequently realized that these were two individual works and they were separated: the former retained its original designation, while the latter was entitled *Factum est*.

Saint Augustine (Aurelius Augustinus, 354–430) was the great Christian bishop of Hippo in northern Africa, and a philosopher. A very prolific author, considered by some to be one of the greatest writers in Latin, he is known for such works as *De Trinitate* (*The Trinity*), *De civitate Dei* (*The City of God*), and *Confessions*.

Saint Cyril (Constantine the Philosopher, 827–69) along with his brother, Saint Methodius (815?–85), were missionaries and teachers of the Slavs, the "Apostles to the Slavs." Fluent in Slavic, they were called upon for the mission to Moravia in 862/63, in response to the request by the Moravian prince Rostislav for missionaries capable of giving religious instruction to the local Slavs in their own language. Because of the task that awaited them, Constantine, in cooperation with his brother and their disciples, invented an alphabet and translated Scripture into Slavic. For more information on the *Lives* of Constantine and Methodius, see M. Kantor, *Medieval Slavic Lives*, pp. 25–138.

2. Concerning the work of Cyril (and Methodius) among the Bulgarians, it is possible that the brothers passed through Bulgaria on their way to Moravia in 862/63 and while on Bulgarian territory engaged in some missionary activity. However, it should be noted that absolutely no mention of this is made in their ancient *Lives*.

3. The introduction of the Slavic liturgy to Moravia by Constantine is a historically established fact. It is described in the *Life of Constantine* (*LC*), the *Life of Methodius* (*LM*), and in papal bulls. It is also a fact that the Slavic liturgy was established in Bulgaria and other Slavic regions, such as Macedonia, Russia, and Serbia.

4. See n. 1 above. This account contradicts the one we find in both *LC* and *LM*. The trip to Rome can be dated around December 867, and both brothers went, since both were invited (*LM*, chap. 6). Furthermore, Methodius was in Rome when Constantine died (*LC*, chap. 18). This is a rather curious contradiction, because *Diffundente sole* draws upon and complements the aforementioned works, the two most important sources of information on events of that time.

5. This is a reference to the so-called trilingual heresy. The trilinguists held that the Liturgy could only be celebrated in Hebrew, Greek, or Latin.

6. After the death of Constantine, Methodius was made a bishop in Rome and was assigned the territories of Moravia and Pannonia. However, the "king" under whom Methodius received his appointment in Moravia was Rostislav. This work, as well as Christian's, does not mention Rostislav by name. Hence the individual referred to as "Svatopluk the First" is in fact Rostislav, while "Svatopluk the Second" refers to his nephew, Svatopluk I. When Methodius returned to Moravia in 870, Svatopluk had already assumed the throne, having treacherously deposed his uncle Rostislav with the help of the Franks.

7. It would appear from the context of this statement that there were seven dioceses in Great Moravia. However, no information about them or their location is available.

8. The Latin term for "Bohemian Slavs" is *Bohemi et Sclavi*, which translated literally means "the Bohemians who are Slavs"—an archaic designation that was used in Latin manuscripts for a number of centuries.

9. The expression "under Arcturus in the climes of the Rhipaen Mountains" simply means "in the north"—i.e., it is a tautology, as both phrases have the same meaning. Arcturus is a star in the constellation Boötes; the Rhipaen Mountains are fictitious "northern" mountains.

10. It is from the Castle Prague (Praha) that the medieval (and modern) center of Bohemia derives its name.

11. This is an echo of the ancient legend concerning the origin of the Přemysl family. As opposed to Christian's work (see n. 13 below), Přemysl is not depicted here as a "ploughman," hence peasant, but as a nobleman and ruler of his people.

12. See *Second Church Slavonic Life*, n. 10.

13. See *Prologue Life of Saint Wenceslas*, n. 4.

14. See *Prologue Life of Saint Ludmila*, n. 2.

15. Hradec is the place associated with the earliest beginnings of Slavic Christianity in Bohemia under the ministration of the priest Kaich. It is present-day Levý Hradec.

16. This is the only early work that mentions Ludmila's baptism by Methodius.

17. A very common pagan reaction over most of Europe to any acceptance of Christianity was to rebel against the ruler responsible for the act. Apparently Bohemia was no exception.

18. See *Second Church Slavonic Life*, n. 10.

19. See *First Church Slavonic Life*, n. 5.

20. See ibid., n. 7.

About the Author

Marvin Kantor is professor of Slavic languages and literatures at Northwestern University. He is the author of *Medieval Slavic Lives of Saints and Princes* (1983) and *The Vita of Constantine and the Vita of Methodius* (1976), as well as several articles on medieval Slavic literature.